POPULAR RADICALISM

STUDIES IN MODERN HISTORY

General editors: *John Morrill and David Cannadine*

This series, intended primarily for students, will tackle significant historical issues in concise volumes which are both stimulating and scholarly. The authors combine a broad approach, explaining the current state of our knowledge in the area, with their own research and judgements; and the topics chosen range widely in subject, period and place.

Titles already published

FRANCE IN THE AGE OF HENRI IV
  Mark Greengrass

VICTORIAN RADICALISM
  Paul Adelman

WHITE SOCIETY IN THE ANTEBELLUM SOUTH
  Bruce Collins

BLACK LEADERSHIP IN AMERICA 1895-1968
  John White

THE TUDOR PARLIAMENTS
  Michael A. R. Graves

LIBERTY AND ORDER IN EARLY MODERN EUROPE
  J. H. Shennan

POPULAR RADICALISM
  D. G. Wright

POPULAR RADICALISM
The working-class experience, 1780–1880

D. G. Wright

LONGMAN
London and New York

LONGMAN GROUP UK LIMITED
Longman House, Burnt Mill, Harlow,
Essex CM20 2JE, England
Associated Companies throughout the world

Published in the United States of America
by Longman Inc., New York

First published 1988

BRITISH LIBRARY CATALOGUING IN PUBLICATION DATA

Wright, D.G.
    Popular radicalism : the working-class
    experience, 1780–1880. – (Studies in
    modern history).
    1. Labor and laboring classes – England —
    Political activity – History 2. Radicalism
    — England – History
    I. Title II. Series
    323.3′2   HD8395

ISBN 0-582-49440-0

LIBRARY OF CONGRESS CATALOGING-IN-PUBLICATION DATA

Wright, D. G.
    Popular radicalism.

    (Studies in modern history)
    Bibliography: p. 191
    Includes index.
    1. Labor and laboring classes——Great Britain——
Political activity——History.   2. Great Britain——
Politics and government——18th century.   3. Great
Britain——Politics and government——19th century.
I. Title.   II. Series: Studies in modern history
(Longman(Firm))
HD8395.W75   1988   322′.2′0942   87-4093
ISBN 0-582-49440-0

Set in 10/11pt AM Comp Edit Times Roman

Produced by Longman Group (FE) Limited
Printed in Hong Kong

CONTENTS

Contents

In Memoriam
Valerie Wright
1939–1987

PREFACE

This book is thematic in that it focusses on political radicalism: attempts, predominantly by the English working class, to bring about changes in political power and the nature and role of the state, mainly in order to redress their economic and social grievances. To that extent it is basically an exercise in political history, rather than being in any sense a social and economic history of 'the making of the English working class', a task recently and splendidly performed by Eric Hopkins in his *A Social History of the English Working Classes* (1979), by John Rule in *The Labouring Classes in Early Industrial England* (1986) and by Richard Price in *Labour in British Society* (1986). Nor is it offered as a work of original scholarship, but rather as a general synthesis based almost entirely on the research of fellow historians. The aim is to assist students to find their way through the various debates and controversies which have enlivened the historiography of popular radicalism, as well as to tackle the major historical monographs and learned articles which have been gutted – not too brutally and misleadingly I trust – in the following pages.

A preface provides a welcome opportunity to acknowledge obligations which all historians necessarily and gratefully incur. Thanks are owed to my MA in History students at Huddersfield Polytechnic, who have taught me more than they perhaps realize; to the Dean of Research for helping to finance visits to the Public Record Office and the British Library; to my colleagues Philip Woodfine and Keith Laybourn for sharing with me their expertise on eighteenth- and later-nineteenth-century labour movements respectively; to Albert Goodwin and Clive Emsley for teaching me a great deal about the effects of the Revolutionary and Napoleonic Wars on British society; to Harry Dickinson for inviting me to present my views on Chartism to the seminar in Modern British and European History at Edinburgh University; to David Cannadine and John Morrill of Cambridge for much encouragement, as well as penetrating, though always courteous and helpful, editorial criticism. And finally to my wife Valerie for tolerating, despite considerable ill-health, the absences and silences involved in writing this book.

Shipley
August 1986

Chapter 1

INTRODUCTION: CLASS AND CLASS CONSCIOUSNESS

In his *Progress in Pudsey*, published in 1887, Joseph Lawson, a sixty-five-year-old former woollen manufacturer and Chartist, complained that 'one serious fault in most of the histories we read when young, and which deeply impressed us at the time, was the everlasting scribble about the kings and queens, nobles and dukes, generals and their feats in various battles, and the consequent wholesale suffering, murder and death. There was very little about the large masses of the people – what they were thinking, doing and suffering'. Were Lawson writing a century later, he could make the same complaint, for it is really only during the last thirty years that there has appeared a daunting, if extremely stimulating, amount of research and writing on 'the large masses of the people'. Nowadays there is as much, if not more, research concerned with 'history from below' as with 'history from above', especially with the emergence of social history as a distinct discipline, rather than being the subordinate of economic history.

The history of the English working class since the eighteenth century does, however, pose a number of difficulties for students. One is the sheer amount of published material and the complexity of the vigorous historical debates which it has prompted. Another is that the topic has, since the 1930s when Marxism first made a significant impact on British intellectuals, been something of an ideological battleground, with historians frequently seeking to employ history as a weapon in present politics. Political axes have been well ground before being wielded in fierce historical disputes on the question of working-class living standards during the industrial revolution, the extent of revolutionary class consciousness during the early nineteenth century, and the alleged *embourgeoisement* of many skilled workers after 1850.

Such controversies remain alive. Even the old 'standard of living' debate, which dates back to the revisionary writings of the 'optimist' Sir John Clapham from the late 1920s, remains far from concluded. Reassessments of the rate of economic growth before 1830 suggest that optimistic assumptions by scholars like T. S. Ashton and R. M. Hartwell

1

of population growth being consistently outpaced by the expansion of the national product rest upon presuming too rapid a rate of economic growth. Hence there is still much to be said for the 'pessimistic' arguments of the Webbs, Hammonds, E. J. Hobsbawm and E. P. Thompson (Rule 1986: 27–43; 379–82). It is therefore not easy to reach anything approaching a detached and balanced view on such contentious issues. Perhaps attempts to do so are misguided. As Margaret Cole once recalled of her childhood: 'Our household was non-political. That is to say, Tory.'

For the historian of popular radicalism, a fundamental historical controversy is that concerned with the existence of a working class; not so much in the sense of large numbers of men and women who owned virtually nothing but their labour power, but of a working class conscious of possessing an identity and interests separate from, and often antagonistic towards, those of the propertied classes. The use of the word 'class' to describe social groups became common only in the early nineteeth century. Although eighteenth-century society was a profoundly unequal one, social cleavages did not yet run along the lines of the more horizontal class divisions discernible by the 1830s and 1840s. When they referred to the major divisions in society, eighteenth-century observers like Archdeacon Paley or Edmund Burke tended to employ the language of 'ranks' and 'orders', as in 'middle ranks' or 'lower orders'. This terminology was deemed appropriate for a hierarchial society of ascending ranks and degrees, held together by bonds of patronage firmly in the hands of those high in the social scale and by ties of dependence which bound those lower down the social scale to those above them: the tenant to his landlord, the labourer to his employer.

This concept of a community of shared interests in agrarian England has also been applied to manufacturing, where a 'vertical' consciousness of 'the trade' bound masters and men, capital and labour, together in a context of shared mutual interests. Although such consciousness did not prevent considerable conflict between capital and labour taking place, such disputes proved short-lived within the parameters of a perceived common interest. Such a view can be taken too far, given the frequency of food riots, turnpike riots and industrial strikes. Alongside the eighteenth-century language of ranks and orders existed another which expressed unambiguous fear of 'the mob'. Nevertheless, it remains true that articulation of a separate labour interest was usually temporary. As Dr Rule points out: 'Bitter exchanges, sometimes violent strikes and sharply articulated hostility often gave way after settlement to an expressed preference for an ordered world in which masters and men both knew their place and the duties that went with it' (Morris 1979: 18; Rule 1986: 384).

After 1780 the language of ranks and orders slowly began to be replaced by the language of class, so that by mid-ninteenth century the old terminology, though still in use, was being substituted by the categorizations 'working classes', 'middle classes' and 'aristocracy', or, even more precisely, 'working class' and 'middle class'. Such a change in linguistic usage implicitly recognized that social conflict had become focused on the clash of interests arising from the distribution of wealth, income and power (Rose 1981: 255; Morris 1979: 9).

THE CREATION OF THE ENGLISH WORKING CLASS

No serious historian, including those most impressed by the gradations and divisions among the working class, denies that a working class, as a descriptive category for people who existed by selling their labour power, came into existence during the late eighteenth and early nineteenth centuries. From about the middle of the eighteenth century, English society was increasingly transformed by a series of virtually simultaneous revolutions: demographic, transport, agrarian and industrial. A sustained increase in population began around 1740, whereby the 5 million people in England and Wales in 1700 rose to 7½ million in 1780, 9 million in 1801, 18 million in 1851 and 26 million in 1881. Such unprecedented growth involved a massive increase in the supply of labour; during the first half of the nineteenth century the labour force more than doubled. It also meant a vastly increased number of people to feed, clothe and house. While it is true that the various revolutions interacted to produce, over the period as a whole, an output of goods and services which outpaced the increase in population, growth took place at an uneven rate and imposed much deprivation and suffering on substantial groups of labouring people. It is important to bear in mind that a good deal of economic growth occurred before the advent of the factory system on any scale. Factories only became dominant in the second half of the nineteenth century. Indeed, the initial impact of the industrial revolution, with only limited application of steam power, was to expand both the numbers and the output of hand-workers in the domestic and small workshop system, workers who continued to outnumber factory operatives until at least 1851.

Between 1700 and 1880 the most significant change in the structure and scale of the labour force was the shift away from agriculture into manufacturing. In 1700 perhaps between a quarter and a half of the occupied population were engaged in manufacture and mining; fifty years later trade and manufacturing together probably employed more workers than agriculture. By 1801 it looks as though over 40 per cent were involved in manufacture and trade, as against 36 per cent primarily engaged in agriculture, although it is difficult to be precise because of the haphazard nature of the occupational censuses and the lack of a clear definition of the 'working population'. There is the further problem of the many people who worked simultaneously in industry and agriculture. According to the 1851 census, 43 per cent of the occupied population were in manufacture and mining. Thereafter the proportion rose only slightly, as the continuous decline in agricultural employment was balanced by an increase in tertiary, rather than manufacturing, occupations, although agriculture, with 1,790,000 workers, was still the largest single occupation in 1851.

In many sectors of the capital goods industry, the expansion of the labour force was accompanied by an increase in the unit of production and the number of workers on each site: in shipyards, mines, quarries, ropeworks, glassworks and brickyards. Technological innovation in these sectors was limited. There was none, for example, in the hewing of coal, yet the number of miners rose from about 50,000 in 1800 to 219,000 in 1851, while the pits themselves employed greater numbers. So far as consumer goods industries were concerned, the bulk of the workforce remained outside the factory system, which as late as the mid-nineteenth century predominated only in the manufacture of cotton and worsted cloth. The 650,000 workforce in East Midlands stocking-knitting and lace-making, as well as 14,000 in the Sheffield cutlery trades, were largely untouched by the factory system. In Birmingham, as in Sheffield, small-scale artisan production persisted in metal goods manufacture, despite the existence of a few large enterprises. The garment industry, including tailors, seamstresses, milliners and glovers, with a total workforce of well over 600,000 in 1851, was small-scale and un-mechanized, as was shoemaking with 243,000. Small masters also predominated in the building industry (600,000) and also, to a slightly lesser extent, in pottery manufacture.

Machine-operatives in factories were therefore only a relatively small minority of the total workforce as late as 1851. The census of that year revealed that there were only 1,750,000 workers in mechanized industry, employing steam-driven machinery, and 5,500,000 in non-mechanized industry. Mechanized industry therefore employed less than a quarter of the industrial workforce even when mining, rather misleading, was classified as mechanized. As in the eighteenth century, industrial production involved the employment of a great deal of female and child labour, with women concentrated in the lighter branches of industry and excluded from the workshop craft trades. On the other hand, it is doubtful whether the industrial revolution meant any significant increase in the female proportion of the workforce, given the ubiquity of women workers in the pre-1780 economy. Child labour is more problematic. Dr Hunt, for example, argues that it was in decline even before 1850 and was probably less extensive than before 1780. But the 1851 census figure of about a third of children aged under fifteen engaged in paid employment is probably a considerable underestimate, omitting the many children who assisted adult workers or were employed in household production.

Industrialization in Britain took place alongside a process of very rapid urbanization. Only London had a population over 50,000 in 1750; but by 1851 there were 29 towns over 50,000 and 9 with over 100,000, while London's population had increased to 2½ million. Between 1801 and 1851, for example, the population of Birmingham rose from 71,000 to 233,000, Manchester 75,000 to 303,000, Sheffield from 46,000 to 135,000 and Bradford from 13,000 to 104,000. A large proportion of the working population had to adjust not only to industrialization, but also to the manifold problems of urban existence, including intense overcrowding and horrific sanitary conditions. The increasing concentration of the workforce in urban areas obviously acted as a stimulant to working-class radicalism; Marx himself argued that urban proximity of work and residence was a major precondition for the emergence of a self-conscious and militant working class.

As it was, changes in the structure and scale of both industry and agriculture involved inexorable proletarianization for a large proportion of the workforce. If hand technology and much small-scale production persisted in industry, then the workers involved were often subject to significant changes, as many of them found it increasingly difficult to maintain their privileges if they were skilled men, as well as to retain control over the labour process or to resist intensification of the pace of work and even wage reductions. The decline of textile handloom weavers and Nottingham and Leicester framework stocking knitters are but two outstanding examples of extreme deprivation and suffering under the impact of plummeting living standards during the first half of the nineteenth century. Occupations like tailoring and shoemaking were subject to 'sweating' as mass-production methods developed, employing cheap labour to produce lower-priced but inferior goods. Capitalist exploitation was not confined to the factory system, since many trades which remained immune to factory production were structurally transformed with the expansion of merchant capitalism and the 'putting out' system. Over many key sectors of industry, workers ceased to own the materials on which they worked or the finished products of their labour, being reduced merely to selling their labour power. At the same time, those brought into the factory system lost control over the pace of the labour process as they became subject to the programmed rhythms of machine industry, to the clock and the factory hooter and no more 'Saint Monday'.

In fact proletarianization, in the sense of people who were obliged to earn their living by selling their labour power, had already made substantial progress as early as 1750, when a substantial proportion of England's population already depended on wages. The crude occupational census of 1811 showed that manual workers of all kinds accounted for four-fifths of the entire population. Wage labour was therefore widespread before the industrial revolution, with groups like East Midlands framework knitters and West Country weavers entirely dependent on work put out by capitalist weavers and clothiers, who collected and marketed the product, paying wages in the form of piece-rate 'prices'. Southern agriculture, rural cloth and metal working, as well as urban printing, tailoring and hat-making depended on a class of wage-earning journeyman labourers. Much domestic and workshop labour involved unremitting toil in wretched conditions by modern standards, although the intensity of labour varied with the amount of work in hand.

It therefore makes sense, as Dr Rule has argued, to speak of the existence of a 'proletariat' by the end of the eighteenth century, even if it were not as yet a self-conscious proletariat capable of mass action on a major scale, given the persistence of multifarious gradations and divisions among the workers. The chances of a journeyman who had served a full apprenticeship being able to set up as a small independent master became progressively reduced. Resentment on the part of skilled artisans at the erosion of their traditions and customary expectations, together with their desire to preserve the privileges and skilled status they were still able to retain, was to place them in the vanguard of both the trade unionism which pre-dated the classic industrial revolution period and the working-class radical movements which coincided with it (Stedman Jones: 1975; Hunt 1981: 7–31; Rule 1986: 1–2, 7–21; Hopkins 1979: 2–16).

THEORIES OF CLASS

A major debate in modern social history focuses on the legitimacy of class terminology and, more specifically, whether the concept of a 'working class' serves as a useful category of historical explanation. Certainly use of the term 'working class' is fraught with historiographical, ideological and semantic difficulties. Even the most committed anti-Marxist historians employ the phrase adjectivally, as in 'working-class housing', 'working-class protest' and so on. The debate itself is complicated by a lack of agreement on what exactly is meant by 'class'. Some historians, like Hobsbawm and Foster, see class as tangible; measurable in terms of income, occupation, relationship to the means of production, area of residence and marriage patterns. Others, including Asa Briggs and E. P. Thompson, put the emphasis on awareness of class and habits of class; with class as the embodiment of common traditions, experiences and values, rather than as an economically homogeneous layer of social stratification.

Any debate on class necessarily has to confront the writings of Marx and ideological differences are at their sharpest over whether a Marxist-Leninist conception of the working class bears any close relationship to historical reality. There are those historians, themselves often left-wing political activists, for whom the Marxist-Leninist conception of class 'forms the adored central mystery of a quasi-religious cult' (McCord 1985). Conservative historians tend to doubt whether the employment of social categories like 'working class' and 'middle class' can be anything other than a handy, if essentially misleading, form of social shorthand, and question whether it is possible to refer in any precise way to a significantly different middle and working class situated on either side of a discernibly sharp discontinuity in the social spectrum. There has therefore been considerable scepticism expressed about the extent to which class consciousness existed in the early nineteenth century, in terms of a recognition of conflicting interests binding together the disparate elements of a particular class in inexorable struggle against other classes. For such sceptics, words like 'bourgeoisie' and 'proletariat' are anathema, to be banished into limbo along with the ghosts of Marx and Lenin.

Such views, of course, represent an extreme case, as does the opposite view that a fully-fledged revolutionary proletariat had emerged in England by mid-nineteenth century. There are more moderate historians who accept readily enough the existence of a working class as a descriptive category for people who were engaged in manual wage labour and had similar lifestyles and material rewards, while at the same time denying the existence of widespread class conflict or the impossibility of collaboration between middle-class and working-class radicalism. There are also those who accept the development of a working-class consciousness in the sense of an awareness of a distinct class identity, while rejecting that this consciousness was 'revolutionary': aiming to overthrow the capitalist system rather than making reformist and opportunist gains within the system.

Marx and Lenin argued that an individual's class was determined by the role he or she played in the production process; the fundamental distinction being between those who owned the means of production and those who owned only their labour power. Marx believed that the emergence of a new mode of production, based on steam power and large-scale capitalism, during the later eighteenth century led to the formation of new class relationships, with a wage-earning and propertyless working class confronting those capitalists who controlled the means of industrial productivity. A characteristic feature of the new mode of production was that workers became subordinated to the monotonous pace of power-driven machines in increasingly large factories, initially concentrated in the textile industry. A growing factory proletariat produced more and more, yet received minimal – even decreasing – wages in return for its labour. The result was surplus value and expanding profits for the capitalist factory owners and a profound sense of alienation for the proletariat. Factory workers became alienated not only from the goods they produced, but also from nature and from themselves.

Marx claimed that the working-class nucleus continued to expand after the beginnings of large-scale industrialization, assisted by the successive proletarianization and alienation of shopkeepers, artisans and peasants. Just as capitalism would absorb an already profit-conscious aristocracy, so the myriad distinctions of skill and status within the ranks of labour would be rendered down to produce a proletariat united against its oppressors. Simultaneously, Marx described what he saw as having happened since the advent of industrialization, and predicted what would continue to occur until the final and inevitable collapse of the capitalist system, doomed by its own internal contradictions.

In other words Marx, not altogether consistently, depicted the working class suddenly emerging with the appearance of the factory mode of production in the 1760s, but also as slowly evolving towards maturity as it came to incorporate other alienated groups. Class conflict and class consciousness necessarily accompanied class formation, though tending to develop rather more slowly. Early attempts to destroy factories and machinery which competed with workers' labour were succeeded by strategies for maintaining and advancing wage levels by means of national trade unions and political campaigns. However, Marx believed that even by the mid-nineteenth century the English working class had failed to reach maturity. Workers occupied a specific socio-economic position without yet possessing much consciousness of an identity of interests. As yet they opposed the bourgeoisie with only rudimentary theories and organizations.

Lenin endorsed Marx's account of class formation, class consciousness and alienation under capitalism, agreeing that workers might succumb to the 'false consciousness' which appeared in the mid-Victorian decades and which diverted attention from outright confrontation with the bourgeoisie. On the other hand, Lenin regarded the initial stage of conflict in industrial society as involving mere 'trade union consciousness', without leading to the victory of the proletariat. Such a victory could only be achieved when political, or 'mature', working-class consciousness emerged at a later stage, under the leadership of a small, disciplined working-class 'vanguard of the proletariat', leading to a struggle for control of the state. In Lenin's view, genuine working-class consciousness appeared for the first time in the Chartist movement (Glen 1984: 2–14).

Historians of the British labour movement writing during the first half of the twentieth century tended to adopt the chronologies laid down by Marx and Lenin. There were some who argued that sustained working-class political or socialist consciousness appeared only during the 1880s, with the foundation of groups like the Social Democratic

Federation (Hobsbawm 1948). It was acknowledged that sporadic revolts against the industrial system occurred between 1760 and 1848, but these were then succeeded, it was claimed, by a process of accommodation whereby workers accepted industrialism without being sufficiently organized and co-ordinated to make a bid for social and political power.

At the same time there were historians like G. D. H. Cole who argued that full working-class consciousness appeared between 1832 and 1848, during the general trade union, Factory, Anti-Poor Law and Chartist agitations. Hobsbawm came to subscribe to this view, although he stressed the fundamental division between the highly-skilled 'aristocracy of labour' and the less-skilled workers, as well as the variety of status levels within the two categories during the classic industrial revolution period. In 1954 Hobsbawm argued that before the 1840s it is doubtful 'whether we can speak of a proletariat in the developed sense at all, for this class was still in the process of emerging from the class of petty producers, small masters, countrymen, etc., of pre-industrial society, though in certain regions and industries it had already taken fairly definite shape' (Hobsbawm 1954: 276; Cole and Postgate 1946: 258–91).

More recent research has resulted in some modification of interpretations derived from Marx and Lenin. Following the pioneering work of J. H. Clapham, economic historians have demonstrated that mechanized industry and large-scale factory production directly involved only a small percentage of the workforce before the 1850s. According to Musson, 'It is evident that the typical British worker in the mid-nineteenth century was not a machine operator in a factory, but still a traditional craftsman or labourer or domestic servant' (Musson 1978: 130–1). In both Birmingham and Sheffield, for example, domestic industry and small-scale workshop production dominated until mid-century, while factories were a comparative rarity. Moreover, factory workers, far from being subject to progressive immiseration, were among the most highly-paid sections of the labour force. The factory proletariat was therefore neither as numerically dominant nor as systematically impoverished as Marx tended to assume (Samuel 1977: 6–72; Smith 1982: 35; McCloskey 1981: 109).

Further reappraisal of Marx's view of a working class manifesting itself in the late eighteenth and early nineteenth centuries was suggested by the work of Asa Briggs on urban social structures. He depicted two main types of urban social and economic development. In many towns and cities, with Birmingham the outstanding example, goods were produced in small artisan workshops, where masters and men worked side-by-side in a context of relatively fluid social and occupational mobility, with only loose control exercised by capitalist merchants. According to Briggs, such urban centres provided less evidence of class formation before 1830 than of co-operation between different social ranks. It was rather in textile factory towns like Manchester and Leeds that there existed by the time of the Reform Bill the class formation and class conflict stipulated by Marx and his adherents. If Briggs was right to suggest that something akin to Marx's proletariat appeared only in a relatively few urban centres, then it no longer seemed realistic to speak of a national working class during the industrial revolution period (Briggs 1952; Briggs 1959: 208–10; Briggs 1963: 85–243).

During the past twenty years or so, historians' attempts to grapple with the problems of class formation and class consciousness during the industrial revolution have received a major stimulus from the writings of E. P. Thompson, Harold Perkin and John Foster. In his seminal *The Making of the English Working Class* (1963), Thompson put forward a vigorous and less crudely economically deterministic reinterpretation of Marxist-Leninist approaches. Like Marx, he saw the working class appearing with the onset of large-scale industrialization. But unlike Marx, he regarded the working class as formed by the 1830s, rather than still being in the process of maturation: 'to step over the threshold, from 1832 to 1833, is to step into a world in which the working-class presence can be felt in every county in England, and in most fields of life' (Thompson 1963: 887). By including skilled artisans, workers in the putting-out system, miners and agricultural labourers in his analysis of working-class formation, Thompson moved the discussion beyond factory workers and urban centres and therefore avoided many of the standard criticisms of Marxist interpretations. On the other hand, he rejected Briggs's claim of relative class harmony in Birmingham, a harmony which turned to discord by the later 1830s, as Behagg has recently confirmed (Behagg 1982: 59–86).

Thompson insisted that class is not a structure, nor even a category, 'but something which in fact happens (and can be seen to have happened) in human relationships'. Class is a relationship which occurs over time. It 'happens when some men, as a result of common experiences (inherited or shared) feel and articulate the identity of their interests as between themselves and as against other men whose interests are different from (and usually opposed to) theirs'. Class therefore involves the existence of conflict relationships. But there are important aspects of class beyond feelings of conflict and their articulation. The conflicts must be acted out by people in their everyday lives. Hence a class for Thompson is also a group of people acting in discernible 'class' ways, and this demands the existence of at least two groups on opposing sides of a conflict situation.

In addition, 'the class experience is largely determined by the productive relations into which men are born – or enter voluntarily' (Thompson 1963: 9–10). In other words, the classes in conflict must be workers who possess only their labour power and capitalists (plus their allies) who control the means of production. To some extent, Thompson agreed with fellow-Marxists like Hobsbawm and Rudé in detecting a tendency for working-class activists to oscillate between trade union objectives and general political agitation, according to the incidence of economic distress. Such oscillation, however, came to an end with the clear formation of the working class by 1832, although he acknowledged that at this stage there did not yet exist a fully formed and generally shared class consciousness among the whole working population. One of the major virtues of Thompson's seminal book is that it traces the foundations for the development of the deeper and more widespread working-class consciousness which emerged during the 1830s after the Reform crisis, even if it eventually proved evanescent (Thompson 1963: 909; Hobsbawm 1954: 126–47; Rudé 1964: 218–19).

Thompson's work has been much criticized. His portrayal of Methodism as 'the chiliasm of the defeated and the hopeless' outraged his conservative and Methodist opponents, but has received support from recent regional studies (Baxter 1974: 46–76; Stigant 1971; Hempton 1984: 55–80; Rule 1986: 164). Other critics of Thompson are sceptical about the size and composition of his 'working class', as well as its orientation towards conflict. And if class conflict is largely a matter of feeling and perception, how then may its existence be adequately tested? His arguments have been dismissed as 'a myth, a construct of determined imagination' negated by 'a surfeit of ideological bias'. It has been objected that too much of his evidence for the existence of a working class refers to artisans, workers in domestic industry and self-employed craftsmen and traders, even though these groups were far more numerous than factory workers and were often themselves creations of industrialization.

Historians committed to the Whig interpretation of history regard social conflict as a form of deviance confined to small minorities, and are at pains to deny the existence of an English revolutionary tradition stretching over several decades. Malcolm Thomis, for example, rejects Thompson's interpretation of Luddism on all counts, arguing that it was a protest against specific industrial grievances, with an absence of political consciousness or substantial links between the three main Luddite areas (Donnelly 1976). However, Thompson's views have received support from Hobsbawm, who came to believe that working-class consciousness did not first appear in the 1880s as he once claimed, but rather 'between 1815 and 1848, more especially about 1830'. Like Thompson, he endorsed a wider occupational composition of the working class, which was not 'a strictly proletarian movement in the Marxist sense' (Hobsbawm 1962: 209, 212–14).

In *The Origins of Modern English Society* (1969), the non-Marxist Harold Perkin studied the formation of a working class within a broad social revolution which resulted in the emergence of a class society in Victorian England characterized by 'the existence of vertical antagonism between a small number of horizontal groups, each based on a common source of income' (Perkin 1969: 176). Perkin's analysis differed significantly from that of Thompson. He doubted whether the Jacobins in the 1790s, or indeed any group before 1815, really gained the support of the workers *en masse*. Instead, he depicted a working class composed of workers from many trades emerging between 1815 and 1820 during the political agitation of the immediate post-war years. For Perkin, class formation is a result of social rather than economic changes. In place of focussing on changing modes of production, Perkin outlined the rise of three classes (working, entrepreneurial and professional), the revival of a fourth (the aristocracy), and the complex inter-relationships between them. Whereas Thompson, dealing primarily with the workers, saw the working class heroically forming itself in new industrial surroundings, Perkin drew attention to influences not exclusively or even substantially the product of workers' collective activities. Sectarian religion, he suggested, both reflected and encouraged declining deference and dependence on the part of the labouring classes. Perkin also emphasized the 'abdication on the part of the governors', whereby traditional notions of paternalism and *noblesse oblige* were increasingly rejected by the aristocracy itself, let alone the nascent entrepreneurial middle class (Perkin 1969: 183–95).

Unlike Thompson, Perkin attempted to trace simultaneously the development of all the major groups in society. He did so, not so much in terms of socio-economic classes, as of people's allegiance to specific 'class ideals', seeing a major theme of the century 1780 to 1880 as the triumph of the middle-class 'entrepreneurial ideal', with its emphasis on thrift, hard work, sobriety, charity and self-help. By implication, the working class ideal was relatively unsuccessful. Perkin was sceptical of Thompson's belief in a major degree of solidarity on the part of the workers and their deep commitment to social conflict during the first half of the nineteenth century. According to Perkin, workers sought a wide range of objectives in the spheres of parliamentary reform, trade unionism and co-operative ventures. And they employed varying methods in their attempts to achieve such aims, ranging from peaceful petitioning to quasi-revolutionary outbursts. Although willing to concede the existence of a working class, Perkin emphasized how 'the divisions of the working class between urban and rural, skilled and unskilled, "aristocracy of labour" and common or garden workers, were proverbial right down the nineteenth century' (Perkin 1969: 231, 236).

Despite the obvious differences, there are some similarities between the views of Perkin and Thompson. Both see the formation of the working class taking place at some point early in the industrialization process, being most visible in urban areas, without being composed primarily of factory workers. Both depict the working class exhibiting class consciousness and conflict orientation. Critics of Perkin, like those of Thompson, doubt the existence of really widespread class consciousness and the extent to which the 'working-class ideal' really was shared by all, or even most. Some readers regard Perkin's emphasis on competing class ideals as over-abstract and too distanced from the economic infrastructure which they see as the prime determinant of class attitudes (Anon. 1969; Morris 1979: 13–14).

In his *Class Struggle and the Industrial Revolution* (1974), largely a study of the textile town of Oldham between 1790 and 1860, John Foster closely followed Lenin's chronological framework in constructing a historical model of class maturation encompassing distinct stages of social change. The first stage, from the 1770s to 1830, was characterized by trade union or labour consciousness of the kind which Lenin postulated, as workers struggled hard to maintain wage levels. This form of consciousness led to 'the involvement of a large part of the labour force in economic struggle'; to an occupational solidarity under the coercive pressure of the Combination Acts which was 'radically new, specifically illegal and in its practical operation a direct challenge to state power'. It also led to the cementing of 'the relationship between the radicals and industrial action' (Foster 1974: 42–43).

Foster and Thompson broadly agree that, prior to the 1830s, trade unions were widespread, with a high degree of solidarity among different trades. These unions were strongly influenced by radical political ideas, helping to provoke numerous collective outbursts. But the two historians disagree over the significance of these findings. Thompson argued that inter-trade links and oscillation between trade union and political activity, often of course involving the same people, were so pervasive both geographically and chronologically as to demonstrate the existence of a considerable degree of class consciousness by 1832. Foster, however, sees collective activities before the 1830s as merely sporadic – 'festivals of the oppressed' in Lenin's terminology. These infrequent outbreaks relied too much on the leadership and support of a weakly organized body of handloom weavers and lacked sufficently firm ideological foundations to ensure permanence. Radicalism before the 1830s involved no concept of a genuinely alternative economic order, as opposed to residual notions of an 'ill-defined Jacobin republic' (Foster 1974: 141, 147). Whereas Foster regards this as an insufficient basis for mature class consciousness, both Thompson and Perkin see it as an important component of an emergent and distinctive working-class ideology.

Foster's second stage, lasting from the 1830s until about 1848, is characterized by full class consciousness, amounting to revolutionary consciousness. This 'fundamental *intellectual* reorientation' by members of a revolutionary vanguard more ideologically advanced than the bulk of their fellow workers, helped to replace sporadic outbursts by a '*permanent* subordination of all sections of the working population to radical control' and, ultimately, by a '*sustained* rejection of bourgeois forms'.

Foster emphasized the increasingly popular ideal of a co-operative commonwealth, supplanting earlier visions of a republic of small, independent producers. Operating in a town where there was only a skeletal system of authority and law-enforcement, Oldham radicals demonstrated the degree to which a large, non-property-owning population, although lacking parliamentary votes, could influence public policy. By the use of exclusive dealing and other forms of intimidation, they were able to influence electors, to commandeer the vestry and to control the policing of the borough, preventing the implementation of the New Poor Law for thirteen years, as well as securing the return of John Fielden as an ultra-radical MP. Foster particularly focuses on the Short-Time Movement, as a continuous and specifically anti-captialist agitation, contributing significantly to the formation of Oldham's mass revolutionary consciousness, manifest in the major strikes of 1834 and 1842 (Foster 1974: 6–7, 146–7, 232–3).

Foster's highly original but provocative book has had many critics and few defenders, despite general admiration for his skilled use of quantitative analysis. Thompson (1974) regards Foster as:

> a platonist Marxist: the model – of the 'true' or 'correct' formation of class organization, consciousness, strategies and goals – precedes the evidence and the evidence is organized in conformity with it ... aspects of the phenomena which do not conform to the pre-existent Leninist model of class struggle are simply dropped from the record and from Foster's terminology.

D. S. Gadian argues that the tradition of co-operation (or collaboration) among different social groups in Oldham remained strong during the industrial revolution period. This was partly because the scale of industrial units was not as large, and the concentration of ownership not so prominent, as in other cotton towns. In terms of the broad contours of social and economic development, Gadian sees Oldham resembling Birmingham more than Manchester, let alone an embryonic Petrograd; with a high degree of social harmony, less political violence and independent working-class activity than in cotton towns like Ashton and Stalybridge.

From a different angle, Gareth Stedman Jones detects a lack of precision in Foster's use of the concepts of class consciousness and trade union consciousness, and remains unconvinced by the distinction Foster makes between them, as well as by his use of the term 'class consciousness' as a virtual synonym for 'revolutionary class consciousness'. He also points out that Foster's argument for the continuity of revolutionary consciousness in Oldham rests chiefly on the considerable local enthusiasm for Owenite co-operation and general unionism in 1834 and for the 'Lancashire Strike' (Plug Riots) of 1842; in other words, on the same kind of sporadic outbursts which characterize his first stage between 1790 and 1830. While Stedman Jones concedes that the Short-Time Movement was anti-capitalist, he does not accept that it was therefore either socialist or revolutionary (Stedman Jones 1983: 25–75).

Other historians have fastened on Foster's claim that the class consciousness which appeared in Oldham during the 1830s and 1840s failed to persist, and that from the end of the 1840s 'the town moved remarkably quickly towards class collaboration'. This seems the least convincing aspect of Foster's analysis and calls into question the whole of its elaborate structure. According to Eric Evans, 'by 1850 revolutionary consciousness was dissipated and, it might be added, the interpretation has moved from the merely unconvincing to the downright mechanistically fanciful: an extreme example of the attempt to fit evidence into a pre-ordained theoretical framework' (Evans 1983: 172). If class consciousness in Oldham evaporated so quickly after 1850, can it ever have amounted to very much? And was opposition to capitalism during the 1830s and 1840s really as intense as Foster claims?

Another significant criticism of Foster's study of Oldham is its failure to be set within any national context. For example, Oldham's experience is not compared with that of neighbouring south Lancashire cotton towns, although he suggests in passing that a 'parallel consciousness existed in other industrial towns', pointing to places like Stockport, Ashton, Rochdale, Bury and Bolton as places with a similar economic experience to that of Oldham. Robert Glen's recent study of Stockport from the 1780s to 1827 challenges Foster's analysis of Oldham as in no way typical, while also rejecting Thompson's views on the making of the English working class, although of course both Foster and Thompson identify the crucial breakthrough to working-class consciousness as occurring after 1830 rather than before 1827.

Stockport was the birthplace of the first effective power-loom and witnessed the early demise of handloom weaving as the town soon became dominated by factory-based industry. By the early nineteenth century, there existed both a prominent and increasingly assertive manufacturing elite and a new industrial proletariat. According to Glen, Stockport provided 'precisely the sort of industrial setting in which a "mature" working class might be expected to emerge'. But he is at pains to refute those historians who, following Engels in his *Condition of the Working Class in England* (1845), argue that class consciousness and class conflict took strong root in the cotton districts. The industrial revolution in Stockport, as Glen sees it, evoked only a limited increase in class feeling and class conflict and 'there is nothing to suggest that anything approaching a majority of the workers in the Stockport district embraced radical views'. The fact that only about 1 per cent of the population of the district belonged to a Jacobin organization during the early 1800s belied the existence of a revolutionary tradition in Stockport. Workers' solidarity was severely circumscribed by a multiplicity of trade organizations, themselves typically concerned with narrow sectional issues. Only a minority of Stockport workers embraced radical political views.

In pointing to the considerable difference which existed between trades, between workers in small and large factories, and between radical groups, Glen lends support to those anti-Marxist historians like McCord and Musson who emphasize the divided rather than the united nature of the early nineteenth-century working population. He depicts the pre-1820 Stockport working class as diverse and relatively incoherent. Even when violent or confrontational tactics were adopted, they aimed at limited sectional goals rather than at overturning the social and economic system. Only a very few radicals, mainly downtrodden handloom weavers seeking inter-trade links and adopting radical politics as a means of compensating for their industrial vulnerability, possessed the kind of conflict mentality which amounted to 'revolutionary consciousness'. At the same time, argues Glen, the solidarity of the middle and upper classes, as well as their hostility towards the workers, has been much exaggerated, not least by Thompson. On the contrary, paternalistic employers did much to defuse potential class confrontation (Glen 1984: 137, 177–80).

Glen's emphasis on the sectarianism, divisions, continuity and modest aims of the Stockport workers is cast in terms of a direct, if rather parochial, challenge to Thompson's thesis that 'In the years between 1780 and 1832 most English working people came to feel an identity of interests as between themselves and as against their rulers and employers' (Thompson 1968 edn: 12). It is not in fact a particularly serious challenge. In the first place, he concentrates on skilled artisans and handloom weavers, largely ignoring not only the vast mass of cotton operatives, but also the declining skilled trades like shoemaking and tailoring whose members were so prominent in radical movements throughout the country as a response to threats to their skill, security and independent status.

Again, Glen's challenge to Foster and Thompson is largely vitiated by ending his study in 1827 and failing to examine the vital years 1829–34 which played such a crucial role in accelerating the class consciousness that was to reach its climax in the Chartist movement, nowhere more so than in the Stockport district. While Thompson certainly claimed that class consciousness existed by 1830, he freely acknowledged that it was only after that date that there matured a more clearly-defined class consciousness 'in the customary Marxist sense'. And, as Kirk has perceptively pointed out, Glen tilts at something of an Aunt Sally, for Thompson has never denied the sectionalism and divisions among the working class or claimed that working-class consciousness must be based on such an abstraction as a total unity of experience. On the contrary, he depicted Chartism as the coming together of working-class groups and organizations which retained their differing outlooks, before taking their separate ways again in the new situation after 1848 (Thompson 1968 edn: 937: Kirk 1986).

A further critique of the view that a class-conscious labouring class existed during the industrial revolution has been put forward by Craig

Calhoun, who, writing from a sociological standpoint, rejects Marxist interpretations, including those of Foster and Thompson. He argues that:

> the populations which were able to mobilize for radical collective action in early nineteenth century England were those socially knit together in local communities or craft groupings. Associations at this level provided the major social foundation for protest. Whatever their ideologies, at no point before Chartism, and only haltingly then, were popular and working class political movements able to work effectively at a national level, or, indeed, at any level very much above the local (Calhoun 1982: 180).

According to Calhoun, radicalism before 1830 was firmly rooted in traditional communities, based on either a locality or a craft, whose members sought to defend their traditional status and values against erosion. Radicalism thrived in small and relatively homogeneous towns and industrial villages, or among communities of urban artisans linked by their craft and workplace and anxious to avoid being pushed down into the ranks of the unskilled proletariat.

Calhoun argues that no united working class, imbued with a common consciousness, appeared on a national scale, given the deep divisions existing among the workers, especially that between artisans and workers in domestic industry on the one hand, and factory workers on the other. Not only was the factory workforce, especially in Lancashire cotton, increasingly female and juvenile, but large urban workplaces were less conducive to the collective mobilization of workers than the small factories and groups of workers in the domestic industry villages, which provided the hard core of Luddism and post-1815 radicalism. Factory workers, with their relatively assured future, were reformist rather than revolutionary, realistically demanding improvements within the burgeoning capitalist system rather than seeking its rejection.

The increasing dominance of the factory in the textile districts – the very heartland of industrial revolution popular radicalism – was arguably a major factor in the decline of insurrectionary radicalism after 1840 and the increasing appeal of reformist Liberalism to working-class activists. Marx erred when he argued that class must eventually supersede all other collectivities of workers, for 'class relations have not, in any advanced capitalist society, been universalized to the point where workers identify primarily with their class, and seek the rational goods of that class' (Calhoun 1982: 229). Workers since the industrial revolution have sought other, less radical, ends than the revolutionary transcedence of capitalism.

It is helpful to bear in mind that occupation and community were much more closely interwoven during the industrial period than in more recent times. Calhoun is right to stress the local bases of social and industrial protest during the early years of the nineteenth century and how such communities, like the Sheffield cutlers, often mobilized in defence of traditional or 'customary' rights. However, he can be criticized for suggesting community as a populist concept more important than class before about 1830. For community and class could certainly co-exist. Many occupational communities, including Sheffield, were also class communities, composed of workers who shared the common experience of selling their labour power to capitalists outside the community. Much early trade unionism was community-based, but it often involved action against masters who did not live within the community. As Dr Rule argues, such action can therefore legitimately be viewed as part of the struggle of labour against capital on a class basis.

If men were motivated by their sense of belonging to a community, as many clearly were, then their actions were often at the same time determined by the shared experience and solidarity of a specific occupation and its place in a shifting pattern of relations of production. Moreover, there is a good deal of evidence (see Ch. 2 below) of at least latent class conflict in eighteenth-century labour disputes and of disputes which spread beyond the local and the communal. Hence Calhoun's chosen date of 1830 for the breakdown of localism and the displacement in many areas of populism by class seems too late. In any case, class and community seem all too often to have been two sides of much the same coin for any clear distinction, let alone opposition, to be made between them (Rule 1986: 158–9).

In a seminal essay published in 1960, Asa Briggs pointed out that the singular term 'working class' appeared soon after the Napoleonic Wars and suggested that the appearance of the term reflected the emergence of the class (Briggs 1960: 43–73). Yet for most of the nineteenth century the plural form 'working classes' was employed at least as frequently as the singular. According to Henry Pelling, 'it would be a mistake, however, to speak of a homogeneous "working class" in Britain at any time before the later nineteenth century. Contemporaries did not use the expression, at any rate in its singular form' (Pelling 1963: 13–14). Marx himself varied his terminology, often referring to the 'working classes' and 'ruling classes' (Giddens 1981:327). In his attack on Foster's version of Oldham radicalism, Musson, as with his critique of Thompson's interpretation, emphasized the sectionalism of occupational groups and argued that the activity of Oldham radicals was essentially a product of trade union and craft preoccupation with wages and hours, rather than with revolutionary politics (Musson 1976; Musson 1972: 29–48).

While nobody has suggested that the working class consisted of one body of workers all exhibiting the same characteristics, many historians have been more impressed by the sectional vitality of working-class institutions than by any integrated consciousness or sense of alienation. Status consciousness was more highly developed, it has been asserted, than class consciousness, while class antagonism tended to be both short-lived and highly-localized (Evans 1983: 173). But it has been shrewdly pointed out that the whole point of class feeling is that it cuts across sectional feeling and united people despite the differences between them. R. J. Morris reminds us that no definition of class consciousness and class relationships could be provided which would satisfy historians like Musson, McCord and Evans:

> Class is a summary of countless day-to-day experiences, not all of which involve the expression of aggressive sentiments of identity and conflict. The people of Nottinghamshire did not all go around smashing machines, but they saw to it that the boys who did were not caught. Trades union leaders were not averse to joining in a petition with the small manufacturer or sitting on a platform with a helpful Anglican parson, but this did not necessarily stop them stoning blacklegs in a strike or sharpening pikes when all else failed (Morris 1979: 45–6).

Historians have suggested ways of distinguishing between different sections of the working class, both sociologically and geographically. R. S. Neale sees two main working-class groups: one comprising industrial workers, both factory and domestic, who were collectivist and non-deferential in their attitudes; the other consisting of agricultural and various low-paid labourers, domestic servants and female workers, all deferential and dependent in their attitudes towards authority. Derek Fraser claims that a contrast may be drawn between the larger metropolitan city of an industrial area and the smaller staple towns with a narrower economic base and therefore a more homogeneous social structure. Class conflict and class consciousness might well have been more evident in places where employment prospects were restricted by a lack of variegated local industry and where market forces were likely in consequence to affect uniformly a large proportion of the town's workforce. By contrast, class tensions would be less marked in cities with a multiplicity of industries, where depression in one trade might be compensated by prosperity in another, and where the social structure was more elaborately graded. 'On this argument class relationships would be more strained in Halifax than in Leeds, in Walsall than in Birmingham and in Stockport than in Manchester' (Neale 1972: 30; Fraser 1979a: 35).

It is difficult to arrive at firm conclusions concerning the existence of a unified working class, or of widespread working-class consciousness during the first half of the nineteenth century. Even in places where both were clearly manifest, as in the South Wales coalfield or the Bradford–Halifax area of the West Riding of Yorkshire worsted industry, links were always maintained with the radical section of the Nonconformist middle classes (Soffer 1965). Kinship, neighbourhood and workplace relationships frequently produced a labour consciousness akin to class consciousness. Yet occupational divisions within the working class remained as striking as any degree of social homogeneity. Engineers' labourers, for example, regarded themselves as superior to bricklayers' labourers, who in turn looked down on general labourers.

Permanent general labourers regarded themselves as a cut above casual general labourers, while the latter shared the general contempt for Irish and female workers. Such social gradations permeated all ranks of the working class, although evidence for major divisions within the working class is more common after 1850 than before.

Moreover, the early Victorian working class was fragmented in that it embraced a traditional elite of skilled artisans not yet in competition with machinery, a new 'aristocracy' of skilled industrial labour, a semi-skilled and unskilled factory proletariat and a 'residuum' of depressed outworkers being squeezed by mechanization, not to mention a mass of deferential domestic servants and itinerant casual labourers, regarded by working-class radical activists with not a little embarrassment. The sheer extent of occupational fragmentation – there were at least ninety different occupations in the Lancashire textile industry during the 1840s for example – is itself sufficient to prompt scepticism about Thompson's assertion that the working class was 'made' by 1832. The term 'working classes' no doubt better reflects the social structure of early Victorian England, with its pluralist class divisions (Hunt 1981: 247–9).

It appears, then, as though the emergence of a working-class consciousness sufficiently endemic to generate a major revolutionary threat was considerably inhibited by occupational and geographical fragmentation. Few cultural links could have existed between, say, the skilled ironworker regularly employed and earning £4 a week by 1850 and the unskilled, casual, migrant London dockworker (Evans 1983: 169). But the sharing of a common experience is a necessary condition for the existence of class consciousness. Working men were just as keenly aware of gradations in status as they were of their solidarity as a class, alienated from the controllers of capital. After all, much trade union activity was devoted to preserving, and even enlarging, differentials of status and income within the working classes. Such a variety of experiences and lifestyles, it has been claimed, proved a major obstacle to the appearance of general, unified, working-class consciousness.

Furthermore, it remains doubtful whether the social perceptions of the working classes were predicated on the inevitable conflict between capital and labour essential for proletarian revolution. Many working-class militants saw the basic conflict as being one between an urban–industrial and a rural landed elite, even in Foster's Oldham (Gadian 1978). Workers should unite to throw off the parasitical burdens imposed by the landed aristocracy and gentry. For many contemporaries, the class war meant not so much the struggle between capital and labour, as the more traditional one developed by eighteenth century radicals and endorsed by the Ricardian theory of rent. This was a conflict between the industrial classes and the landed classes; between industrial producers and idle consumers; between urban enterprise and rural landed estates, notwithstanding the close involvement of the landed aristocracy and gentry in transport, mining, banking and urban development.

This traditional conflict, with its assumption of a common urban interest, was undermined to a considerable extent by economic depression, trade union agitation, Owenism, the Factory Movement, resistance to the New Poor Law and Chartism. Nevertheless, working-class support for the Anti-Corn Law League after 1842, the exaltation of Peel to the status of a popular hero after 1846 and a degree of reconciliation between working-class and middle-class radical movements after 1850, all suggest that the idea of such a common interest revived after the antagonisms and splits of the 1830s and remained both viable and influential (Fraser 1979a: 38).

WORKING-CLASS RADICALISM

It is the argument of this book that, although organizations of labouring men to secure higher wages or better conditions existed long before the industrial revolution, there began in the 1790s a tradition of working-class radicalism which was partly inspired by the outbreak of the French Revolution, while drawing at the same time on an English radical tradition dating back to the seventeenth century. This popular radical tradition increased in strength and appeal, though not at an even rate, during the first half of the nineteenth century. In an important sense, the study of this tradition is the study of the prehistory of the Chartist movement, when the world's first national labour movement appeared in Britain. Furthermore, this popular radical tradition was based on growing class consciousness, even if it were confined to specific sectors of the total workforce. Much of this radicalism was directly concerned with trade issues and the defence of livelihoods against the forces making for proletarianization; but there was at the same time a growing tide of popular opinion aimed at procuring a more democratic constitution and a state machine less firmly in the grasp of property-owning elites. It was a movement which governments between 1793 and 1820, and again in 1829–32 and 1838–48, saw as constituting a revolutionary threat which placed established institutions and the social order in jeopardy. In the event, the revolution which Marx confidently predicted failed to take place, but there were a number of occasions when the much-vaunted essential stability of English society looked distinctly shaky.

Despite the views of those historians who have been more impressed by the diversity of working-class occupations than by any uniformity deriving from a common status as wage-earners, the argument of Edward Thompson that by 1832 widespread class consciousness was beginning to appear has been able to withstand considerable criticism. It was not only the speeches and writings of working-class leaders which recognized the significance of a new working-class presence, but also the opinions (and manifest fears) of many higher in the social scale. Although contemporaries in both the middle and the working classes recognized the diverse and heterogeneous nature of the working class, they did not go so far as to deny its existence. Similarly, the fact that working- and middle-class radicals were often able to combine in a common cause, such as mounting pressure for a Reform Bill after 1829 or for the repeal of the 'taxes on knowledge' in the 1830s and 1840s, did not preclude that the two movements possessed some distinct aims and tactics. When working-class radicalism reached its climax in the first phase of Chartism in 1839–40, accompanied by a considerable amount of arming and drilling, middle-class radicals either kept their heads well down or restricted themselves within the narrow confines of the Anti-Corn Law League.

But Chartism was not only the world's first independent labour movement, it was also, despite the presence of a number of leaders of superior social status, a class-based movement. That revolution on working-class terms, peaceful or otherwise, did not come about, was not so much because of the fact that working-class radicalism was never able to attract the majority of the working population – after all, revolutions are made by minorities – but because of the inherent stability of the British state and the skill of governments in applying a subtle blend of concession and coercion.

If Edward Thompson and some of his supporters have exaggerated the extent of revolutionary class consciousness in the troubled years before 1848, that is not to say that it did not exist and received at least tacit support from considerable numbers of working people. Too much time, energy and hard cash were devoted by the propertied middle classes after 1848 to defusing working-class consciousness and popular radical politics for them to have been part of a historical myth created by Marxist historians. After 1848 working-class consciousness was admittedly more subdued, as distinct working-class radicalism seemed almost to disappear. But, it will be argued, both the consciousness and the radicalism were still present, if rather more subtle in both approach and tactics; only seriously being weakened in the years between the 1867 Reform Act and the socialist revival of the 1890s.

The aim of this book is to offer what must inevitably be a personal and selective assessment of the nature and strength of working-class radicalism between 1780 and 1880, as well as to offer a guide to the fierce controversies which have taken place on the structure, if not the very existence, of the working class in this period. Why popular radicalism was important, as well as the extent of its achievements, remain important historical questions which continue to promote a great deal of historical research and writing. It is hoped that the following chapters provide some helpful answers.

Chapter 2

ORIGINS 1770–89

During the year 1792 the influence of the French Revolution on English politics intensified, as Paineite radicalism spread across the country and popular Reform societies proliferated in the provinces. Historians of working-class radicalism agree on the significance of this year as 'the *annus mirabilis* of the English popular movement' (Goodwin 1979: 171). According to Gwyn Williams, it was in 1792 'that "the people" entered politics', demanding universal suffrage and annual parliaments, ready, if need be, to act alone without either aristocratic Whig or Dissenting middle-class support. Edward Thompson sees the formation of the London Corresponding Society in January 1792, with its rule that 'the number of our Members be unlimited', as 'one of the hinges upon which history turns. It signified the end of any notion of exclusiveness, of politics as the preserve of any hereditary elite or property group'. By December 1792 up to 2,000 artisans had become active members of Reform societies in London, Derby, Sheffield, Manchester and Norwich (Williams 1968: 4; Thompson 1968 edn: 24; Harvey 1978: 79).

If it was only in 1792 that genuinely independent working-class radicalism became possible, popular participation in politics to some degree existed throughout the eighteenth century. Early Hanoverian England was ostensibly more democratic than early Victorian England, with a considerable number of working men able to vote at parliamentary elections. On the other hand, it was only during the 1760s that the landed elite faced a determined challenge to their political dominance for the first time since the mid-seventeenth century. The re-birth of popular radicalism during the early years of the reign of George III, largely among skilled workers who were often small property-owners, was largely focussed on the metropolis, relied on a lead being taken by those higher up the social scale and tended to exclude the unpropertied masses. It needed nearly thirty years of radical agitation over various issues, especially the political debates prompted by the American War of Independence, before a distinctive working-class radical tradition could emerge and take root in the provinces as well as in London. This chapter is concerned with the background and context which made such an emergence possible.

THE FREEBORN ENGLISHMAN

While those radical artisans who rushed to join the Reform societies in 1792 were clearly inspired by events across the English Channel, as well as being provoked by rapid inflation at home, they were also able to draw upon a vigorous native tradition of resistance to ruling oligarchies by 'the freeborn Englishman' (Cunningham 1981: 10–11). What have been termed 'the peculiarities of the English' went back a long way. Certainly in the eyes of Continental observers, eighteenth-century England appeared a very peculiar country indeed, with a pattern of development quite different from that of any other nation. There was clearly something very unusual about a country where, within a decade in the 1640s, successful war had been waged against the king; abolition of the House of Lords and the bench of bishops had been carried through; and Charles I – the Lord's anointed – decapitated in the name of his people. Englishmen's determined championship of their Protestant mixed constitution, of their rights and liberties as well as their property, much impressed foreigners.

During a visit to England in 1729, Montesquieu wrote to a friend: 'I am here in a country which hardly resembles the rest of Europe. . . . This nation is passionately fond of liberty . . . every individual is independent.' Englishmen's freedoms, including trial by jury, were guaranteed under English law. The Revolution settlement of 1688 had confirmed parliamentary government, *habeas corpus* and religious toleration, as well as property rights. Statutory censorship of books and the press lapsed in 1695. Parliamentary reporting in the newspapers dated from the 1730s, while attempts to extend standing armies, erect military barracks, or centralize police forces and tax-collection, invariably aroused fierce opposition (Porter 1982: 271–2).

ECONOMIC AND SOCIAL STRUCTURE

England's distinctive political tradition was partly a consequence of her unique social and economic development. While some historians have seen the development of capitalism as a result of the seventeenth-century revolution, it has been argued that the disintegration of English feudalism and the origins of capitalism date back at least to the thirteenth century (Macfarlane 1978: 163). It has already been noted that by 1700 mining and manufacture already occupied between a quarter and a half of the adult population, with about half the working population being wage labourers. The occupational structure of eighteenth-century England was therefore more industrial than was formerly assumed, with industrial growth occurring throughout the century and nor merely during the last quarter (Berg 1985: 29, 316). In a society which had long been more highly developed and widely monetized than its Continental neighbours, income per head in the second half of the century was higher than anywhere else in Europe, despite cruelly long working hours in conditions that were frequently horrific and dangerous, as well as the frequent incidence of industrial disputes, which often spilled over into 'collective bargaining by riot', as trade societies sought to maintain wage levels, rules of apprenticeship and control of the supply of skilled labour (Rule 1981: Ch. 6; Dobson 1980: 19–37; Crouzet 1982: 5).

Rapid population growth, much of it in urban centres like Birmingham, Leeds, Liverpool, Manchester and Bristol, was sustained by major economic expansion in agriculture, industry and commerce. Although rapid urban growth was more a nineteenth than a eighteenth century phenomenon, the fact remains that in 1600 just under 10 per cent of the English population lived in towns of over 2,500 inhabitants: by 1801 this had risen to slightly over 30 per cent at a time when there were fifteen provincial towns of over 20,000 population (P. Clark 1985: 13; Rule 1986: 16–17). Economic growth did not, of course, always prove beneficial to wage-earners. The expansion of the eighteenth-century textile and metal industries, for example, depended as we have seen on the recruitment of large quantities of cheap female and child labour.

Crucial for the development of political radicalism was the fact that such changes nurtured the growth of an increasingly acquisitive middle class, whose members, amounting to about a million out of a population of 7 million in 1760, became sufficiently wealthy and educated to demand increased social status and political influence. This demand became more acute as the economic policies of the landed elite shifted the burden of taxation from the great landowners to those who produced, sold or purchased many items of popular consumption, such as beer, leather, candles and soap (Dickinson 1985: 1–2). At the same time, government policies could result in wars which severely dislocated trade, or in legislative restrictions on the activities of traders and manufacturers. Discontent with the influence and policies of the aristocratic elite was not confined to the urban 'middling orders', but included many small shopkeepers and tradesmen, skilled craftsmen and artisans. Even the labouring poor, often hard-pressed by declining wages or rising prices, could express deep hostility towards the landed classes, as well as towards their employers.

THE ROOTS OF POPULAR UNREST

Growing discontent was partly sustained by the spread of a libertarian political ideology which harked back at least to the mid-seventeenth century. Many working-class radicals in the 1790s, lacking accurate knowledge of recent history, frequently appealed to the bogus historical myth of 'the Norman Yoke': that English liberties and forms of constitutional government had been of Anglo-Saxon origin, nurtured by Alfred the Great before being repressed by William the Conquerer and his evil barons (Hill 1958: 50–122). Other reformers, invoking the doctrines of Milton, Harrington and Locke, harboured a widespread, and rather more accurate, belief that the fundamental rights and liberties of Englishmen had been destroyed much more recently, when Walpole's imposition of single-party rule after 1714 involved the gradual strangulation of the electorate by the executive and the avoidance of parliamentary contests.

Seventeenth-century England had been more democratic than the Augustan age. During the reign of the early Stuarts, the electorate was substantially enlarged in both boroughs and counties, so that by 1640 there existed something akin to a political nation, admittedly still partially controlled and manipulated, but no longer merely co-extensive with the will of the gentry. The electorate, it has been estimated, consisted of between 27 and 40 per cent of adult males. Even 'men of the meanest sort', especially small farmers and craftsmen, became actively involved in political affairs (Hirst 1975: 105; Manning 1976: 137, 184). Between 1653 and 1660 there were more parliamentary elections than during the previous thirty years, as genuine consultation took place between parliament and substantial numbers of ordinary people. During the Putney debates of 1647, the Levellers advocated votes for all adult males, except servants, apprentices and beggars; terms which caused Cromwell and Ireton to wince with horror.

Continued growth of political consciousness could not be checked during the reigns of Charles II and James II, both deeply suspicious of parliament. After the Glorious Revolution of 1688, essentially a political compromise, politics became dominated by the rage of party, as most boroughs of any size, plus many villages (in Suffolk, for example), became divided on Whig versus Tory party lines, with a considerable proportion of floating voters, less influenced by their social superiors than many of them were to become in Hanoverian England. At the accession of George I, perhaps 5.5 per cent of the total population possessed the parliamentary franchise, compared with 2.6 per cent in the years immediately prior to the 1832 Reform Act and 4.7 per cent immediately after. In other words, England in 1715 was more democratic than it was to be again until well into the reign of Queen Victoria. Not that contemporaries aspired to modern notions of democracy, given high turnover at elections, the lack of contests and the fact that many who possessed the vote failed to exercise it (Plumb 1969, 1967; Speck 1977: 16; Clark 1985: 15–22).

During the first half of the eighteenth century it proved difficult for the radical tradition to develop and flourish, even though there was a degree of popular involvement in politics, especially in London when the 'mob' supported Jacobitism in 1715 and demonstrated over Jenkin's Ear in 1739. In Queen Anne's reign, England had been ruled by two rival elites grouped into the Whig and Tory parties, elites which under the reign of the first two Georges were to coalesce into a ruling class, as faction weakened party and fragmented the political nation in the constituencies, themselves increasingly in the grip of oligarchic control. Hence politics became more exclusive. While the population increased by 18 per cent between 1715 and 1754, the electorate grew by only 8 per cent, and that mainly in the county constituencies, as election costs rose and contests became less frequent.

WILKES AND LIBERTY

Although before 1760 there were always dissidents from elite politics ready to make opportunistic forays on behalf of popular grievances like the excise and indirect taxes, it was only with the political crisis of the first decades of the reign of George III, culminating in the loss of the American colonies, that the social and economic grievances of the 'middling classes' provided the impetus for a serious challenge to the dominance of the landed elite and for substantial reform of the political structure (Colley 1981). Indeed, it was widely believed that the King himself was at the centre of a sinister plot to increase the power of the Crown and thereby subvert the balance of the constitution.

Initial opposition to the Court and Cabinet of George III focussed on the City of London and originated in the crisis over the Middlesex elections of 1769–70 (Sutherland 1959). The City, with its surrounding metropolitan area, formed the greatest concentration of urban population in the country, amounting to about half a million people and constituting the home of one person in every ten and the workplace of one adult in every six at some time in their lives. Serious economic dislocation and industrial unrest, reaching a peak in the late 1760s, was channelled through the City's ancient corporate institutions of municipal self-government, sufficiently privileged and independent to be capable of effective political intervention.

Within the City, political predominance was exercised by the 12–15,000 freemen. These 'men of the middling sort' possessed incomes of between £50 and £400 a year and included lesser merchants, tradesmen and master craftsmen. Relative economic self-sufficiency enabled them to act independently of the 'monied interest' of powerful City financiers. While political leaders in the City entered into an alliance with aristocratic opposition groups in parliament, Alderman William Beckford, City MP and Lord Mayor, resorted increasingly to a petitioning movement and extra-parliamentary pressure in order to obtain the redress of grievances and a more representative House of Commons, a tactic that was to persist until 1848. Such 'pressure from without' soon came to include the London 'mob', whose members tended in fact to be wage-earners, artisans, lesser craftsmen and apprentices, rather than criminals, vagrants, or the very poor (Rudé 1962: 15).

This metropolitan radicalism was inherited and exploited by the mercurial rake John Wilkes when he was excluded from the House of Commons in 1768 and then campaigned to retake his seat, to get rid of general warrants and to secure the reporting of parliamentary debates. Political discontent in the metropolis was fanned by the high price of corn and unprecedentedly numerous industrial disputes. Hence the cry of 'Wilkes and Liberty!' attracted not only the allegiance of opposition groups in the City, but also that of large numbers of the metropolitan unenfranchised: small property-owners as well as Spitalfields silk weavers, East End coal-heavers and Wapping sawyers. Admittedly the London 'mob' was extremely volatile, with groups like the merchant seamen and London journeymen vociferously protesting their loyalty to the Crown and attacking the Wilkite crowds (Dobson 1980: 83, 122).

Neither the rebirth of popular radicalism nor the Wilkite phenomenon would have been possible without a flourishing provincial press and a thriving indigenous political culture, enabling thousands of literate and semi-literate men and women to identify with, and become absorbed in, events outside their own immediate experience (Colley 1981; Dickinson 1976). Total sales of newspapers were as high as 12.5 million by 1775. Four daily and five or six tri-weekly papers circulated in London by 1760, while the 25 provincial papers of 1735 rose to 35 in 1760 and 50 in 1782, at a time when about 60 per cent of married couples in many regions could sign their names on the marriage register and about 75 per cent of the middle classes were literate (Stone 1969). The *York Chronicle*, for example, had a circulation of 2,000 in the 1770s, with a readership of about 12,000. The impact of an expanding press was assisted by the mass of political and satirical prints which thrived from the beginning of the reign of George III (Porter 1986).

It was not merely a matter of the press. As early as 1740 London had 550 coffee houses, besides clubs and debating groups of all varieties, each subscribing to the political press and helping to disseminate political ideas and mould political opinion. There was a similar pattern of political and other clubs in major provincial cities. In Birmingham such clubs ranged from the elite Lunar Society to the country gentlemen's clubs and the tavern fraternities of artisans and small tradesmen. As in the capital, so in Birmingham the expansion of printing, publishing and libraries helped to generate a more widely diffused political awareness and to promote the political articulacy of the common people. The small masters and artisans of Birmingham were able to make their voices heard at the 1774 general election: 'Even if they had no voting rights in their own region, it is clear that they were neither indifferent to politics nor lacking the sort of organization which reflected their interest' (Money 1977: 109; Money 1971).

The lead in the creation of the Wilkite movement was taken by the growing commercial middle classes, in an agitation independent of traditional client relationships and patrician patronage. The dinners, the feasts, the production of Wilkite ceramics, handkerchiefs, buttons, cuff rings, snuff boxes and twenty-six different coins and medals marked the commercialization of politics, for 'the opening up of politics and of enterprise went in tandem' (Brewer 1982). A flood of pamphlets, newspapers, political cartoons and handbills destroyed the view of politics as the preserve of the parliamentary classes. Edmund Burke's *Thoughts on the Cause of the Present Discontents* (1770) sold 3,250 copies, but was perhaps read by 100,000 – that is, one person in every thirty-five. The Wilkes affair of 1763–4 provided a focal point for hitherto amorphous groups of radicals in both the metropolis and the provinces, a function later served by conflicts over the American colonies and parliamentary reform. With his style, wit, charm and sheer effrontery, Wilkes was a godsend to the radical movement. Although an indifferent speaker, he was a publicist of unusual skill, who carefully cultivated the press in associating his own person with the abstract cause of liberty and in portraying political power as emanating from the people. In a remarkably successful opportunistic attempt to identify his cause with that of the ordinary citizen, a good deal of Wilkes's message was shrewdly tailored to the tastes of the common people, in chap-books as well as bawdy handbills (Brewer 1976: 164–79).

The bulk of support for the Wilkite reform and petitioning movement came from London, but its adherents were by no means confined to the capital. There were 55,000 signatures on the Wilkite petitions in 1769. When he was released from King's Bench Prison, illuminated windows, fireworks, wax tapers and processions were seen throughout England; for example in Derby, Birmingham, Newcastle, Leeds, Hull, Durham, Hexham, Bradford, Tadcaster, Chester, Wakefield and Halifax. After 1760 public opinion increasingly mattered in politics; parliamentary politicians could no longer be inoculated against the people. If, in both London and the provinces, the Wilkite movement was organized and led by merchants, manufacturers and other members of the 'middling orders', then the crowds which demonstrated and rioted in defence of Wilkes – for example on St. George's Fields on 10 May 1768 when six were shot – were largely composed of wage-earners: apprentices, weavers, domestic servants and labourers.

It is true that these volatile plebeian ranks as yet lacked a common ideology; nevertheless they derived enormous vicarious pleasure from teasing and goading the high and mighty as they made Wilkes the centre of the elaborate ritual and pageantry of the London crowd, according him symbolic status as a quasi-monarch, a lord of misrule. Wilkes therefore left an indelible mark on British politics, especially when his supporters developed a nationwide political network for organizing petitions to parliament, thus creating the machinery to facilitate the expression of extra-parliamentary opinion (Christie 1982: 63).

THE EARLY PARLIAMENTARY REFORM MOVEMENT

Between 1776 and 1783, the years of the American War, radical publicists began to concentrate on the issue of parliamentary representation, a concentration which can largely be attributed to ideological contamination from the American debate over British attempts to tax the thirteen colonies, which included the explosive slogan 'No taxation without representation' (Bonwick 1977: Ch. 1; Beloff 1949: 39–40). Americans like James Otis argued that English representation ought to be reformed and seats given to Manchester, Birmingham and Sheffield. The Society of the Supporters of the Bill of Rights, founded in 1769 as an offshoot of the Wilkes agitation, had strong American connexions, which led it to demand a taxpayer franchise. The American War of Independence therefore generated fierce criticism of the British government, as the colonists' demands encouraged British radicals to question the nature of their own representation at Westminster.

Some of the more extreme radicals went so far as to commit themselves to universal male suffrage, employing the same arguments, based on natural justice and natural rights, which the American colonists had borrowed from prominent British radical Dissenters like Richard Price and Joseph Priestley. In 1776 Major John Cartwright published *Take Your Choice*, in which he advocated universal manhood suffrage, the secret ballot, annual parliaments, equal single-member constituencies, payment of MPs and abolition of the property qualification for sitting in the House of Commons. Such a programme appealed only to the most extreme metropolitan radicals, though it was to be taken up by the working-class Reform societies in the 1790s and later re-emerged as the six points of the Charter in 1838. Most radicals in the 1770s, however, were more cautious, equating citizenship with economic independence. To enfranchise the economically-dependent was seen as self-defeating, since such men would merely cast their votes at the behest of their masters and superiors.

At the end of 1779, however, a new Reform movement appeared as a result of Britain's indifferent performance in the American war, of suspicion of financial waste and war-profiteering, of resentment at heavy taxation and fear of an over-mighty executive undermining the balance of the constitution (Goodwin 1979: 56–66). Unlike the Wilkes agitation, the 'Association Movement' had provincial origins, being led by a Yorkshire squire, the Rev. Christopher Wyvill, himself eager to eliminate financial waste, reduce Crown expenditure and safeguard the independence of parliament by the creation of a hundred additional county representatives and the holding of triennial rather than septennial general elections (Christie 1962: 70–4). The device of county meetings and petitions, pioneered by Wyvill's Yorkshire Association of freeholders, landed gentry, Anglican clergy and Dissenting ministers, was imitated in Middlesex, Westminster, Surrey and the City of London, with substantial support in the provinces. Nearly forty counties had petitioned parliament for 'economical reform', meaning reductions in placemen, pensioners and government expenditure, by April 1780. The Westminster sub-committee, in the hands of extreme radicals much influenced by American pamphleteers, like Major Cartwright and Dr John Jebb, adopted the programme outlined in *Take Your Choice*, before founding the Society for Constitutional Information (SCI), which within three years had published 88,000 copies of thirty-three radical pamphlets and recruited members from twenty-seven towns outside London (Royle and Walvin 1982: 30).

In the event, the Association Movement soon lost impetus as internal quarrels developed and parliament rejected the petitions. The Reformers were then brought into disrepute by the Gordon Riots of June 1780, whose death toll of 300 made them the most serious civil commotion since the Monmouth Rebellion. It was the Gordon Riots which implanted a deep dread of popular demonstrations among the governing elite, while frightening many lukewarm Reformers into silence (Rudé 1956). Between 1783 and the outbreak of the French Revolution, the weakened Reform cause was upheld by the SCI and the London Revolution Society, composed of Dissenters who had championed the American colonists and who now campaigned for the repeal of the Test and Corporation Acts (Goodwin 1979: Ch. 3).

One must, however, be wary of too ready an acceptance of the radical critique of the electoral system in the half-century before 1832, a critique endorsed by the Whig historiography of the Victorian age. Recent research casts some doubt on the view that 'elections were determined by a small minority of voters – the educated and politically alert class of landed proprietors, with a sprinkling from the upper fringes of various professional groups' (Christie 1958: 155). Not only did the rate of contested elections in borough seats begin to recover from 1761, but between 1780 and 1831 there were no less than thirteen general elections. The electorate itself appears to have increased from 282,000 to somewhere between 410,000 and 450,000 during the same period, almost in line with population increase.

While in the last analysis the Hanoverian oligarchy was able to control the electoral system and preserve the dominance of the landed elite, it none the less met considerable resistance. The 'pool' of electors was always wider than the numbers voting at a particular election, given the high rate of turnover and replacement, perhaps amounting to over a million individuals by the early nineteenth century, roughly equivalent to 30 per cent of adult males in England and Wales. Moreover, the unreformed electorate contained a significant proportion of voters from the middling and lower orders. O'Gorman (1986) estimates that elite groups – landlords, gentry, big tenant-farmers and freeholders – accounted for about 14 per cent of the electorate, with retailers 20 per cent and semi-skilled or unskilled workers about 14 per cent.

Nor was the unreformed electorate as passive and deferential as it has often been portrayed. Fickle and demanding voters had to be persuaded and the power of patrons, outside a few score nomination boroughs, was far from absolute. Not only was there a high level of communal involvement at contested elections, but, after the American War, hitherto dominant local concerns had political, constitutional and religious issues superimposed on them. Elections, argues O'Gorman, were as much a matter of negotiation, principally between the landed elite and the middling orders, as they were a matter of domination and manipulation from above in any direct manner.

Although more of the common people formed part of the political nation in the late eighteenth century than was once realized, it has also been persuasively argued that the more determined radicals and Rational Dissenters who endorsed Cartwright's programme of reform were less democratic than might appear to modern eyes (Dickinson 1977: 228–30). Many of them would have been well satisfied with a householder or ratepayer franchise which would exclude large numbers of wage-earners, and hardly anticipated the labouring classes taking any active political role apart from petitioning and casting votes. All the Reform groups, even the SCI, were dominated by middle-class men of property and education. In their desire to increase the political influence of urban commercial interests and the 'middling orders' *vis-à-vis* the great landowners: 'they did not envisage a political society in which the poor would actually wield power'. Labouring men were assumed to be naturally deferent to those of superior fortune and education, and therefore unlikely to take part in the process of political decision-making or themselves seek election to the House of Commons.

If the radicals sought to make the Commons more representative, then they had no wish to erode the special privileges of the monarchy or the House of Lords. Neither did they envisage any substantial redistribution of wealth. Their emphasis on lower taxation and cheap government precluded discussion of legislative schemes to increase poor relief or lessen social and economic inequality and injustice. Private property rights were still sacrosanct. The fact remains, however, that radical opinion from at least 1780 had endorsed the principle of the sovereignty of the people, transforming the nature of political argument and involving many more people in both political debate and political organization. In the general election of 1784, for example, Dissenters and radical Reformers played an active role shaping public opinion and imposing electoral pledges on candidates, thus helping to erode traditional electoral 'independency' (Kelly 1972). The fact that many artisans and craftsmen played an active role in eighteenth-century elections and radical campaigns, and were certainly less deferent than many contemporaries cared to admit, does not mean that distinct working-class radicalism was more than embryonic. It needed the impact of the French Revolution to permit the common people to move from the wings towards the centre of the political stage and to create a genuinely popular democratic movement.

ECONOMIC CHANGE AND LIVING STANDARDS

The outbreak of the French Revolution took place at a time when Britain was subject to dynamic flux and rapid change as it became the first nation in history to undergo the process of industrialization. By the standards of the eighteenth century, Britain was already a heavily urbanized country, about 15 per cent of her population being town-dwellers in 1750 and 25 per cent by 1801, with two-fifths of workers employed in manufacturing and ancillary occupations (Evans 1983: 101). In the Black Country, for example, the balance between agriculture and industry became so upset that by the 1780s no more than a sixth of the population earned their living on the land. Rapid economic development undermined traditional patterns of life for many people in both town and countryside.

If the accelerating process of enclosures in agriculture brought economic opportunities for many farmers, it adversely affected most squatters and poorer commoners, whilst substantial numbers of formerly independent cultivators were thrown into direct dependence on wage earning. In southern England and East Anglia the proletarianization of farm labour was well in progress as early as 1750 and its momentum quickened, leading to extensive pauperization after 1790 (Chambers and Mingay 1966: 86–99; Turner 1984: 64–76; Wells 1979). Although the situation and living standards of agricultural workers varied enormously from area to area, ranging from the comfortable to the horrific, as the century drew towards its close many people in the countryside became a burden on the poor rates, not least because of over-population in rural areas. Hence there was to exist considerable tension in agrarian England at times of dearth and crisis, although never so intense as in Ireland or parts of Continental Europe (Mingay 1963: 167–72; Wells 1983: 3–5).

Burgeoning industrial enterprise acted as the locomotive of social and economic change during the eighteenth century. New methods in textile, iron and pottery production created more wealth, but even before 1800 began to pose the threat of technological redundancy in traditional cottage industries. Economic growth was itself constantly and profoundly affected by the impact of war during the twenty years after 1792. The loss of French and Dutch markets severely damaged textiles and consumer hardware, industries which depended heavily on export outlets, with consequent spells of severe unemployment in the Black Country, the East Midlands, East Anglia and the Clyde Valley. Hence commercial depression furnished one of the prime causes of radical anti-war sentiment. Rapid population growth also began to affect food supplies, so that in years of poor harvests supply failed to meet demand in some areas as grain prices soared, fuelling the inflation of the war years.

One consequence was an increase in the incidence of food riots, the classic form of pre-industrial popular direct action throughout eighteenth-century Europe (Geary 1981: 26). These riots could take a number of forms: simple looting expeditions; the prevention of the removal of grain from a district in order to avoid local scarcity and famine prices; the coercion of market dealers and shopkeepers into selling at 'fair' fixed prices; and attacking the property of millers and farmers in order to force them to release allegedly hoarded foodstuffs on to the market and thereby a fall in prices. Such direct action, usually entirely lacking any political motivation, was often successful and treated relatively leniently by magistrates, troops being called in only when a riot got completely out of hand (Stevenson 1979: 91–112; Thompson 1971; Wells 1977; Christie 1984: 150–2; Rule 1986: 348–53).

If the unpropertied wage-earning common people played little more than a peripheral part in politics before the 1790s, they were not slow to take direct action in defence of their interests. Besides food riots, there were frequent eighteenth-century demonstrations against the re-organization of the militia, on behalf of 'Wilkes and Liberty!', against Roman Catholics and Nonconformists, against turnpikes, tariffs and excise officials, against employers and new machinery, and against attempts to arrest smugglers, wreckers and poachers. The only effective weapon against popular disturbances was the creation of efficient police forces, but that was prevented by widespread and characteristically English anti-militarism.

At the same time, it was generally recognized that rioting provided a necessary outlet for the frustrations of those at the bottom of society unable to safeguard their interests by trade combinations and other conventional means. While the authorities had no compunction against using the sword and gallows against rioters and criminals when it was deemed necessary, they were on the whole more moderate and less savage than their counterparts in Ireland and Continental Europe (Hay 1975: 22–3, 43). Ian Christie argues that 'there was a general awareness among the political class that occasional violent demonstrations should not be taken too seriously, that they usually arose over particular material grievances, and that they were not directed against the social system in general' (Christie 1984: 35). Such *sang-froid* was, however, much less common after 1792 and the publication of Paine's *Rights of Man*, which was clearly and vigorously directed against the whole social system within a context of declining deference and potential revolution.

It remains a vexed question how far the expanding economy of the eighteenth century, especially in its later decades, involved increased prosperity for the mass of the working population. Some historians are wary of undue pessimism, pointing to evidence that improvements in agriculture, machinery and transport meant higher wages and living standards for workers in leading sectors of the economy, wages which were often supplemented by women's earnings and joint family income (McCord 1979: 18–19). Even during the Revolutionary and Napoleonic Wars, punctuated by economic crisis, total output continued to rise, with an increasing proportion channelled into home consumption.

On the other hand, statistics have to be treated with caution, if not suspicion. It has been well said that 'there is no field of quantitative history as treacherous as the study of real wages' (Winter 1986: 231). Matters are complicated by the comparative rarity in this period of a straightforward money wage offered in exchange for measured labour time or for piecework. Both wages and prices fluctuated wildly and were subject to considerable regional variation. Hence averages which demonstrate that wages advanced broadly in line with prices are suspect, especially after 1790 when working-class incomes appear to have lagged behind wheat prices in many areas amid conditions of wartime inflation. Certainly there were significant numbers of people whose living standards were reduced by the effects of harvest failure, population pressure and uncertain overseas markets, as well as by technological innovation. Living standards, in the sense of increased consumption per head, grew only slowly prior to the 1820s, given the inability of the economy to achieve high rates of growth of productivity or major changes in the capital–labour ratio. Only by 1850 was it unambiguously evident that output of goods and services had outpaced population growth (Flynn 1974; Lindert and Williamson 1983; Crafts 1985: 104; Rule 1986: 27–43).

EARLY TRADE UNIONISM

Working people were not, however, mere passive victims of economic forces. If the mass of the unskilled were able to defend their economic interests only through 'collective bargaining by riot', this was not true of the skilled operatives. Only recently has it been demonstrated that, if the separation between capital and labour long pre-dated the industrial revolution, so did tension and conflict between them and the development of effective trade unions (Dobson 1980; Rule 1981). Pre-industrial craftsmen, artisans and skilled labourers were able to preserve, or even improve, their living standards and working conditions by their ability to combine in trade unions and friendly societies, intended to accumulate funds for benefit purposes or for the pursuit of labour disputes. C. R. Dobson has located nearly 400 such disputes in the British Isles between 1717 and 1800. Trade societies tended to be small and localized, although there is evidence of regional and even national organization among some trades, woolcombers for example. The number of societies and the frequency of disputes about wages, hours and how many apprentices were permissible increased sharply during the later decades of the century. London shipwrights were only one group of skilled craftsmen able to develop sound organization and effectively defend their trade practices and real incomes (Prothero 1981: 22–50; Rule 1986: 255–65).

Strong union organization among skilled men was not confined to the metropolitan area. In north-east England, for example, Tyneside miners, keelmen, shipwrights and seamen were able to conduct successful collective bargaining for higher wage rates (McCord 1979: 80–4; Foster 1974: 105). Of course, such skilled men comprised only a small minority of the total workforce and numerous disputes in other sectors resulted in victory for the employers and victimization for the men. Nevertheless, the harsh laws against trade combinations were seldom fully applied, if only on grounds of cost and delay. The basic inequality at law between masters and men was narrower in practice than has sometimes been acknowledged (Rule 1981: 172–8). Magistrates did not invariably take the side of employers in labour disputes and were often willing to act as arbitrators and mediators (Dobson 1980: 74–92; Aspinall 1949: 33–4). Indeed, it is possible that the widespread existence of trade combinations among skilled craftsmen and artisans provided something of a safety valve for working-class discontent, thus blunting the edge of revolutionary fervour during the Napoleonic Wars and confining it to a minority of the workforce (Christie 1984: 150).

If it is generally agreed that an independent working-class radical movement dates from 1792, then it is equally clear that its foundations were laid long before the French Revolution. Although the initiative in eighteenth-century radical movements was invariably taken by those higher in the social scale, there was, as has been seen in this chapter, considerable political involvement on the part of the common people. It was not merely a matter of participation in general elections, where wage-earners accounted for a significant minority of the electorate. Political awareness among the 'lower orders' was stimulated by urbanization, by industrialization, and by the proletarianization of large numbers of labouring men, with a consequent growth of antagonism between capital and labour. The increase in literacy among skilled workers, the proliferation of political clubs and tavern fraternities, as well as increased opportunities for popular political participation during the early years of the reign of George III all contributed to the spread of libertarian political ideology.

Middle-class metropolitan opposition to the Crown in the 1760s, combined with economic distress and popular unrest in the capital, brought in its wake a new political consciousness among the mass of craftsmen, artisans and wage-earners, who were further stimulated to political action by the Wilkes affair. While most radicals in the 1760s and 1770s had no desire to see real political power in the hands of working men, the more extreme among them adopted a programme of universal manhood suffrage which was eventually to prove the rallying cry of popular radicalism, based as it was on the potentially explosive principle of the sovereignty of the people.

Until the 1790s, the characteristic form of much working-class protest was direct action and rioting, especially food riots. But the combination of increasing political awareness and the economic pressures which resulted from enclosures, new technology and the increasing separation of labour and capital proved sufficient to lay the foundations for the beginning of a shift from non-political direct action over economic issues to working-class radical political campaigns. Such a shift was to spread over decades and the working-class radical campaigns of the 1790s attracted only a minority of the workforce consisting of the skilled and better-paid artisans, with a leavening from the middle class and maverick radical gentry.

With the outbreak of the French Revolution in 1789, it was once again aristocratic and middle-class Reformers who mounted the initial campaigns for a more democratic, though not a fully democratic, society. But *Take Your Choice* and the Westminster programme of 1780 had let the genie of full democracy out of the bottle for good. By 1792 working-class radicals were ready to make an attempt, though it turned out not to be an entirely successful one, to escape the tutelage of their social superiors. In its 'Address and Resolutions' of 24 May 1792, the London Corresponding Society, usually seen as the first working-class political organization, was sufficiently confident to issue an uncompromising challenge: 'THE NATION IS UNREPRESENTED ... THE PRESENT SYSTEM IS TOTALLY UNCONSTITUTIONAL ... every individual has a right to share in the government of that society of which he is a member.'

Chapter 3

ARTISANS AND JACOBINS
1789–1815

Between 1793 and 1815 English radicalism faced the daunting task of attempting to flourish in a country at war. Although wartime governments were not so vicious and repressive as depicted by the Hammonds in *The Skilled Labourer* (1919), they took the threat of revolution extremely seriously, given that radicals openly adopted the ideology of an enemy who had abolished both the monarchy and the aristocracy. A massive government-inspired campaign of counter-revolutionary and loyalist propaganda, mixed with selective repressive policies, attracted more support from patriotic Englishmen than the radicals were ever able to achieve. It seems likely that more of the poor and unskilled joined loyalist mobs than joined the democratic clubs and societies.

How far a genuine threat of revolution in England actually existed during the war years is a question which has exercised many historians. Despite the heroic efforts of Edward Thompson and his supporters in arguing for the existence of a 'revolutionary underground', particularly after 1797, it does not seem that those attracted to violent and revolutionary tactics were ever anything other than a small and geographically scattered minority. In recent years the received picture of English radicalism in this period has undergone considerable revision. Not only was the renowned London Corresponding Society less proletarian than was once thought, but most radicals, including the 'English Jacobins', were careful to abjure violence and refrain from attacking the monarchy, the House of Lords or the institution of private property. Questions of economic inequality never really gained a place on the radical agenda.

Working-class radicals were overwhelmingly members of artisan elites who made no attempt to recruit the trade societies, let alone the labouring poor. These groups only became involved in the minority network of United Englishmen between 1797 and 1800. After 1800 working-class popular radicalism was seriously weakened by a combination of government repression and propaganda, as well as by an increasing tide of patriotism which was determined to resist Napoleon Bonaparte and viewed radicals with contempt as traitors to their country. During the 1800s the radical tradition was kept alive more by gentry and middle-class Reformers than by artisans and wage-earners. Mass working-class radicalism became possible again only after 1813, when it was clear that Britain and her allies were going to win the war.

THE IMPACT OF THE FRENCH REVOLUTION

The outbreak of the French Revolution in 1789, a time when, according to Wordsworth, 'Reason seemed the most to assert her rights', created an atmosphere of intense political excitement in Britain. Initially, news of the Revolution was generally welcomed, even by many conservatives who were not displeased to see absolute monarchy destroyed, a major competitor crippled and a revolution taking place which at first seemed little more than a Continental version of the Glorious Revolution of 1688. More positively, British radicals saw the French Revolution as offering the unexpected chance to create a Jerusalem below and realize the perfectibility of man (Cobban 1950: 3–4). Richard Price, the veteran Unitarian Reformer, declared:

> I have lived to see the rights of man better understood than ever; and
> nations panting for liberty which seemed to have lost the idea of it ...
> And now methinks I see the ardour for liberty catching and spreading; a
> general amendment beginning in human affairs; the dominion of kings
> changed for the dominion of laws, and the dominion of priests giving way
> to the dominion of reason and conscience.[1]

The campaign for the repeal of the Test and Corporation Acts was re-stimulated by events across the Channel; the Society for Constitutional Information (SCI) came back to life and began to disseminate radical reform propaganda. Some liberal Whig Reformers established the Society of the Friends of the People in April 1792 and campaigned for a moderate measure of parliamentary reform (Goodwin 1979: Chs. 3, 4).

If the French Revolution revived the activities of veteran Reformers like Major Cartwright, Richard Price, Christopher Wyvill and Horne Tooke, and stimulated the existing middle-class Reform societies, it also led to the creation of new radical groups with more ambitious aims, groups whose members included many from lower down the social scale. These admired the efforts of the French Revolutionaries and were not averse to being dubbed the 'British Jacobins'. But in April 1792 France went to war with Austria and Prussia, and with Britain in February 1793. War not only immediately raised the possibility of radicals being seen as traitors, but also involved the dislocation of foreign trade and domestic production, as it created inflation, widespread unemployment and, for many, lower real wages. The necessities of war finance meant a growing tax burden, especially indirect taxation on items of popular consumption. For most of the eighteenth century, the government had appropriated about 20 per cent of its citizens' *per capita* income. But during the French Wars the proportion rose to an extraordinary 36 per cent. Economic distress reached a peak in 1795–6, when harvest failure in 1794 increased food prices to record levels and provoked a plethora of petitions demanding peace (Brewer 1984; Emsley 1979a: 41). Throughout the 1790s economic hardship acted as a major recruiting agent for the radical societies.

POPULAR RADICAL SOCIETIES

The most important of these societies was the London Corresponding Society, founded in January 1792 by a small group led by the shoemaker Thomas Hardy, who became secretary and treasurer. Membership was open to all who paid a penny at each weekly meeting. Although the LCS had been initially established to discuss increasing poverty and high prices, it soon adopted the full radical political programme: manhood suffrage, annual parliaments and redistribution of parliamentary seats from rotten and nomination boroughs to large towns. The influence of the LCS was soon felt, as branches or divisions spread across the metropolis, with at least thirty members in each branch. By May 1792 there were about a hundred members in each division, sending a delegate to a general committee which in turn elected a small executive (Hardy 1832: 13, 102).

The precise size of the membership of the LCS is not easy to ascertain. A total membership of 5,000 was claimed by the Society itself, but this clearly includes occasional attenders. The number of hard-core activists appears to have been about 650 in late 1792 and through 1793, fluctuating considerably in 1794 and early 1795, before rising to a peak of over 1,500 during the autumn of 1795. Total membership may have been as high as 3,000, falling to 1,000 by late 1796, then to 600 in 1797 and to about 400 in 1798 on the eve of its forced dissolution (Thale 1983: xxiii–iv). LCS membership was therefore confined to a very small minority of the London working population, even if large numbers of sympathizers were drawn to its open-air meetings and its programme was widely approved by the London artisans affected by the sharp rise in prices and decline in real wages.

The LCS was not in fact as proletarian as has often been assumed. Admittedly some of the leading activists were tradesmen: Hardy the shoemaker, Francis Place, a tailor and John Binns, a plumber. An analysis of 347 activists reveals that about half were artisans in the London trades, the other half being made up of the 'middling classes': medical men, booksellers, clerks, shopkeepers, printers and attorneys (Thale 1983: xix). Such leading members as Gerrald, Gale Jones, Margarot and Thelwall came from these higher status groups. Artisans and tradesmen therefore played an important role in the central management of the LCS, but never a dominant one, although no doubt they bulked larger among the rank-and-file membership. There is no evidence to suggest, however, that the LCS succeeded in attracting the unskilled labourers or the very poor (Dickinson 1985: 11).

Similar radical societies appeared in the provinces, most notably the Sheffield Society for Constitutional Information, founded by a group of five or six 'Mechanicks' in December 1791 against a background of class antagonism and conflict between artisans in the cutlery trade and their masters. A visitor in July 1791 noted that the Sheffield journeymen 'stuck up all over Sheffield printed Bills with the Words *No King* in large characters. This I suppose is one mode of exerting the *Rights of Man*' (Donnelly and Baxter 1975). By June 1792 there were 2,500 members, including about 600 militant activists, meeting weekly in public houses to discuss radical parliamentary reform and elect delegates to a general executive committee which distributed political literature. The committee also kept in touch with the LCS and SCI in London, besides stimulating the development of radical societies in towns like Leeds, Derby, Nottingham and Stockport.

Although the Sheffield SCI had some leaders from higher social groups, most of the active members were small masters and skilled journeymen in the workshops of the steel industry. Hostility to the war against the French was manifest when between 5,000 and 6,000 met in the open air in February 1794 to pass resolutions in favour of peace abroad and liberty at home. As Gwyn Williams has commented: 'there was a power in Sheffield, an intransigence, a sense of identification with a local community, which were rare' (Goodwin 1979: 159–70; Williams 1968: 59).

In towns like Manchester, Birmingham, Norwich, Derby, Leicester, Nottingham, Leeds, Newcastle, Stockport, Edinburgh, Dundee and Stirling, the radical societies followed the lead either of the old Reform societies or the LCS and Sheffield SCI. They were nearly all composed predominantly of small merchants and masters, professional men, shopkeepers and tradesmen. Only some of them succeeded in attracting urban artisans and other workers. In Manchester there was a society for the middle classes and two others catering for artisans, tradesmen and a few labourers (Handforth 1956).

A Revolution Society founded in Norwich in 1789 by middle-class Dissenters, merchants and professional men encouraged the growth in 1792 of more radical clubs set up by artisans, tradesmen and shopkeepers and containing 2,000 members. By the autumn there were forty separate radical clubs.[2] Members issued a handbill in November 1793:

> Be assured that Liberty and Freedom will at last prevail Tremble O thou Oppressor of the People that reigneth upon the Throne, and ye Ministers of State, weep for ye shall fall, weep oh ye Conductors of this vile and wicked War, ye who grind the Face of the Poor (Jewson 1975: 33, 38, 43).

In some towns, like Birmingham and Leicester, the Reform cause was seriously divided between extreme radicals and moderates reluctant to support manhood suffrage and unable to withstand the onslaught of conservative reaction between 1793 and 1795. And there were major provincial centres like Bristol, Hull, Liverpool, Plymouth and Portsmouth incapable of sustaining even short-lived radical societies. Support for radical parliamentary reform therefore remained uneven, both geographically and socially (Dickinson 1985: 13).

Artisans and British Jacobins in the 1790s adopted the six points of parliamentary reform advocated by the Westminster Association in 1780, although in their addresses, resolutions and petitions they concentrated on manhood suffrage, annual elections and equal constituencies. The right to vote ought not to depend on property qualifications, but rather on the natural rights of man.[3] Less appeal was made to dubious historical precedent. Thomas Paine, in the first volume of his *Rights of Man* (1791), provided the classic popularization of democratic principles in straightforward and uncomplicated language capable of reaching a mass readership. He uncompromisingly rejected the legacy of the past, including the Glorious Revolution of 1688 which he dismissed as sanctifying oligarchy and property, rather than liberty. All men were created equal and possessed the natural rights of life, liberty, property and the pursuit of happiness. Governments should be subject to the sovereign will of the people and a written constitution. Hereditary titles, honours and privileges were iniquitous. Paine, it has been claimed, 'unshackled radicalism from its subaltern role in the unofficial opposition' (Belchem 1981; Fennessey 1963: 168–73).

Even though the new rhetoric of liberty involved an unmistakable note of insubordination, relatively few members of the Jacobin societies were prepared fully to adopt Paineite principles, for any overt assault on monarchy and aristocracy would alienate the propertied elite, most of whom remembered the Gordon Riots, read horrific accounts of the September Massacres of 1792 in Paris and regarded anarchy as having succeeded the abolition of monarchy and aristocracy in France (Butler 1984: 5; Dickinson 1985: 15). While most radicals could see little virtue in hereditary monarchy and aristocracy, it appears unlikely that very many of them wished to see a genuinely democratic government, with unskilled labourers exercising real political influence. The majority of radicals were members of the middle classes or the skilled working classes and tended to assume that men of property and education should govern in the name of the labouring masses. Women, regarded as dependants incapable of independent judgement, were deemed unworthy of the franchise.

The emphasis was on parliamentary reform, rather than on the economic and social programme outlined by Paine in volume two of his *Rights of Man* (1792). Criticism of the legitimacy of private property was generally ruled out as likely to provoke the propertied elite and encourage the poor to attack the property of the middle classes and tradesmen. In any case, many artisans were themselves employers and small property-owners. Most radicals believed that social and economic inequalities were the result of an unjust political system, rather than of the maldistribution of wealth. Distress and misery were produced by excessive taxation, levied to enrich a spendthrift monarchy and aristocracy, as well as to fight ruinous wars. Parliamentary reform, by contrast, would produce a just government which would then get rid of the crippling tax burden by savings on political corruption, aggressive wars and the armed forces. Other measures could then be pushed through a reformed parliament: abolition of tithes, repeal of the game laws, removal of newspaper stamp duty, reform of the law of debtors.

On the whole, radicals were anxious to avoid charges of social and economic levelling, accepting that a degree of economic inequality was natural and inevitable. Even the cutlers and filesmiths of the Sheffield SCI stressed that: 'We are not speaking of that visionary equality of property, the practical assertion of which would desolate the world, and replunge it into the darkest and wildest barbarism' (Dickinson 1977: 255). Paine himself feared social revolution and only advocated a tax on property in order to pay for his programme of child allowances, maternity benefits and marriage grants. William Godwin, in his *Enquiry Concerning Political Justice* (1793), hoped that the rich would voluntarily transfer a portion of their wealth to those in need, while he opposed any violent or even legislative expropriation. Only Thomas Spence went so far as to produce a scheme for the abolition of private landowning: 'the pillar that supports the temple of aristocracy' (Dickinson 1982: 74; Parsinnen 1973a; Knox 1977).

In fact a radical reform of parliament was just about all that the British Jacobins could agree upon in terms of final aims. Few of them were Paineite republicans or adhered to a common package of social and economic reforms. While they agreed on the necessity of appealing to reason and organizing a propaganda campaign to raise the political consciousness of the people and expose the abuses of an unjust political system, there was much less agreement on the tactics to be adopted if substantial parliamentary reform could not be brought about by rational persuasion. Only a minority were ready seriously to contemplate physical violence or armed revolution, even when government repression and loyalist witch-hunts pushed most of the popular reform campaign underground.

All radicals, however, were determined to educate the people in their political rights, while many believed that a propaganda campaign would prove sufficient to achieve substantial political change. The Address of the LCS to the French Legislative Assembly in September 1792 proclaimed: 'Information makes rapid progress among us, curiosity has taken possession of the public mind; the conjoint reign of ignorance and despotism passed away. What is Freedom? What are our rights? Frenchmen, you are already free, and Britons are preparing to become so' (Veitch 1913: 222).

RADICAL PROPAGANDA AND CAMPAIGNING

To further their aims, all radical societies organized meetings for political discussion and helped disseminate printed political propaganda. Members of the forty radical clubs in Norwich, for example, met in cellars to hear readings from Paine's works (Jewson 1975: 38). Like the other major radical societies, the LCS issued broadsheets, pamphlets and addresses, also publishing a couple of magazines. As its name implies, it corresponded regularly with radical groups in both Britain and France. Provincial radicals also issued political propaganda and sometimes published weekly newspapers, like Joseph Gales's *Sheffield Register*, the *Manchester Herald*, the Norwich *Cabinet* and the *Leicester Herald* (Read 1961: 69). None, however, was able to survive the repression of 1793–5.

Some radical theorists and publicists manfully set out to reach a mass audience. John Thelwall, a former lawyer and businessman and disciple of Horne Tooke, embarked on an extensive series of lecture tours. By 1794 he was 'regarded by friend and foe alike as the spokesman for English radicalism', with his lectures, in which he launched bitter attacks on an increasingly repressive government, attracting large crowds (Royle and Walvin 1982: 53). Others relied on cheap printed literature like Daniel Isaac Eaton's *Politics for the People* or Spence's *Pig's Meat*. Of all the political pamphlets issued, none could rival Paine's *Rights of Man*, one of thirty-eight replies to Burke's *Reflections on the Revolution in France*, but one which sold tens of thousands of copies in cheap editions. Paine's unadorned style, clear arguments and radical views had widespread appeal for a mass readership. Godwin's *Political Justice*, on the other hand, with its doctrine that man possessed 'the faculty of being continually made better and receiving perpetual improvement' influenced radical intellectuals, but was too difficult for the less well-educated.[4] Radicals also continued to employ the traditional weapon of petitioning.

Despite all these efforts, the response to Charles Grey's motion for parliamentary reform in 1793 was disappointing. The House of Commons received 36 petitions, 24 of them from Scotland. Sheffield mustered 8,000 signatures, but London only 6,000 and Norwich a mere 3,700. No county petitions were received. As Dickinson comments: 'These certainly indicated that there was a considerable body of people desiring parliamentary reform, but they failed to demonstrate anything like mass support or an irresistible tide in favour of change' (Dickinson 1985: 21). By 1795 there was more impressive support for a nationwide protest against the government's repressive legislation, organized in conjunction with the Foxite Whig opposition in parliament and moderate reforming opinion in the country. The ninety-five petitions presented to parliament, defending free speech and free assembly, contained over 130,000 signatures.

Other radicals urged the calling of a 'National Convention': an 'anti-parliament' representing the true wishes of the sovereign people more fully than the corrupt parliament at Westminster. This proposal had been first put forward by radicals in the 1770s, including Cartwright in *Take Your Choice* and Paine in *Common Sense*, before being reiterated in the early 1790s by Paine and Joseph Gerrald of the LCS, who recalled the alleged Saxon precedent of the 'folk-mote' (Parsinnen 1973b). Proposals that a National Convention meet to draw up a written constitution and challenge the established government, as in America and France, were rejected as too extreme. But there was considerable support for a Convention where the radical societies would be able to unite behind a Reform programme which would then be put before parliament and the people.

REPRESSION

In Edinburgh, the Scots Reformers held a convention of 160 delegates in December 1792, after which Thomas Muir was found guilty of sedition after a travesty of a trial and transported to Botany Bay for reading out an address from the United Irishmen in Dublin. The Convention reassembled on 30 April to plan a larger conference in the autumn to which English delegates were invited, including Margarot and Gerrald from the LCS. It was these English delegates who played the leading role in the Convention's proceedings and alarmed the Scots authorities into closing it down and arresting the leaders. Skirving, Margarot and Gerrald were convicted of sedition before the biased and uncouth Justice Braxfield ('Let's awa' an' hang the buggers'), although they had not advocated violence. Radicals had seriously underestimated the fears which a Convention would provoke among those in authority, for whom the very word had connotations of revolution: from the

Convention parliaments of the 1660s to the Convention currently sitting in Paris. Hence 'Convention' conjured up images of popular revolution: the September massacres, war and a republic of regicides (Goodwin 1979: 284–306).

Despite the fears and alarms among the ruling elite, radical tactics during the 1790s were remarkably restrained. There was no attempt to co-ordinate popular riots in order to mount pressure on the government. Violent revolution was never seriously considered. Neither were trade societies and the labouring poor rallied *en masse* behind the cause of parliamentary reform. Most radical leaders shared a middle-class background, were committed to doctrines of individual liberty and eschewed violent action as likely to provoke a backlash from the propertied classes. Their aim was political equality rather than the improvement of living standards and working conditions for the mass of their fellow countrymen. The idea of harnessing the power of trade unions and employing strike action to achieve political ends did not occur to them. Even though Thelwall, Paine and Godwin acknowledged the crucial role of labour in the creation of wealth, they developed no coherent theory of distribution and failed to see the potential of industrial strikes for wringing concessions from the ruling elite. Strikes in the 1790s were concerned primarily with economic rather than political issues (Dickinson 1985: 22–3; McCord and Brewster 1968).

After the government embarked on a policy of major repression from 1795, the LCS increasingly resorted to mass open-air protest meetings. At Copenhagen Fields on 26 October and 12 November 1795, speakers like Thelwall and Gale Jones spoke in favour of political reform and peace with France, protesting against high food prices and the passing of the Seditious Meetings Act and Treasonable Practices Act. But these meetings, despite government apprehension, were not intended as preliminaries to violent rioting (Goodwin 1979: 391–8). While it is true that political slogans often appeared during food riots, for example at Sheffield in 1795 and more generally in 1800, these were unco-ordinated and sporadic. When it became clear that the government preferred firm repression to conceding reform, most radicals were reduced to near-silence. Only a small minority was prepared to conduct an undergound conspiratorial movement involving serious consideration of violence and even treason.

COUNTER-REVOLUTIONARY PROPAGANDA AND LOYALISM

From the autumn of 1792, the time of the September massacres in Paris and the victories of the Revolutionary armies at Valmy and Jemappes, radicals in Britain faced a veritable flood of counter-revolutionary propaganda (Hole 1983: 55). Skilfully adapted to appeal to a variety of social levels, it attacked Paine's 'levelling' doctrines and poured scorn on French revolutionary principles, while defending the British monarchy, aristocracy, property and tax system. Between September 1792 and January 1793 a mass outpouring of counter-revolutionary tracts, ballads and cartoons was prompted by widespread fear of a radical plot to seize London with French assistance and of assaults on property by 'cunning, low-minded men who had nothing to lose. Actuated by the lust for power and gain, under the mask of Equality'.[5] An idealized, stable, prosperous and contented Britain was contrasted with revolutionary France – racked with civil conflict, hardship for the poor, violence, atheism and turmoil. French revolutionaries were portrayed as the deceitful cannibalistic creatures depicted in Gillray's vicious cartoons.

The second half of the decade was dominated by Hannah More's *Cheap Repository Tracts* which reached a larger audience than Paine's publications. By 1798 nearly 2 million half-penny tracts had been sold, emphasizing man's fallen corrupt nature and the impossibility of human perfection through radical, Paineite or revolutionary schemes. The Reform movement in the 1790s was therefore crushed by an outstandingly successful propaganda campaign, as well as by legal repression. The defence of the existing social and economic order mounted by the opponents of Reform convinced the majority of the English people. Even the provincial press inclined more towards the conservatives than the radicals. Modern research, in demonstrating that the French Revolution was a disaster for the majority who had to live through it, has conferred a degree of retrospective legitimacy on those who refused to be taken in by 'French Liberty' (Forrest 1981).

Conservative ideology in the 1790s possessed 'considerable appeal, endurance and intellectual power' (Dickinson 1985: 26). British radicals and Jacobins were portrayed as dangerous, dissolute, jealous and subversive malcontents, bent on using parliamentary reform as the first step towards the destruction of monarchy, aristocracy, property and all social distinctions, as well as the rule of law and benign British paternalism. Propertied men deserved to be represented in parliament because they contributed disproportionately to the wealth of the nation, while exercising the vote with genuine concern for the welfare of the unpropertied and unrepresented, themselves too ill-educated and volatile to resist the blandishments of self-seeking demagogues. Natural equality was utopian nonsense, given the obvious inequalities in body, mind and application, and could only be imposed by a degree of violence which would inevitably create anarchy. Men of education, property and leisure could alone be entrusted with the delicate art of government. The British constitution was a glorious and near-perfect one, because it was the product of trial and error over centuries, rather than the result of abstract political theories and the absurdities of pure reason (Harvey 1978: 106–14).

These arguments were first put forward by Burke in his *Reflections on the Revolution in France* (1790), which depicted the Revolution as essentially destructive, leading inexorably to bloodshed and anarchy. Radicals wished to impose the same horrors on England. Events in France between 1792 and 1793, including war, terror, the execution of Louis XVI and the creation of a republic, as well as the spread of popular radicalism at home with the same ideology, seemed to confirm Burke's dire prognostications so far as the bulk of the propertied classes and the political nation was concerned. Like Burke himself, many moderate Whigs broke with Fox and the minority still committed to parliamentary reform and lined up behind Pitt's administration (Goodwin 1979: 365–6).

A good deal of anti-radical propaganda was subsidized and distributed by the loyalist associations which spread across the country after 1792, direct successors of the Church and King clubs founded in many areas to resist the Dissenters' campaign for the repeal of the Test and Corporation Acts, a campaign increasingly based on appeals to natural rights. The Church and King movement, though frequently sponsored by Anglican magistrates, was not confined to a social elite, but drew on the fears and prejudices of the middle and lower ranks. This was demonstrated in the Birmingham riots of July 1791, when Dissenters' houses, including that of Joseph Priestley, were destroyed and radicals put to flight, and in the Manchester anti-radical disorders of December 1792. Throughout Lancashire, with its strong Tory tradition, there were over thirty-five violent Church and King disturbances (Rose 1960; Money 1977: 223–38; Booth 1983). The sympathy of the authorities was revealed by the fact that few members of the violent loyalist mobs were brought to justice.

The loyalist associations formed an essential component of a government-inspired nationwide campaign in late 1792 to unite conservative and patriotic opinion against the radicals by means of loyal addresses and the implementation of the May 1792 royal proclamation against seditious writings. In November, John Reeves, a government employee, founded the Association for the Preservation of Liberty and Property against Republicans and Levellers at the Crown and Anchor tavern in London. Within a few months, hundreds of similar associations had been established across the country, actively managed and orchestrated by local bigwigs, but gaining considerable support from men of little or no property whose hatred of the French needed little encouragement and who almost certainly outnumbered those attracted by the radical societies.

The loyalists more than matched the radicals with their own tactics: dinners, processions, addresses and resolutions, correspondence between the various associations and, above all, dissemination of a mass of printed and pictorial propaganda extolling the virtues of the British constitution and condemning the horrors of anarchy in France. The Manchester loyalist association, for example, distributed 10,000 copies of its own address and 6,000 copies of other conservative political pamphlets. In a typical broadside of 1791, John Bull says: 'I never liked anything in my life that came from France – painted faces, fans, fashions, frippery and foppery, all these spoil our persons – and now a cargo of Revolution Froth to poison our minds' (Dozier 1983: 53–69, 76–97; Mitchell 1961; Ginter 1966). Loyalist associations had no hesitation in employing violence and intimidation, as they recruited local thugs and encouraged major riots in industrial Lancashire. They also organized banquets, processions and bonfires for burning effigies of Tom Paine and copies of his works and set up witch-hunts for rooting out radical and pro-French sympathizers. Innkeepers were threatened with the loss of their licences if they permitted radical meetings on their premises.

Moreover, the loyalist associations played a key role in rallying support for the war effort against France, providing extra clothing and supplies for the army in Flanders and encouraging local militias as a defence force against foreign invasion, a force which would also serve as a supplementary police force in the suppression of riots and industrial disorders. Increasingly alarmed by fears of invasion from abroad and subversion at home, the government created the Volunteers in March 1794, often based on existing loyalist organizations and encouraged to raise private funds (Western 1956). These proved forthcoming on an impressive scale, so that by 1803 the Volunteer force was about 450,000 strong. While many of the Volunteer corps were plebeian, with elected officers and committees, aiming at active citizenship and even willing to participate in food riots in some places, there were some Volunteer groups willing to act as a surrogate police force. When invasion failed to materialize, they concentrated on distributing propaganda, preserving internal order and drumming up displays of patriotism and anti-radicalism. In Stockport, for example, Volunteers put down riots in the 1790s and helped suppress the 1808 weavers' strike (Emsley 1979a: 104; Williams 1968: 105; Glen 1984: 51, 57; Colley 1986). It needed extremely committed and determined radicals to withstand such an onslaught.

PITT'S 'REIGN OF TERROR'

However powerful the loyalist movement may have been, the government was unwilling to take any risks and summoned its full executive, legislative and judicial powers to weaken, and if possible destroy, British radicals and Jacobins. Thus was inaugurated 'Pitt's reign of terror'. An elaborate counter-revolutionary organization was created under the auspices of the Home Office, the London police and the Alien Office, besides a small secret service section. Justices of the peace throughout the country supplied the Home Office with information concerning radical activities and 'suspicious persons'. The Post Office tampered extensively with the mails. Customs officials kept a close watch on movement in and out of the ports. Diplomats abroad, especially in Hamburg, reported on the English and Irish radicals active on the Continent, while a host of private individuals, including landlords and employers, clergymen and innkeepers, informed the Home Office about radical activities in their localities. Such information required careful sifting, for Home Office officials were not so naive as to believe everything they were told. Spies and paid informers were extensively employed to infiltrate groups like the LCS and the United Englishmen, especially when genuine conspiracies were hatched in the late 1790s (Wells 1983: 28–43; Emsley 1979b; Harvey 1978: 83–5).

Judicial and legislative powers were employed against radicals by a government conducting a war abroad and convinced that it faced revolutionary conspiracy at home. After the success of the Scots treason trials in 1793–4, Pitt and Dundas decided to move against the English radicals in late 1794. Forty-one men, including Hardy, Horne Tooke and Thelwall, were arrested and charged with high treason. Brilliantly defended by Thomas Erskine before an unpacked jury, Hardy was acquitted to popular rejoicing after the reliability of the government's key witnesses had been undermined and the purely circumstantial prosecution evidence treated with contempt. Twenty days later, a jury took only six minutes to find the insouciant Horne Tooke not guilty. Despite the second rebuff, the government went ahead with the trial of Thelwall. When he too was acquitted, Pitt abandoned the treason trials and had the other prisoners released. Yet the trials dealt a blow to the radical societies from which they never fully recovered. Harsh prison conditions took their toll of the accused, while their families were reduced to penury.

Once released, radicals faced increasing hostility and victimization from those who believed the government's distorted evidence purporting to show that English democrats were English Jacobins, treacherously plotting to betray their country to the evil French. If the administration had little success with trials for treason during the remainder of the decade, action against those charged with publishing seditious libels or uttering seditious words was more effective, despite problems with furnishing satisfactory evidence and convincing juries. Those who could not afford bail were kept in prison for prolonged periods before being released without being brought to trial. At the same time, increasing use was made of special juries.

However, although most of those accused of seditious libel were convicted, Pitt's policy hardly amounted to a reign of terror, especially in the eyes of modern readers recently accustomed to the Prevention of Terrorism Act, packed juries in 'political' cases and the secret activities of the 1,249 Special Branch officers in England and Wales in 1985. During the whole decade of the 1790s there were fewer than 200 convictions (Emsley 1981). Among those who were convicted, however, were leading radicals like Thelwall, Spence, Thomas Walker of Manchester and James Montgomery, editor of the *Sheffield Iris* (and author of 'Angels from the Realms of Glory'). Paine was convicted *in absentia*, while the threat of prosecution drove radical leaders like Joseph Priestley and Joseph Gales into exile.

Repressive legislation followed the presentation of a mass of written and oral evidence, much of it from informers, to House of Commons Committees of Secrecy in 1794 and 1799. In practice, the legislation turned out less effective than anticipated. *Habeas corpus* was only suspended from May 1794 to July 1795 and April 1798 to March 1801, and even then few were imprisoned without trial. The notorious Two Acts of 1795 (the 'Gag Acts') proved less than effective weapons. Under the Treasonable Practices Act of 1795 outspoken criticism of the government could be regarded as treasonable. But the Act, designed to intimidate, was never actually invoked against anyone. The Seditious Meetings Act of the same year gave magistrates power over the holding of public gatherings, but failed to prevent an increasing number of meetings organized by the LCS; while only John Gale Jones was convicted under the provisions of the Act after a meeting in Birmingham (Hone 1982: 17–20). There was only one prosecution under a 1797 Act making it a capital offence to incite mutiny in the armed forces, while the banning of the leading radical societies by law in 1799 was otiose, they being on their last legs by then (Prochaska 1973).

In 1799 and 1800 parliament passed the notorious Combination Acts, making illegal all combinations of workers or trade unions, if followed by industrial action, as conspiracies in restraint of trade. These laws were passed by aristocratic politicians in a spirit of vindictive hostility towards workmen seeking to defend or improve their pay and conditions, partly with the aim of preventing trade unions spreading from well-entrenched skilled artisans to the workforce at large. In fact they were rarely used, since employers preferred to take action against trade unions under common law. The Combination Acts did not make trade combinations any more illegal than they already were under both statute and common law, but were nonetheless much resented by working men as potent symbols of 'class legislation'. An employer resorting to the Combination Laws was likely to lose the goodwill of his employees and fail to get much support from fellow employers and competitors (Glen 1984: 105; Rule 1981: 180–1; Goodwin 1979: 454–6; Christie 1984: 147–8). The Acts appear to have been largely ineffective in restraining the growth of trade unions. In Nottingham and district, for example, a great variety of trade combinations flourished during the twenty-five years of the Acts' existence. Strikes occurred on at least fifteen occasions, but the Combination Laws were invoked against strikers only on five. Clearly, the Combination Acts were often ignored at times when they could have been applied (Thomis 1969: 60).

It remains true, of course, that although the government's repressive legislation was not often invoked, it remained a threat hanging over the heads of radicals and trade unionists, as well as marking a serious infringement of traditional civil liberties. Even if the government refrained from arresting large numbers of radicals, it had no hesitation in prosecuting, harassing and intimidating most of their leaders, thus depriving the radicals of effective leadership as prominent publicists were silenced. At the same time, most of the rank-and-file were themselves intimidated into deserting the Reform movement (Dickinson 1985: 41–2).

Yet the collapse of the popular radical movement in the late 1790s was not simply a matter of repression by the government and local magistrates. Effective conservative propaganda convinced substantial sections of the population that the radicals were subversive traitors. Events in France caused many to cherish the relative stability which existed under the British constitution, whilst war with the French from 1793 aroused deep-seated traditional British patriotism. Chauvinistic songs and stage representations enjoyed a considerable vogue and even George III gained considerable popularity, with celebrations organized in provincial towns on his recovery from illness in 1789 and for the 1809 Jubilee. Not all radicals and Reformers were uncritical observers of the French Revolution (Money 1977: 92; Colley 1984; Glen 1984: 63–64; Cunningham 1982). Except at moments of extreme economic crisis, there was never much prospect of radicals gaining support from the mass of the population in wartime.

A THREAT OF REVOLUTION? UNITED IRISHMEN AND ENGLISHMEN

Although very few radicals ever advocated the violent overthrow of the state, the government remained convinced of the existence of a genuine threat of revolution, presenting further evidence of Committees of Secrecy in 1801 and 1812. The 1801 Committee referred to 'a dangerous and treasonable conspiracy for the subversion of the constitution and the government ... in concert with a foreign enemy'. Much of this evidence is suspect, having been gathered by panicky local magistrates or unreliable spies and informers with a vested interest in exaggerating the extent of revolutionary activity. Historians have found it difficult to interpret the evidence. While revolutionary plots certainly existed, there is the problem of deciding whether they were confined to tiny groups of unstable misfits, or whether they symbolized widespread popular hostility to the social and political order.

Some historians have dismissed any genuine threat of revolution (Veitch 1913; Cannon 1973; Thomis and Holt 1977). Ian Christie, for example, argues that 'despite occasional fears and alarms, there was no danger of revolution in Britain in the 1790s'. A. D. Harvey accepts that there existed revolutionary groups in contact with each other, but claims that they 'reflected not an actual revolutionary underground, but an illusion of one' (Christie 1984: 93; Harvey 1978: 95–6). Other scholars, usually from a left-wing perspective, see revolutionary groups as more widely supported (Baxter and Donnelly 1974; Thompson 1963; Wells 1983). There are also those who accept the existence of a revolutionary movement, but question its degree of popular support (Dinwiddy 1974; Goodwin 1979; Stevenson 1979). Problems of interpreting the evidence regarding what was essentially a secret movement make it unlikely that final agreement will ever be reached.

Although the government wilfully exaggerated the threat of subversion, partly in order to justify its repressive legislation and pacify the propertied elites, domestic conspiracy and foreign undercover activity certainly existed. Rumours of a plot in late 1792 caused the government to call additional troops up to the capital (Emsley 1978). But it was in 1797 that the conspiratorial wing of the English radical movement began seriously to contemplate insurrection and became linked to the United Irishmen and thereby with the French. Intense and widespread loyalism, however, meant that there was really very little chance of French or Irish agents successfully fomenting a major revolution in England. The Irish clerical secret agent William Jackson warned his employers in 1795 that the English 'are not friends of the French Revolution. And if they complain somewhat, it is only because of the economic situation' (Elliot 1983). Ireland seemed a better prospect for a French government eager to stretch Britain's military resources and gain revenge for English assistance to French royalists. The Directory therefore sent five naval expeditions to Ireland between 1796 and 1798 plus untold quantities of arms. Had Hoche made a successful landing in December 1799, with his 15,000 experienced troops, then England would probably have been obliged to make peace with France in order to contain the threat from across the Irish Channel.

In Ireland itself, however, no united and coherent revolutionary movement existed. The United Irishmen were plagued by internal dissension, sectarian divisions and lack of mass support. The 1798 rebellion, put down with fearsome savagery, was not one prompted or controlled by the United Irishmen, but rather a spontaneous rising of Catholics against the violence of the Orange order, after which the cause of the United Irishmen rapidly waned. Emmet's attempted rising in 1803 was little more than a fiasco (Elliott 1982: 163–4).

In 1796 the United Irishmen had established an undercover organization in London as well as in Paris, in the hope of stirring revolution in England, or at least of pinning down forces which might otherwise be sent to Ireland. They attracted considerable numbers of sympathizers in England, especially in Lancashire, as well as in central Scotland. Many of the 40,000 Irish resident in London gave their support. Two United Irish leaders, Arthur O'Connor and Rev. James O'Coigley, were active in England from early 1797, adding a new note of urgency to English revolutionary activity at a time when militants in England and Scotland were being driven to consider extreme measures in the face of government repression and the severe economic hardship caused by food shortages, dislocation of trade and high taxation (Stevenson 1974: 43–52). An organization of United Englishmen, committed to using force if necessary to achieve manhood suffrage, sprang up in north-west England before spreading to the West Riding of Yorkshire and the East Midlands, though some of them seem to have been as concerned with trade union as with political aims. However, the leaders were soon arrested after evidence was gathered by the government's increasingly professional counter-insurgency agencies (Bythell 1969: 188; Wells 1983: 28–43).

Unlike most of the British Jacobin societies, membership of the United Englishmen included a substantial number of poor labourers, as well as impoverished Irish and English weavers, spinners, tailors and shoemakers. In the capital, militant members of the LCS like John and Benjamin Binns made contact with O'Connor and the United Irishmen, before proceeding to establish between twenty and forty clandestine revolutionary groups and to collect arms in anticipation of simultaneous rebellion in Ireland and England, with French assistance. Relying on an increased flow of information from agents and spies, the government took swift action in 1798 against what proved to be a series of unco-ordinated revolutionary associations whose plans stood little chance of success. Most of the leaders in London, Lancashire and Scotland, including O'Connor, O'Coigley and the whole general committee of the LCS, were arrested. Few could be convicted without revealing the extent of the government's spy network both at home and on the Continent; so in the event only O'Coigley was convicted and executed for treason. The conspiracy was crushed for the time being. There was no simultaneous English insurrection at the time of the 1798 Irish rebellion, even though some revolutionary groups remained in being, holding occasional surreptitious nocturnal meetings (Thompson 1968 edn: 187–94; Harvey 1978: 85–97; Goodwin 1979: 430–50; Hone 1982: 41– 57; Wells 1983: 121–30).

Exceptionally high food prices, general war weariness and economic depression provoked widespread discontent between 1800 and 1802, manifested in riots, arson and petitions demanding the repeal of the 1799 Combination Act. The year 1800 marked the apotheosis of the anonymous threatening letter and handbill (Thompson 1975; Emsley 1979a: 86; Wells 1983: 178–81; Rule 1986: 33). A Somerset handbill urged 'half Starv'd Britons':

> Then raise yr drooping spirits up
> Nor Starve by Pitt's decree
> Fix up the sacred Guillotine
> Proclaim – French Liberty

In Wiltshire in 1802 the highly organized shearmen (croppers), with strong local support, were able by means of strikes, arson, intimidation and destruction of mills to delay the introduction of gig mills and shearing frames until after 1815 (Randall 1982).

It was against such a background of discontent that agents and informers reported renewed meetings and armed drilling by United Irishmen and United Englishmen in Lancashire, the West Riding and London, prompting the government to root out the underground revolutionary groups by a series of swift arrests. Spies discovered that Colonel Despard, an aggrieved Irish officer who had been arrested and subsequently released for conspiracy in 1798, was plotting in London to infiltrate the regular army garrisoned in the capital and then seize the Bank of England, Woolwich Arsenal and the King himself, before summoning the north-west revolutionary cells to insurrection. Plans would only be put into action after a further Irish rebellion and French invasion.

But the government was unwilling to take chances and arrested Despard and his associates before the full extent of the plot was discovered. Although all the ramifications of the conspiracy were never traced, it seems likely that there was substantial provincial support, while the execution of Despard and his colleagues in February 1803 effectively destroyed Anglo-Irish Jacobinism and eroded whatever support there might have existed in England for violent revolution (Elliott 1977; Thompson 1968 edn: 18–28; Hone 1982: 105–13).

Forwarding a handbill to the Home Office, Earl Fitzwilliam, Lord Lieutenant of the West Riding of Yorkshire, wrote in a covering letter: 'loose Conversation, taking its rise in the pressure of the Times, from scarcity & dearness of provisions, & from want of employment, has certainly been holden by the lower Orders of the People, & they talked of revolution, as the remedy for Famine'.[6] There is no doubt that the plots, drillings and nocturnal meetings after 1796 were related to economic disruption and distress, although the exact relationship remains problematic. Political slogans appeared in both food riots and industrial strikes (Emsley 1979a: 85–8). In *The Making of the English Working Class* (1963), Edward Thompson argued that an underground revolutionary tradition existed in Britain for twenty years or so after the suppression of overt agitation in 1796–7, breaking the surface at the time of the naval mutinies in 1797, the disorders of 1799–1801, the 'Black

Lamp' disturbances of 1801–2 and the Luddite disorders of 1811–13. Thompson has gained some support for taking very seriously the threat of insurrection on these occasions (Baxter and Donnelly 1974; Donnelly 1976; Wells 1983).

Other historians have, on the contrary, seen the disturbances as basically economic protests, motivated by distress rather than desire for a popular rising. Only a small minority in Lancashire and Sheffield contemplated revolution (Dinwiddy 1974; Christie 1984: 53; Cannon 1973: 134–43). A considerable degree of apprehension on the part of magistrates and the Home Office suggests that there was a genuine challenge to domestic peace, though insufficiently powerful in England itself to form the basis of a widespread popular rising. It has been questioned whether the relationship between political radicalism and economic disturbances was in fact all that close. Revolutionary radicals appear never to have developed an effective means of capitalizing upon the deprivations of the labouring masses or upon the impressive network of trade societies (Dickinson 1985: 55).

The 1797 mutinies in the British navy – the vital 'wooden walls' of England's defence against France – alarmed the government more than any other threat of subversion during the war years. There seems little doubt that the sailors were chiefly motivated by low pay and the horrific conditions and draconian discipline on board a man-o'-war. Petitions demanding improvement made no impression on the Admiralty. The Channel Fleet at Spithead refused to sail in April 1797 unless grievances were met; the North Sea Fleet at the Nore mutinied the following month. Government concessions swiftly quashed the first mutiny, but the better organized Nore seamen, who set up a central committee under Richard Parker composed of ships' delegates, proved more difficult to deal with. After the government had cunningly offered a programme of limited concessions in order to split further the already-divided mutineers, more rifts among the men led to the surrender of many in June 1797 when the government struck hard, hanging Parker and thirty-five other 'ringleaders' and handing out lesser sentences to hundreds.

Government alarm stemmed not only from England's military vulnerability, but also from suspicion that the seamen had been incited by Jacobin agitators. Although the language of the sailors' protests was often remarkably similar to that of the corresponding societies and popular democrats, Home Office investigators proved unable to establish clear links between the mutineers and revolutionary radicals. Most historians writing in the Whig tradition blamed the mutiny entirely on bad conditions in the Navy and dismissed any political motivation (Lewis 1960: 124–7; Lloyd 1970: 183; Dobrée and Mainwaring 1935: 100–5). By contrast, Thompson sees the naval mutinies as representing a major popular revolutionary crisis, where the mutual grievances of the majority became linked to the revolutionary aspirations of a minority of dedicated political radicals.

In his *Insurrection: the British Experience*, Roger Wells supports Thompson's interpretation, pointing out that at least 15,000 out of the 114,000 in the Royal Navy in 1797 were Irish quota men, many of them being former United Irishmen pressed into service as a means of repression. He demonstrates that cells of United Irishmen existed in the Channel Fleet and sent delegates to incite Irish seamen at the Nore. United Irish leaders were keen to encourage the mutinies and improve the chances of a French invasion of Ireland. French agents were active issuing propaganda to Irish sailors (Wells 1983: 83; Elliott 1983: 46). There is some evidence that representatives of the LCS visited the fleets and attracted support from those shopkeepers, tradesmen and artisans who had enlisted in order to use the financial bounties offered by local authorities to pay off their debts. There seems little doubt, however, that the politically disaffected were a minority among the sailors, most of whom mutinied over pay and conditions, as was demonstrated when support for the mutiny quickly folded after Admiralty concessions on terms of service.

In a similar vein, Thompson claims that the 'Black Lamp' agitation in West Yorkshire in 1801–2 was a mixture of industrial protest and revolutionary conspiracy. But Dinwiddy argues equally forcefully that clandestine nocturnal meetings aimed at improving the living standards of the workers rather than promoting insurrection and that Thompson's evidence for plotting in Sheffield is both thin and suspect. Again, one is driven to conclude that conspirators and United Englishmen were active in Sheffield and in touch with the Despard conspirators in the capital, and that economic protest and demands for political reform cannot be neatly separated. Once again, however, it is clear that the conspirators failed to attract genuine mass support.

If Thompson's underground revolutionary tradition existed, then it remained well underground for at least a decade after the 'Black Lamp' agitation, under the weight of government repression and infiltration by spies and informers. In the meantime, radical agitation was kept alive mainly in the metropolis, despite the disintegration of the reforming section of the Whig party. Veteran Reformers like Wyvill, Cartwright and Horne Tooke again became involved in the cause. But in the provinces only small groups of Reformers in major towns managed to keep active, while it proved impossible to drum up nationwide support for a parliamentary reform campaign. For the obstacles facing reform were considerable, not least the universal excuse of 'national security'. Intense patriotism was consolidated by events on the Continent. Many former enthusiasts for 'French liberty' were led to modify their views when, in line with Burke's gloomy forecast, the French Republic was transformed into an Empire and the real nature of Napoleonic rule in Europe became apparent.

A good deal of radicalism was therefore undermined by the general anxiety to resist the invader. This process was assisted, not only by firm repression on the part of conservative groups who regarded the French Revolution as the unleashing of anarchy culminating in military dictatorship, but also by a flood of patriotic propaganda, including the cartoons of Gillray, himself in receipt of a government pension, depicting 'Little Boney' vainly waving his sabre or attempting to sail his little boat across the Channel against a steadfast John Bull, Jack Tar or 'bold volunteer' (Emsley 1979a: 112–23; Dickinson 1986: 17). Much propaganda was devoted towards convincing the poor that they had as much to lose as anyone else by a French victory or Spencean assaults on property.

An anti-war movement always existed, despite the patriotism of the majority (Cookson 1982). This was partly a matter of principle and partly a result of the burdens of war. New taxes, vast loans and the massive expansion of military recruitment caused much resentment. In 1808, for example, 150,000 supported the peace agitation in Lancashire and Yorkshire alone (Harvey 1978: 334–7; Emsley 1979a: 106–9). War finance lined the pockets of bondholders, contractors, government officials and officers in the armed forces, so that 'the ruling oligarchy and the war establishment formed an unholy alliance at the expense of the middling and lower orders' (Dickinson 1985: 65). A wartime inflation rate of about 3.3 per cent per annum meant that the labour force had a declining share of the nation's increasing prosperity. Even many of the middle classes, especially manufacturers in the Midlands and the North, resented the expansion of the war establishment and the imposition of government regulatory policies. Hence the vigorous and eventually successful campaigns in 1807–8 and 1812 against the Orders in Council prohibiting neutral ships, often carrying British exports, from trading with the enemy (Read 1964: 54– 60).

BURDETT AND METROPOLITAN RADICALISM

Military failures and government corruption led to renewed pressure in the capital for parliamentary reform. In 1807 the rather aloof patrician Sir Francis Burdett, who had condemned Pitt's repressive legislation and exposed the harsh treatment of political prisoners in the Cold Bath Fields prison, was elected for Westminster. Burdett's imprisonment in the Tower of London in 1810 for castigating recent military failures and clashing with the House of Commons over its privileges, was followed by riots in London, plus a rash of petitions from the provinces reminiscent of the days of Wilkes (Hone 1982: 156–61). The campaigns against the Orders in Council and on behalf of Burdett represented a revival of the radicalism which had been largely crushed in 1796–7. These campaigns were orchestrated and led by gentry and middle-class Reformers, but this did not prevent Burdett being supported by demonstrations that were largely plebeian in character.

Although Burdett was flexible on Reform, never regarded universal suffrage as a *sine qua non* and seeing the gentry as the natural leaders of any national campaign, he was a consistent Reformer since the 1790s. Moreover, he attracted working-class support by the way he presented parliamentary reform as a means of reducing taxation, still the chief preoccupation of the lower orders (Dinwiddy 1980). Burdettite radicalism was more significant and widespread than has sometimes been suggested, yet it never amounted to a persistent campaign for parliamentary reform covering the whole country. That only became possible once it was clear that the Napoleonic Empire was certain to be overthrown and the threat to Britain's security removed.

In the meantime, most middle-class radicals remained constrained by fears of revolution and concern for property rights. Besides, there was little agreement on the exact nature of parliamentary reform. There were some who simply aimed at curtailing government patronage; there were those who desired merely a moderate extension of the franchise to taxpayers and small property owners; and there were those who would accept nothing less than the six-point programme of the 1780 Westminster Committee. In parliament itself, moderate Reformers numbered only a couple of dozen or so, while the Opposition Whigs remained lukewarm and the radical movement in the country lacked a firm organizational base outside Burdett's electoral machine at Westminster.

Before the end of the war in 1815 political radicalism was largely a manifestation of the increasing conflict between men of modest property and a governing elite of wealth, rank and influence, with the 'lower orders' in a relatively subordinate role. It was the veteran Reformer Major Cartwright who began to change the situation by insisting that mass support was necessary for a programme of radical Reform based on universal suffrage, and that to confine the movement to Hampden clubs restricted to men of property was a recipe for failure. When leading Reformers in the capital remained unconvinced, he turned to the provinces and working men of little or no property. From 1812 he stumped the country, visiting manufacturing centres like Manchester and Halifax. During the following year he covered 900 miles in twenty-nine days, visiting thirty-four urban committees to promote petitions for annual parliaments and at least a taxpaying householder franchise (Miller 1968; Osborne 1972: 76–103). Cartwright's efforts were to be rewarded after 1815, when economic depression and intense popular discontent created the mass support which he deemed essential.

LUDDISM

The Luddite disturbances of 1811–13, which at their peak coincided with the middle-class agitation against the Orders in Council and the most severe food crisis of the entire war period, are extremely difficult to interpret and have created fierce historical controversy. Historians like the Hammonds (1919), F. O. Darvall (1934) and Malcolm Thomis (1970), plus Robert Glen writing specifically about the Stockport district, argue that Luddism played no part in popular political radicalism, but that the Luddites were engaged in a purely industrial struggle, without being involved in wider political conspiracies to overthrow the government by force. But Thompson (1963) sees Luddism as both an economic agitation motivated by chronic distress and as a 'quasi-revolutionary movement' which verged on political insurrection (Hammonds 1919: 210–74; Darvall 1934: 174; Thomis 1970; Thomis 1969: 77–99; Thomis and Holt 1977: 33–4; Thompson 1968 edn: 569–659; Glen 1984: 166–84; Rule 1986: 366–75).

There is little debate about the economic roots of the Luddite outbreaks in Nottinghamshire, South Lancashire and West Yorkshire. Framework knitters and handloom weavers in Nottingham and Lancashire were subject to low wages, truck payments, high frame or loom rents, unemployment and dilution from cheap, semi-skilled labour turning out inferior work. As the Duke of Newcastle, Lord Lieutenant of Nottinghamshire, wrote concerning the knitters in villages near Mansfield:

> [They are] in much distress at this moment from not being able to get work at their business ... the high price of every thing necessary for their subsistance presses now still heavier upon these poor people as they are out of employ. They certainly are very much to be pitied.[7]

In West Yorkshire, the skilled croppers feared that the spread of the gig mill and shearing frame would reduce them to the status of semi-skilled labourers and weaken their trade organizations. As Rule has put it: 'An element in the great machinery debate of the early nineteenth century, not always stressed as it should be, is the resort to machinery as a means of breaking the hold of unions able to exploit an essential manual skill' (Rule 1986: 279). Attacks on property and machinery in all three regions came only when peaceful demands by means of petitions and workers' associations had been rejected and the government refused to introduce protective legislation. Thomis, who adheres to a somewhat artificial scheme of compartmentalized workers' activity, claims that workers turned to violence as a final desperate attempt to exert pressure on intransigent employers by inflicting substantial financial losses by the destruction of stocking frames which produced the cheap 'cut ups', the wrecking of gig mills, shearing frames and steam looms. The key question is whether Luddism was anything more than a varying compound of hostility to powered machinery with a more complex set of grievances related to changing industrial conditions and pressure on living standards? Did the disturbances merit the 12,000 troops brought in to deal with them?

The collection of arms and their occasional use, as well as the celebrated attack on Cartwright's mill at Rawfolds and the murder of William Horsfall of Marsden in 1812, are viewed by Thomis as the actions of men desperate for the redress of their economic grievances, or the activity of gangs of criminals seizing their opportunity in Luddite areas where law and order had temporarily broken down. Evidence of secret meetings appears dubious, often owing as much to the imagination as to the precise observation of government spies anxious to remain in employment and therefore willing to rely on rumour and hearsay evidence. If there were groups of radicals plotting political revolution, then they were isolated and enjoyed no support from most Luddites or the local population. The Luddite threat, claims Thomis, was to law and order and employers' property, not to the central government and the constitution. Local magistrates, baffled by the opaque nature of Luddite organization, were unnecessarily alarmist. Craig Calhoun, in emphasizing the importance of community as a basis for 'populist' action rather than social class as a basis for revolutionary action, has recently argued that Luddism was essentially local in its manifestation, capable of developing an insurrectionary mode of discourse and action, but unable to generate stable, co-ordinated revolutionary organization (Calhoun 1982: 61).

Edward Thompson, on the contrary, takes the evidence for the existence of political disaffection much more seriously, regarding arms collection and drilling as preparations for insurrection. While he accepts Thomis's view that Nottinghamshire Luddism was an industrial struggle motivated almost entirely by economic grievances, he insists that the revolutionary underground was active in South Lancashire and West Yorkshire, bent on political subversion in the manner of the Despard conspiracy and the Black Lamp agitation, much of it enshrined in local oral tradition recorded by the late Victorian historian, Frank Peel.

After a recent thorough re-examination of the evidence, Dinwiddy concludes that Thompson was right to suggest that industrial protest or sabotage, political reform and revolutionary conspiracy, should not be seen in total isolation from each other as Thomis tends to do (Dinwiddy 1979). Workers frustrated by the failure of industrial action often turned to political action, especially in Lancashire where weavers' petitions for parliamentary reform and peace with France in 1811–12 were rejected, resulting in clandestine activity as a product of frustration. Secret oaths, political committees, arming and nocturnal drilling certainly existed in the Manchester and Bolton areas in 1812. Similar underground political groups were active on the other side of the Pennines, in Leeds, Sheffield, Barnsley, Huddersfield and Halifax.

However, it does not appear that the revolutionary movement was very extensive or that a broadly-based national conspiracy was afoot, or that armed insurrection was other than a long-term aim. But Dinwiddy, who discounts the existence of a 'Black Lamp' subversive agitation in 1801–2, accepts that there existed groups of workers with revolutionary aims in South Lancashire and West Yorkshire, even if such groups lacked considerable numerical support or failed to pose a genuinely serious danger to the ruling elite and the government. There was a political dimension to northern Luddism and the Luddite years marked an important stage 'whereby workmen came to regard democratic control of the state as an essential means to the improvement of their condition'.

It seems reasonable to conclude that, although the redress of economic grievances was not the sole aim of all the Luddites, or the naval mutinies of 1797, or the Black Lamp agitation, Thompson and his supporters tend to exaggerate the scale of the revolutionary underground and the extent of its support in the industrial districts in the early years of the nineteenth century. There are strong grounds for believing that British institutions took the strain of wartime discontent without too much real difficulty and that those institutions were defended by a government which displayed considerable skill and a degree of restraint, in England if not in Ireland. Radicalism was faced with the countervailing force of patriotism and national consciousness. In 1803 the British ruling class was sufficiently confident to distribute firearms among over 200,000 unenfranchised, poverty-stricken civilians in the Volunteer corps and still retain its authority intact (Colley 1986).

Arguably, what is more significant than the existence of a revolutionary underground, linking 1802 to 1812, is the survival of an open and predominantly peaceful tradition of radical reform which contrived to remain within the law, despite the hostility of government and magistrates and of a large proportion of patriotic public opinion for whom the war with France was paramount (Royle and Walvin 1982: 106). In the face of repressive legislation and a tidal wave of conservative propaganda, the radical tradition had been kept alive by men like Cartwright, Francis Place, Henry Hunt and Thomas Attwood. Industrial workers, threatened by increased capitalistic control of the work process, learned from the artisan Jacobins to demand parliamentary reform as a cure for their ills. Once the war was over, the Reform agitation, released from the burden of treachery to the national cause, was able to enter a new phase of vigorous growth in popular radicalism.

NOTES AND REFERENCES

1. Richard Price, *A Discourse on the Love of our Country, delivered on 4 November 1789*, 50–1.
2. Norwich Revolution Society to the London Corresponding Society, 16 October 1792. PRO, TS.11.965.3510.A.
3. *Sheffield Register*, 27 June 1794.
4. William Godwin, *Enquiry Concerning Political Justice*, 3rd edn, 1798, ed. K. Codell Carter, 1971: 58–59.
5. *The Englishman's Catechism*, 1792.
6. Fitzwilliam to Portland, 18 April 1801. PRO, HO 42/61.
7. Duke of Newcastle to Home Office, 26 November 1811. PRO, HO 42/117.

Chapter 4

RADICALS AND REFORMERS 1815–30

During the five years following the end of the Revolutionary and Napoleonic Wars popular radicalism gained the degree of mass support in both London and the industrial districts of the north and Midlands which had been lacking since the turn of the century. Outbursts of mass radical activity in these years, as in the 1790s, alarmed both the government and the propertied classes at a time when middle-class radicals remained quiescent. A new infrastructure of political clubs and a thriving radical press, assisted by widespread economic hardship, produced once again Luddism, riots, mass meetings and plots. Events like the Spa Fields riots, the Pentrich rising, Peterloo and Cato Street have been the subject of considerable controversy among historians and still require interpretation.

However, the extraordinary – and somewhat neglected – Queen Caroline affair of 1820–1 heralded the decline of mass popular radicalism during the 1820s, a decline caused by a combination of the failure of direct action, government repression and relative economic prosperity. Until the beginning of a mass reform agitation in 1829, working-class radicals were pushed back to trade union organization, a rich variety of minority clubs and associations, and, at a theoretical level, the development of a challenging alternative to orthodox political economy.

POST-WAR DISTRESS AND DISCONTENT

The end of the war in 1815 coincided with an upsurge of popular unrest, exacerbated by serious economic difficulties. Markets for British goods slumped in a devastated Europe as competition was renewed from countries freed from the British or Napoleonic blockade. Industries like iron and ship-building, which had expanded to meet wartime needs, now swiftly contracted. In Shropshire, for example, 7,000 ironworkers lost their jobs. Poor rates soared alarmingly. It seems likely that the real earnings of an average working-class family were lower between 1815 and 1819 than they had been in the 1780s (Deane 1965: 247). The 1815 Corn Bill, prohibiting imports of foreign wheat until the domestic price reached eighty shillings a quarter, was passed amid widespread rioting in both London and the provinces (Stevenson 1979: 190–3; Darvall 1934: 151). This was a topic on which middle-class reformers and working-class radicals could agree. The middle classes regarded the Corn Law as a blatant example of the self-interest and political strength of the landed elite, even though landowners bore the brunt of direct taxation. Working-class radicals blamed the Corn Law for the high bread prices which provoked renewed rioting later in the year.

Further outbreaks of Luddism in the East Midlands were accompanied by food riots in manufacturing districts and substantial 'collective bargaining by riot' in East Anglia where crowds, accompanied by horn, fife and drum, protested at high flour and bread prices, demanded higher wages and enhanced levels of poor relief, set fire to property and destroyed the threshing machines which threatened winter employment. Five men went to the gallows. Such economic riots, based on direct and often very destructive action, were in fact on the verge of a progressive decline, the last major food disturbance taking place in Cornwall in 1847 (Thomis 1969: 93–99; Peacock 1965; Stevenson 1974). Luddite machine-breaking flared up again in 1816 in West Yorkshire, Leicestershire and Nottinghamshire. Eventually, however, traditional 'pre-industrial' forms of rioting slowly started to give way to a more thoroughly organized and less immediately violent deployment of labouring strength, exemplified in trade union activity and strike action, aimed at humanizing rather than abolishing the new industrial society (Geary 1981: Ch. 2).

Organized political protest among artisans and workers spread rapidly after the peace, as a result of economic distress, the emergence of industrial centres and small-scale industrial communities with dense and stable social networks, and the diffusion of political awareness among the working classes by means of Hampden Clubs and Union Clubs, as well as the burgeoning radical press. In an anonymous pamphlet, *The State of the Nation*, published by members of the Liverpool government in 1822 a large share of the blame for post-war agitation and violence was blamed on the radical press and 'that general circulation of their cheap and seditious tracts, which were the first movers of the popular turbulence' (Gash 1986: 38). In November 1816 Cobbett issued his *Political Register* as an unfolded two-penny sheet ('The Tu'penny Trash'), avoiding the fourpenny newspaper stamp and achieving a circulation of 40,000–60,000 instead of the 1,000–2,000 when the paper had cost just over a shilling. One contemporary observer suggested that crude circulation figures should be multiplied by thirty to give an accurate indication of the numbers who read each paper printed. This may be an exaggeration, though a factor of ten or so seems reasonable.

Men made remarkable efforts to get at the news. They clubbed together to buy single copies; old newspapers circulated through entire streets; coffee houses and pubs provided papers for their customers. The 'pothouse oracle' read aloud from the newspapers, commenting on what he had read. Access to newspapers could also be gained in Political Reading Societies, reading rooms attached to bookshops, hiring and lending arrangements and by hearing the newspapers read out at large public meetings (Webb 1957–8; Aspinall 1949).

Readers of radical papers like the *Political Register*, Wade's *Gorgon*, Wooler's *Black Dwarf* and *Sherwin's Weekly Political Register* became leaders of radical opinion in their own communities and key figures in the development of the popular radical campaign for parliamentary reform, with its attacks on privilege and 'Old Corruption': the parasitic ruling class of aristocrats, priests, pensioners, placemen, borough-mongers and fundholders, all living off taxes levied on working men. Only a radically reformed parliament would reduce taxation and allow men to climb out of poverty by keeping for themselves the fruits of their labour (Hollis 1973: 3). As Cobbett put it:

> The real strength and all the resources of a country, ever have sprung and ever must spring, from the *labour* of its people ... with what indignation you must hear yourselves called the Populace, the Rabble, the Mob, the Swinish Multitude ... But suppress your indignation, until we return to this, after we have considered the *cause* of your present misery and the measures which have produced that cause ... It is the *enormous amount of taxes*, which the government compel us to pay for the support of its army, its placemen, its pensioners etc., and for the payment of the interest on its debt ...[1]

The common people still tended to regard themselves primarily as consumers, noting how £27 million out of a Budget of £50 million by 1834 was raised mainly by levies on food and drink. It was to take subsequent analysis of the capitalist system by Ricardian socialists and journalists like Bronterre O'Brien to shift the focus from taxation to profits.

The Hampden Clubs which, according to Samuel Bamford, 'were now established in many of our large towns and in the villages and districts around them', were originally stimulated by Cartwright's provincial tours, but soon became self-generating reading and discussion societies for working men. They proved capable of concerted action; for on New Year's Day 1817 delegates from twenty-one Lancashire clubs met at Middleton and organized local petitions for annual parliaments and universal suffrage. A reformed parliament, it was hoped, would reduce the influence of the House of Lords and the Church, as well as repeal the Corn Laws.

A subsequent meeting organized by the London Hampden Club saw Henry Hunt and the Lancashire delegates carry a motion for universal suffrage against those moderates, including Cobbett, who wanted to go no further than household suffrage. At the end of the month petitions containing 50,000 signatures were put before parliament (Bamford 1844: 11–14, 18–22). At this stage the Reform movement was broadly divided into three groups: the parliamentary radicals like Burdett and Cochrane; the constitutional radicals like Cartwright, Cobbett and Hunt; and the mass of popular radicals, including the London artisans and provincial members of the Hampden clubs, who saw Hunt as being most sympathetic to their aims and tactics (Thompson 1968 edn: 668–90).

From the foundation of the London Corresponding Society in 1792 to the final fling of Chartism in 1848, popular radicals always faced the problem of confident governments ready to resist popular pressure, even when ministers themselves faced physical danger. In 1815, for example, the Corn Bill led to Castlereagh being chased through the streets to his London residence, while Robinson's house was besieged. 'There is a great clamour out of doors', wrote Peel, the young Irish Secretary, on 7 March, 'and last night in the neighbourhood of the House of Commons we were indebted to the military for the preservation of peace. Some members were most vehemently hissed and hooted, and some did not make their escape without the loss of half their coats and a little personal injury'.[2]

Yet the disturbances did nothing to deflect the government from its policy of resisting popular pressure and pushing the Corn Bill through parliament. Even when the autumn brought bank failures, unemployment in the London trades, as well as in the port and its industries, because of the loss of wartime contracts, increasing prices as a consequence of a poor harvest, and an escalation of metropolitan destitution as discharged servicemen were turned on the streets, the Liverpool administration kept its nerve. Indeed 'in leaving the meeting of parliament until 1 February, a later date than usual, the Cabinet reflected optimism if not confidence' (Bentley 1984: 34–5). Such ministerial intransigence faced radicals with the dilemma of whether to adopt 'constitutional' or 'revolutionary' tactics; whether to embrace or forswear illegal methods; whether to support 'moral' force or 'physical' force. For many, the dividing line was always to prove a fine one.

SPA FIELDS AND BLANKETEERS

The dilemma had to be faced in 1816. The illegal conspiratorial tradition which had emerged during the war years, surfacing in the Despard conspiracy and the activities of the United Irishmen, resurfaced after 1815 – especially among the disciples of Thomas Spence on the extreme left of London radicalism who believed that the abolition of private property was infinitely preferable to mere parliamentary reform. The Society of Spencean Philanthropists, whose 'divisions' met in various London taverns, supported Henry Hunt as a popular leader and champion of the 'mass platform' against the rival 'constitutional' approach of Burdett and Cobbett. Hunt's rhetoric often appeared to endorse violence, unlike the moral force of Cartwright and Burdett, who relied on public meetings and petitions (Belchem 1978).

In the bitter autumn of 1816 the Spenceans planned a series of mass meetings to petition against distress and for Reform, with Hunt in the chair, though he insisted on no mention of expropriation of the land. Already, it appears, the Spenceans were hatching revolutionary schemes. Hunt dissuaded them from making the occasion of the Spa Fields meeting of 15 November the starting point for a march to Carlton House to petition the Regent. Although most of the crowd took Hunt's advice to disperse peacefully and put their faith in petitioning, a small group marched through Westminster, smashing the windows of foodshops in protest at high prices (Prothero 1981: 90–1).

According to government informers, a section of the Spenceans now began to plan a metropolitan rising, which would include attacks on the Bank of England, the Tower and debtors prisons. Firm evidence that arms were collected, the *tricoleur* flown, together with banners calling on soldiers to join in the rising, caused the government to station troops and police at strategic points during the second Spa Fields meeting on 2 December, when the Spenceans arrived early and persuaded a breakaway group of a hundred or so to follow Arthur Thistlewood and the drunken James Watson junior in a march on the city, plundering gun shops *en route*. Some of the crowd fled after running up against the Lord Mayor and a party of constables at the Royal Exchange; another group was chased towards the East End by dragoons. The section of the crowd which succeeded in reaching the Tower was soon dispersed by cavalry, with subsequent arrests of the leaders and seizures of arms. In fact the riot was less dangerous than it appeared, for although the rioters acquired over 200 muskets and pistols, besides swords, pikes and three cannon, few had any idea how to use the weapons and failed to make a concerted attack on a Tower garrison which had run out of ammunition (Stevenson 1979: 193–6; Parisinnen 1972; Thompson 1968 edn: 691–7).

The full truth about the Spa Fields riots will probably never be known. Hunt later claimed that he had nothing to do with any planned insurrection, though Thistlewood alleged that the rising failed because of Hunt's caution. Even the question of whether the riot was a semi-spontaneous insurrection or a premeditated, well-laid plan admits of no certain answer, given the ambiguity of the evidence. Whichever it was, it provided government committees of secrecy with the opportunity to demand repressive legislation, claiming that 'a traitorous conspiracy has been formed in the metropolis for the purpose of overthrowing, by means of a general insurrection, the established Government, Laws and Constitution of this kingdom, and of effecting a general plunder and division of property'. Radicals in the provinces expected the non-arrival of mail coaches as the sign of a successful rising in the capital. The demands for repressive legislation were strengthened at the opening of parliament on 28 January 1817, when the Prince Regent was hissed and his coach windows broken by stone-throwers. Claiming that a conspiracy existed to subvert the country's institutions, Castlereagh introduced bills suspending *habeas corpus*, renewing sections of the Treason Acts of 1795, making subversion of the armed forces a capital offence, and forbidding 'seditious meetings' (Thompson 1968 edn: 699–701; Cookson 1975: 107–12). Radicals could now be imprisoned without trial, prompting Cobbett to flee to America for two years.

In Lancashire there were groups of weavers who sympathized with extreme London radicalism. Joseph Mitchell, Samuel Bamford and William Benbow established close relations with Hunt and his followers, besides contacting the Spenceans. On his return to Lancashire, Benbow helped to organize a hunger march of Lancashire weavers to London, in order to petition the Prince Regent to relieve their distress. Local magistrates, however saw the initial meeting of 4,000–5,000 weavers in St. Peter's Fields, Manchester, on 10 March as potentially seditious and promptly sent in the cavalry to arrest the ringleaders. About 200 'Blanketeers' were seized at Stockport. Four or five hundred marchers reached Macclesfield in small groups, while fewer than 100 continued to Leek and Ashbourne with their blankets under their arms (Glen 1984: 207; White 1957: 155–7). Spies and *agents provocateurs* were infiltrated into scattered groups of reformers throughout the industrial districts. The discovery of plots to march on Manchester, perhaps stimulated by *agents provocateurs*, was used to justify the arrest of leading Reformers, as the Hampden Clubs were broken up and peaceful agitation for Reform rendered nugatory. Samuel Bamford left an especially graphic account of the effect of repression on Middleton Reform Society (Bamford 1844: 43–5; Thomis and Holt 1977: 40–2).

PENTRICH

No rising took place at Manchester, however. Given the tainted nature of the evidence, it remains unclear how far support ever really existed for such a rising. Instead, Bamford embarked on a provincial tour in the company of W. J. Richards, alias 'Oliver', the notorious government spy whose credentials had been vouched for by Joseph Mitchell, one of the Lancashire weaver delegates at the London Hampden Club in January. Proceedings at delegate meetings at Huddersfield and Wakefield, designed to plan a general rising, were faithfully relayed by 'Oliver' to his paymasters at the Home Office (Royle and Walvin 1982: 115). Actual risings occurred only in the Holme Valley near Huddersfield, and Pentrich near Nottingham, both fiercely Luddite areas in 1812. It was the arrest of ten Yorkshire delegates, betrayed by 'Oliver', at a secret meeting at Thornhill Lees near Dewsbury on 6 June, which panicked hundreds of cloth workers, including many of the croppers formerly involved in Luddism, to launch a premature march on Huddersfield, under the leader who told them: 'Now, my lads, all England is in arms – our liberties are secure – the rich will be poor, and the poor will be rich.' But the insurgents were stopped at Folley Hall, just outside the town, by a small detachment of troops with no loss of life.

On the very same day, Jeremiah Brandreth, who had witnessed Despard's execution, was making final plans at Pentrich for his celebrated fourteen-mile march on Nottingham on 9 June; according to Thompson 'one of the first attempts in history to mount a wholly proletarian insurrection, without any middle-class support' (Thompson 1968 edn: 733). Spies had ensured that the authorities were fully prepared to deal with the two or three hundred desperate stockingers, quarrymen, ironworkers and labourers, armed with a few guns, pikes, scythes and bludgeons. Many of the insurgents had slipped away before Nottingham was reached, despite promises of roast beef, rum and a hundred guineas a man. A small force of hussars put the remaining men to flight before eventually rounding them up.

In June, Edward Baines exposed the methods of 'Oliver' and the spy system in his *Leeds Mercury*, creating general revulsion against the government and a new willingness on the part of middle-class radicals to embrace Reform. This revulsion was, however, unable to save the lives of Brandreth (who had killed a servant when firing through an open window) and two more of the thirty-five men arraigned at Derby in October for high treason before a hand-picked and compliant jury (Thompson 1968 edn: 723–4; White 1957: 162–75; Stevenson 1979: 209–10). Although the Hammonds in their *The Skilled Labourer* (1919) depicted the Pentrich Rising as provoked and instigated by 'Oliver', whose name was carefully kept out of the October trials, modern scholars from both ends of the ideological spectrum are agreed that 'Oliver' may have exploited the rising but did not initiate it. Not all the conspirators were unlettered labourers. Some were skilled and literate men, while others were experienced revolutionaries rather than being the simple dupes of the wily 'Oliver' (Thompson 1968 edn: 731–3; Thomis and Holt 1977: 43–61; Thomis 1974).

PETERLOO

The events of 1817 and anxiety about spies deeply divided the ranks of the Reformers, persuading the majority of radicals to take the constitutional and legal path to Reform, via petitioning and peaceful meetings. In 1817 there were 700 petitions from over 300 towns, and over 1,500 the following year (Fraser 1961). Such tactics were further encouraged by a good harvest and an uplift in the economy later in the year (Hilton 1977: 69). Early in 1818 *habeas corpus* was restored and political prisoners released, as a new campaign for parliamentary reform developed, with political unions founded in Lancashire, Yorkshire, the north-east, the Midlands and the West country.

In London the Spenceans remained committed to revolution, despite the disapproval of 'constitutional' Reformers like Burdett, Cartwright and Francis Place, who were conscious of the damage which the events of 1817 had inflicted on their cause. Yet the Spenceans were convinced that the mass of the people were exploited by a small elite who staffed the political system, as well as being robbed and oppressed by unjust laws and exorbitant taxation. The government was composed not only of plunderers and borough-mongers, but also of traitors to the historic constitution (Belcham 1981-9). The sovereign people therefore had the right to change the political system and resist oppression, ignoring laws emanating from rulers in whose selection they had had no say. There were those who felt that the time for insurrection was ripe, believing that workers in many areas of the country would support a rising, and that the government was seriously weakened by its isolation from public opinion. This isolation, it was argued, was the result of government use of a standing army against peaceful protestors, its employment of spies, its passing of the Corn Bill as a further device for taxing the poor, and its reckless issue of paper money through the Bank of England (Prothero 1981: 91-2).

In September 1817, Watson, Preston and Thistlewood, firm believers in decisive action by a small, resolute group, began planning a rising for October, when a Committee of Public Safety would be established in order to declare the land the property of the people. Thistlewood's scheme in February 1818 to murder Lord Sidmouth, the Home Secretary, and some other ministers, met with opposition from Watson, who now favoured a mass popular movement of 'the industrious classes'. This dispute produced further splits among the Spenceans, some of whom moved closer to Hunt after Thistlewood was imprisoned for a year in May for challenging Sidmouth to a duel. In the meantime Watson's followers gained influence in Lancashire, with the help of Hunt, pressing for the mass-meeting strategy, as at Spa Fields in 1816. Although Thistlewood planned a London insurrection immediately on his release in May 1819, Hunt took the chair at the Smithfield meeting on 14 July and prevented it becoming the launching-point of an insurrection (Prothero 1918: 112–14).

Hunt's close contact with the Spenceans meant that he was playing with fire and aroused deep suspicion among the authorities. When he agreed to address a mass protest meeting of Lancashire Reformers on St Peter's Fields, Manchester, on 9 August, he was threatened with arrest. The manner in which contingents marched to the meeting in disciplined columns also aroused suspicion that it was at the very least designed as a display of the power of the unrepresented, as well as of anger at the Manchester magistrates' use of the Combination Laws (Rule 1986: 274). It was probably Hunt's presence, as well as the spinners' and weavers' strikes of 1818 which had silenced 60,000 looms and led to some disorder, plus the fact that many radicals had indulged in quasi-military drilling, which caused the authorities to regard the Manchester meeting as subversive, rather than peaceful and constitutional. In fact the Manchester meeting was designed as Lancashire's contribution to a whole series of meetings held in the north of England since January, many of which elected 'legislative attorneys' for the unrepresented towns (Parssinen 1973b). The language used by speakers at these meetings often hinted at imminent insurrection. Even so, the Manchester meeting had something of a carnival atmosphere, with many women and children among the 60,000 or so present (Read 1958: 103–5, 128–31).

Like magistrates elsewhere, those in Manchester were over-anxious to employ troops for the maintenance of order despite Home Office discouragement. Twelve days before Peterloo, Henry Hobhouse, Permanent Under-Secretary at the Home Office, informed the Manchester stipendiary magistrate that it would be advisable simply to gather evidence of what took place at the meeting, to ignore illegal proceedings for the time being and avoid the use of force: 'But even if they really should utter sedition, or proceed to the election of a representative, Lord Sidmouth is of opinion that it will be the wisest course to abstain from any endeavour to disperse the mob, unless they should proceed to acts of felony or riot'.[3] Hence the attitude of the Manchester magistrates and the government differed, although both believed that the radicals were bent on eventual revolution.

Surveying the meeting from a nearby house, the magistrates decided, soon after proceedings commenced, to arrest Hunt and the other speakers. Nadin, the deputy constable, warned that 200 special constables were insufficiently powerful to execute the warrants. The yeomanry cavalry therefore advanced through the crowd before panicking and slashing indiscriminately with their sabres. Before his arrest, Hunt – always skilled at keeping on just the right side of the law – urged the crowd not to resist. Regular troops, adept at using the flat of their swords, then moved in to restore order. Eleven people were killed and over 600 injured. This was the notorious 'Peterloo Massacre'. When the government had little alternative but to confer retrospective approval on the conduct of the magistrates, public opinion was outraged. Even the relatively pusillanimous Whigs moved to attack the Liverpool administration. Attempts to defend the magistrates, by portraying them as muddle-headed, apprehensive men; or to insist that the government was eager for a showdown with the radicals, remain equally unconvincing (Walmsley 1969; Thompson 1968 edn: 750–1).

Peterloo did much to shatter the moral authority of the old unreformed order, as it became a sacred day in the radical calendar after enormous press publicity. A series of public protest meetings in various parts of the country was the product of a wave of revulsion, on the part of the Whigs and the middle classes as well as the working-class Reformers. Whole communities were outraged. On 15 November 1819, for example, three months after Peterloo, a procession of 200 Haslingden men marched to Burnley for a radical meeting bearing a flag with the words: 'Thou was covered with anger and persecuted us. Thou has slain us and hast not pitied us. Cursed be their anger, for it was fierce, and their wrath, for it was cruel' (Calhoun 1982: 185).

CATO STREET AND THE SIX ACTS

Widespread anger provided the context in which the Spenceans renewed their plotting, now that the strategy of mass open-air meeting was no longer possible. By December 1819 the Thistlewood group in London had resolved that, like Despard in 1802, they must strike a dramatic blow in order to provide a positive lead for their supporters in the provinces and spark a spontaneous rising. Urged on by an *agent provocateur* in the pay of the Home Office, Thistlewood and a small group of fellow conspirators planned to assassinate members of the Cabinet as they attended a dinner at Lord Harrowby's house in Grosvenor Square on 22 February. Fully informed by their spy of these plans, the government pounced on the eighteen conspirators as they assembled in Cato Street. Thistlewood and four accomplices were executed for high treason on 1 May 1820, when five others were transported (Thompson 1968 edn: 769–79; Prothero 1981: 127–31; Hone 1982: 305–7).

The Cato Street Conspiracy was not quite the wild and isolated gesture it has sometimes been portrayed. Some evidence exists to suggest links between the London Spenceans and those who led disturbances elsewhere later in the year. In Scotland, Reformers had established Union Societies and adopted Peterloo slogans. After a strike in Glasgow, a group of radicals from Stratheven marched on Glasgow on 5 April, dispersing when further support failed to materialize. At the same time, a group of twenty-five men left Glasgow for Stirlingshire, resisting troops at Bonnymuir until finally overwhelmed. On 11 April there was a march of 300 or so men from Barnsley to Grange Moor, which fizzled out when reinforcements proved unforthcoming. Some of those involved had plotted revolution in 1812. Further rumours of a concerted rising, however, came to nothing (Thomis and Holt 1977: 70–84).

As in 1817, insurrectionists found themselves waiting in vain for support which never arrived in sufficient quantity to offer a chance of success. Yet it is clear that revolution appealed to a determined minority. One reason for this was government provocation in the form of the Six Acts, which became law at the beginning of 1820. These gave magistrates extensive powers to restrict public meetings and conduct searches for arms. Unauthorized military training was prohibited (Stevenson 1979: 347). The radical press was circumscribed by the Blasphemous and Seditious Libels Act. All cheap periodical publications were henceforth deemed newspapers and liable for the fourpenny stamp duty in an attempt to place them beyond the pockets of working men.

The year 1820 was the last of post-war 'alarm' and of abortive attempts at revolution, as well as rumours of many more. With their leaders in prison or in exile, their organizations infiltrated by spies, the minority who embraced the 'language of menace' had no immediate future. On the other hand, the Six Acts failed to impede the further development of peaceful protest and forms of extra-parliamentary pressure which the government could hardly regard as treasonable. Spies were powerless in the face of open organization. Moreover, government repression was relatively mild by Continental standards. English rioters were never blown to pieces by cannon fire, while Lord Liverpool, prime minister from 1812, rejected the pleas of many country gentlemen that all discontent be put down by the military, besides flatly refusing to augment the army at home. Neither had Wellington any desire to use the army as a political weapon (Hilton 1977: 81–2).

THE QUEEN CAROLINE AFFAIR

Post-war radicalism reached its climax, not at Peterloo, but in the curious Queen Caroline Affair which, according to John Stevenson, marked the last of the great agitations in the tradition of Wilkes in which 'a largely metropolitan-based movement dominated the political scene' (Stevenson 1977: 204). The attempt by George IV to divorce his estranged wife, Caroline of Brunswick, after he became king on 29 January 1820 offered a golden opportunity for opponents of the government to orchestrate the most sustained and widespread agitation in the capital since the days of 'Wilkes and Liberty!' Caricaturists had a field day, as six to ten satirical pieces appeared each week, compared with the usual three to five (Dickinson 1986: 13). Pamphleteers and pornographers made fat profits. Many joined the campaign as a way of discrediting the administration, but it soon became self-generating, arousing a mighty wave of popular feeling as the attempt to deprive Caroline of her royal title because of her sexual misconduct became a symbol of the attack on English liberties.

From the time of her triumphant arrival in London on 6 June, the 'Queen's cause' provided a focus for radical groups, leading to a temporary alliance between the Whig opposition in parliament and the popular street agitation. Having failed to bribe Caroline into remaining abroad, the government was driven to mount a 'trial' of the new queen before the House of Lords. Caroline had powerful allies, her campaign being managed by Alderman Wood, who had been a key organizer of Burdett's election campaigns and could summon up the resources of City radicalism and the trade societies. Cobbett was her speechwriter, able to bring the radical press to her side. Henry Brougham and Thomas Denman (who had defended the Pentrich rebels) were her Whig legal advisers. During the summer and autumn the capital was much enlivened by numerous colourful parades and processions organized by the queen's supporters.

Addresses and resolutions poured in from all over the country. In Leicester, for example, an Opposition dinner at the Bull Hotel was followed by illuminations and a procession (Patterson 1954: 129). The fact that the king and government had not only been defeated, but also made to look ridiculous, compensated Reformers everywhere for their recent defeats and repression. Bonfires and celebrations took place in several provincial towns. When the government decided to abandon the intended trial and Bill of Pains and Penalties against the queen in October, streets all over London were illuminated.

Yet it proved difficult to keep the affair on the boil. When the Whigs failed to gather sufficient support among the country gentlemen and other independent MPs to topple the administration, divisions appeared among the radicals, while many Whigs themselves began to desert the movement (Mitchell 1967: 143–58). Support for Caroline faded rapidly from January 1821, when she accepted an annual pension of £50,000. Locked out of the king's coronation, she was accompanied by only a 'thin and shabby mob'. Her health broken by this humiliation, the queen died on 6 August. The government hoped to avoid further demonstrations by disposing of her remains as quickly and discreetly as possible. It was resolved to send the cortège to Harwich, for ultimate interment in Brunswick, by a circuitous route north of the City. However, despite the presence of Horse Guards escorting the funeral procession, mobs blocked the route with carts in an attempt to force the cortège through the City. In Hyde Park, the troops were pelted with dirt and stones, later charging the crowd and shooting two men. All alternative routes were barricaded, obliging the procession to go through the City with the Lord Mayor as escort. The troops were dismissed, while the magistrates in charge sought refuge in the Home Office. Although the disturbances were on a relatively minor scale, they nevertheless marked a notable defeat for the government, as the radical press and the London trades arranged an elaborate public funeral for the two men killed, as well as whipping up anti-military resentment (Stevenson 1977; Prothero 1981: 132–55; Hone 1982: 307–18).

The Queen Caroline Affair demonstrated, as the Reform crisis was to do a decade later, that large numbers could only be moved to political activity in a context of general political excitement created by those in much more influential positions than were the radicals. And large numbers were certainly involved. As Hazlitt noted, the Caroline affair 'excited a thoroughly popular feeling. It struck its roots into the heart of the nation; it took possession of every house or cottage in the kingdom' (Stewart 1986: 158). The various manifestations of popular discontent in the post-war years had tended to inhibit middle-class radical reform campaigns. To a considerable degree, working-class radicals had to 'go it alone'. Yet the manner in which Peterloo and the Caroline affair helped to discredit the government and put new heart into the Whig opposition encouraged middle-class groups to speak out in favour of greater representation, especially now that attempts at popular insurrection seemed finally quelled.

THE DECLINE OF MASS RADICALISM

In the event a mass Reform movement could not be sustained during the 1820s, in spite of the continued existence of political unions in various parts of the country. Although considerable economic distress affected substantial sectors of the working population, such as agricultural workers in southern England, Spitalfields silk-weavers and domestic textile-workers in the Midlands and the north facing increased capitalistic control over the work process and the effects of technological innovation, the economy in general began to recover from the distorting effects of a long war. Relative prosperity was much assisted by a succession of good harvests until the end of the decade (Pollard 1981: 21–4; Rostow 1948: 116–17).

The developing boom caused general interest in Reform to wane, a process reflected in parliament. In April 1822 Lord John Russell moved to deprive the 100 smallest boroughs of one member each and to distribute them to the counties and the unenfranchised towns. Although the Whigs were soundly beaten by 269 votes to 164, support for Reform was greater than at any time since Pitt's motion in 1785. In the following year, however, an almost identical motion by Russell suffered a much more resounding defeat, dissuading him from further moves during the next two years (Cannon 1973: 184–5). When, in 1827, he moved that the corrupt seats of Penryn and East Retford be transferred to Manchester and Birmingham, he was again defeated. In the meantime the London Hampden Club had collapsed and Wooler was obliged to close down the *Black Dwarf*.

Organized groups of radicals nevertheless continued in existence, receiving a political education through the radical press at a time when the freedom of the press itself became an urgent political issue, and one for which Richard Carlile spent the years 1819 to 1825 in gaol for blasphemous and seditious libel, having published the works of Paine (O'Boyle 1967–8; Thompson 1968 edn: 791–4). It was men like Carlile whose courage and determination undermined the *ex officio* informations and special juries employed by both the government and by the Constitutional Association and the Society for the Suppression of Vice in their private prosecutions. After 1824 the number of press prosecutions declined and the policy of trying to silence the radical papers solely by the laws of libel was quietly abandoned (Wickwar 1928: 228–38). Carlile himself provided a bridge between freethinkers, republicans and radical political Reformers on the one hand, and the popular millenarian sects which flourished during the post-war years, as well as the various 'Zetetic' educational and mutual improvement societies (Wiener 1983; Royle 1974: 31–8; Harrison 1979: 135–60).

Radicals like Carlile stood very much in the old artisan Jacobin, Paineite tradition, which tended to emphasize abstract individual political rights at the expense of the economic and fiscal grievances of the industrial working class (Belchem 1981: 29–30). Popular radical associations in the 1820s therefore mainly recruited from skilled artisans and small shopkeepers. For working men, anxious to regulate wage rates and working conditions, the trade societies and trade unions possessed broader appeal, although there always existed considerable overlap between political and economic organizations. Trade societies, which provided a system of finding work by means of houses-of-call for tramping artisans, performing a friendly-society function of mutual aid in hard times, had flourished since the early eighteenth century (Dobson 1980: 38–46). The Combination Acts had failed to suppress them, as they sought to maintain or even improve wage levels and preserve the privileges of skilled labour by restricting access to a particular trade through limiting the number of apprentices (Prothero 1981: 51–61; Glen 1984: 68).

After 1815 there occurred a number of attempts to form federations of trade unions in order to strengthen labour's bargaining position, by strike action if need be. John Gast, the political leader of the London shipwrights, organized the short-lived 'Philanthropic Hercules' in 1818 to link the London trade societies. At the same time, the Lancashire cotton spinners established a 'Philanthropic Society' as a general union based on an existing federation of local spinners' unions, launching a strike in a bid to restore wage reductions imposed since 1816. The collapse of this strike was one of the reasons why Lancashire workers moved into political agitation in 1819 (Prothero 1981: 68–70; Kirby and Musson 1975: 14–27). These abortive initiatives were to prove forerunners of the more ambitious attempts at general federations of trade unions in the 1830s and 1840s.

Francis Place, the master tailor who had been prominent in the London Corresponding Society during the 1790s, was led through his rationalism and preference for operating behind the scenes to embrace the utilitarian and orthodox economic views of Bentham and James Mill, although always concerned at the plight of the working man. It was Place more than anyone who engineered the repeal of the Combination Laws in 1824, believing as he did that legal restrictions on journeymen's combinations encouraged secrecy and conspiracy (Wallas 1898: 239). If the Combination Laws had failed to stem the growth of trade unionism, while creating much bitterness and stimulating illegality, then they should be repealed. In 1818 Place and Bentham helped John Wade, a woolcomber, to found the *Gorgon* as a trades paper: 'not only to prove that the situation of the working classes is much worse than it has been, but also to establish the mischievous tendency of low wages'.[4]

Place himself became the key intermediary between trade union leaders and radical politicians in the Commons like Joseph Hume and J. C. Hobhouse. A number of petitions led to the appointment of a parliamentary Committee of Inquiry in 1824, which interviewed a procession of witnesses meticulously drilled by Place. It was persuaded to support Bills introduced by Hume, which not only repealed the Combination Laws of 1799 and 1800, but also removed the common law prohibition on combinations and conspiracies. Place's considerable wire-pulling skills disguised from the majority of MPs the significance of repeal. Yet when a series of strikes followed, parliament was quick to restore the laws against conspiracy, although associations for the regulation of hours and wages remained legal. Despite an ambiguous legal position which persisted until the 1870s, trade unions could henceforth organize and campaign more freely (Prothero 1981: 172–82; Thale 1972: xii–xiv; Thompson 1968 edn: 563–9).

POPULAR POLITICAL ECONOMY AND THE UNSTAMPED PRESS

Other than some outbreaks of Luddism in 1826, there was little popular agitation between 1824 and 1830 (Thomis and Holt 1977: 82–3). It was in these years, however, that there took place intellectual developments which helped to provide a theoretical base for the more widespread working-class radical movements of the 1830s. Carlile's revival of Paineite republicanism in his *Republican* was paralleled by the beginnings of socialist thought and a radical critique of the orthodox political economy of Ricardo, James Mill, Torrens, McCullogh and Senior. Between 1824 and 1827 there appeared a serious alternative political economy with the publication of William Thompson's *Inquiry into the Principles of the Distribution of Wealth most Conducive to Happiness* (1824) and *Labour Rewarded* (1827), Thomas Hodgskin's *Labour Defended Against the Claims of Capital* (1825) and *Popular Political Economy* (1827), and John Gray's *Lecture on Human Happiness* (1825).

What these writers had in common was an attempt to develop a labour theory of value, in order to account for the exploitation of labour by capitalists and middlemen, as well as the persistent economic crises of capitalism (Thompson 1984; Royle and Walvin 1982: 135; Hovell 1918: 41–7). Earlier socialists like Charles Hall and Robert Owen also saw the problems of exploitation in economic and industrial terms, rather than as a question of natural and traditional rights. But Hall, in his *The Effects of Civilization* (1805), recognized only the 'physical evils' of industrialism, chiefly the lack of the basic necessaries of life, while Owen was neither anti-industry nor anti-capitalist, believing that in a rational moral order the interests of workers and employers would be identical. Such an order could be created by education and co-operation (Thompson 1984: 65–81; Dinwiddy 1976; Treble 1971).

The alternative political economy of Thompson, Hodgskin and Gray became widely disseminated in the radical press, whose editors were prepared to devote much space to discussion of the causes of exploitation and poverty, the reasons for poverty in the midst of abundance, the repercussions of mechanization, the consequences of free trade, the origins of glutted markets and redundant labour, and the effectiveness of trade unions in improving the condition of the labouring masses. Cheap unstamped newspapers like *The Crisis*, the *Pioneer*, *The Voice of the West Riding*, the *Destructive* and the *Poor Man's Guardian* in the early 1830s were anxious to resist the efforts of propagandist popularizers of orthodox classical political economy like Harriet Martineau, James Mill, Henry Brougham, Charles Knight and Francis Place – dismissed by Marx as 'the hired prize fighters'. As Bronterre O'Brien wrote in the *Poor Man's Guardian* in 1833: 'the battle of labour against capital is not to be fought with guns and swords . . . it will be of enlightened against foolish labourers, who are ignorant dupes of the capitalist'.

The popular unstamped press strongly challenged orthodox political economy which, in the hands of the classical writers, seemed designed to act as a buttress of an inequitable social system; a theoretical relationalization of the improvishment of labour based on Malthusian principles (Thompson 1984: 21; Hollis 1970: 220–46; Wiener 1969: 122). As William Thompson had put it: 'Some of the partisans of the diffusion of knowledge, use all their exertions to shut out from the consideration of the Industrious Classes all views and matters of social science, particularly on detached and still disputed points of political economy, which do not exactly square with their notions.'[5]

Drawing upon the works of Thompson, Hodgskin and other socialist and anti-capitalist writers of the 1820s, journalists in the 'pauper press' argued that orthodox political economists depicted an economic system riddled with evils and injustice as rational, fixed and immutable. Especially resented was the Malthusian assumption that labourers must necessarily exist at subsistence level, that questions about the rate of capital accumulation and the expansion of output were much more important than the issue of the distribution of the national product. In the eyes of radical economists, this was to deprive economic questions of their ethical and moral dimensions by relegating man to the status of a mere instrument of production lacking essential human attributes (Checkland 1964: 403–10).

If the working-class unstamped press almost unanimously rejected classical political economy, there arose the question of what should be put in its place in order to tackle the problem of the maldistribution of wealth and to guarantee that working men be awarded a substantial proportion of the produce of their labour. A labour theory of value was assumed, plus a theory of economic crisis originating in deficient working-class demand. Radical alternative solutions took the form of attempts to transform the system of exchange and distribution, rather than challenging the relations of production or the rights of private property. Labour banks, labour notes, co-operative trading societies, equitable labour exchanges leading to producers' unions – all would ultimately provide the means for labour to purchase its own capital goods, thus making itself independent of capitalists.

Most of the classical political economists regarded the recurrence of economic crisis and depression after 1815 as a result of merely temporary problems of excess supply or of surplus population. Radicals, on the contrary, argued that slumps followed a glut caused by production for profit rather than for use. The existing monetary system expressed a standard of value which attached no weight to the social utility of commodities. This was why, claimed theorists like Thompson and Gray, money and market values deviated from genuine labour values, while the monopoly control exerted by bankers and rentiers shored up Old Corruption and Cobbett's demons: 'tax-eaters', 'war-mongers' and 'idle parasites'.

This radical alternative to classical political economy reached the peak of its influence in 1830–4, when the cheap unstamped press attained its maximum circulation at a time of deepening class hostility

(Hollis 1970: 95–106). After 1834 the attention of popular radicals was increasingly diverted from economic theory by practical concerns such as factory reform, the Anti-Poor Law agitation and the struggle for the People's Charter. Despite the articulation of alternative conceptions of society, economy and politics in the speeches of labour and radical leaders, it took some considerable time to persuade the mass of working men that it was the capitalists, rather than the tax-collectors, fundholders, priests, landlords, placemen and borough-mongers, who were the prime exploiters of those who laboured by the sweat of their brow. And, of course, radical political economy suffered from theoretical deficiencies, as it sought a reform of the mechanisms of exchange rather than the abolition of the private ownership of the means of production. It needed Marx to argue in *Das Kapital* (1867) that under capitalism, even if commodities exchanged at full labour value, there would still be 'surplus value' and hence exploitation (Thompson 1984: 219–28; Elster 1985: 165–233).

It is impossible to ascertain how far the radical economic ideas put forward in the unstamped press were either endorsed, or even understood, by its working-class readers. Editors and writers were as concerned to educate and mould working-class opinion as they were to reflect it. Even if it is accepted that the relationship between radical leaders and the rank-and-file was exceptionally close and that after 1815 radical economic and political ideas sold newspapers, the fact remains that for many popular radicals universal suffrage and political rights took primacy over schemes to transform the economic system. Moreover, Owen's ideas of rational harmony and community-building gained a wide following, while there were groups of workers like the Nottingham framework knitters who sought a remedy for distress in demanding traditional legislative regulation of the trade (Johnson 1979; Pollard 1960; Church and Chapman 1967). Above all, parliament – the seat of power in English politics – was still the major target of most popular radicals. The wealth produced by the 'industrious classes' was siphoned off by corrupt politicians, to be squandered on wars, sinecures, places, pensions and servicing the national debt. If the aristocracy controlled the vital instrument of parliament and used it both to tax the poor and to legislate against their interests, then parliamentary reform should assume priority over schemes to revolutionize production, distribution and exchange.

Between 1815 and 1829 working-class radicalism had followed a clear trajectory. The intensity of the post-war depression and the dis-appearance of the risk of treason in wartime produced the recruits for mass radical activity who had largely been missing since the 1790s. Both the technique of the mass platform and the conspiratorial tradition had been revived, though in both cases with relatively little effect. The mass platform reached its climax at Peterloo, while the Cato Street conspiracy demonstrated that the conspiratorial tradition could neither attract sufficient numbers nor prevent secret meetings and plots being infiltrated by government spies, which helped to rob it of any chance of success in the face of a determined Tory government which had behind it the bulk of 'respectable' opinion.

After 1820, with the upsurge in the economy, it was largely a matter of consolidation after major defeats. Significantly, radical opinion throughout the country was more deeply stirred by the Queen Caroline affair than by Spa Fields, Peterloo or Cato Street. In other words, the most favourable circumstances for the progress of working-class radicalism, apart from economic depression, was when the stability of government was shaken and both Opposition MPs and middle-class radicals were willing to join in an alliance with popular radicalism. By a fortuitous series of political crises facing Tory administrations after 1828, this was to happen again, although the development of the unstamped press and an ideology which challenged orthodox political economy was to make the renewed, and indeed much stronger, alliance still very much one of convenience rather than conviction.

NOTES AND REFERENCES

1.   *Political Register*, 2 November 1816.
2.   C. S. Parker, *Sir Robert Peel*, 1899, i, p. 168.
3.   Hobhouse to Norris, 4 August 1819. PRO H.O.41/4.
4.   *Gorgon*, vol. 38, 1819: p. 299.
5.   W. Thompson, *Labour Rewarded: The Claims of Labour and Capital Conciliated by One of the Idle classes*, 1827: p. 46.

Chapter 5

REFORM AND CONFLICT 1830-8

Historians who argue for the widespread existence of class consciousness during the early nineteenth century rest much of their case on the 1830s, a decade when, in contrast with the 1820s, popular radicalism advanced on a broad front. The Reform agitation, the campaign against newspaper taxes, the Factory Movement, trade-union activity on an enhanced scale and the Anti-Poor Law agitation: all represented a deepening sense of class hostility among large numbers of working people in both London and the industrial districts. Although many of these campaigns involved alliances between working-class radicals and some from the middle and landed classes, it may safely be asserted that by 1838 political awareness among urban wage earners generally, as opposed to somewhat restricted groups of skilled artisans, was much more widespread than it had been ten years previously. So were the organizational and agitational skills that, together with intensified class consciousness and a more sophisticated ideology, were to make Chartism the greatest mass movement in English history.

While all this seems indisputable, the various agitations of the 1830s have inevitably produced a good deal of historical controversy. Just how far did there exist a genuine threat of revolution in 1830-2? Did the unstamped press purvey a coherent ideology more suitable to a critique of industrial capitalism than of the increasingly outmoded 'Old Corruption'? Was the Factory Movement primarily concerned with the welfare of little children? Has the movement for general unionism in 1834 been exaggerated, and was its collapse all that damaging to the trade societies? And why was the Anti-Poor Law agitation so short-lived? This chapter attempts to provide a satisfactory assessment of the problems and controversies raised by such questions.

THE REFORM AGITATION AND THE GREAT REFORM ACT

Although universal manhood suffrage was the prime aim of the vast majority of working-class radicals from the 1790s, there was never any chance of it being enacted by a nineteenth-century parliament. Norman Gash has pointed out how the Reform Acts of 1832, 1867 and 1884 'were passed by men who had no belief in the kind of political democracy implicit in universal suffrage and equality of electoral districts and who feared that the introduction of such a system would lead to the tyranny of the illiterate many over the cultured few and of a numerical majority over the interests of minorities'. Most politicians and educated people regarded the parliamentary vote as a trust, the exercise of which demanded a certain degree of education and social responsibility. Even after the Third Reform Act of 1884, something like 40 per cent of working men remained disfranchised under the registration and residence qualifications, a situation remedied only in 1918 (Gash 1986: 55).

Grey and most of his colleagues who came to power in the Whig-dominated coalition government of 1830 were aristocrats who used the word 'democracy' as we would use 'anarchy'. Grey's son, Viscount Hawick, noted in his diary in October with some distaste how 'ye most violent democratical principles are daily spreading and are avowed and proclaimed by bodies of respectable people in a manner not a little alarming' (Mitchell 1967: 245). Trade unions were regarded as seditious; extra-parliamentary organizations were distrusted. Most members of the new administration thoroughly approved of the draconian sentences meted out to the Swing Rioters, 19 of whom were executed and 481 transported to the Antipodes (Ziegler 1976: 136–7). The relative humanity and restraint displayed by both police and law courts on the occasion of the Merthyr rising of May 1831, when forty people were killed, did not meet with general Whig approval (Williams 1978: 165–78). Grey himself told his fellow peers in November 1831: 'There is no one more decided against annual parliaments, universal suffrage and the ballot than I am. My object is not to favour, but to put an end to such hopes and projects.' In his speech in the Commons in defence of the Reform Bill in March 1831, Macaulay argued that 'the labouring classes' could not be entrusted with the suffrage because they were subject to insecure employment, low wages, dear food and large families:

> We know what effect distress produces, even on people more intelligent than the great body of the labouring classes can possibly be. We know that it makes even wise men irritable, unreasonable and credulous; eager for immediate relief, heedless of remote consequences ... that it blunts their judgement, that it enflames their passions, that it makes them prone to believe those who would flatter them and to distrust those who would

serve them ... I oppose universal suffrage because I think it would produce a destructive revolution.[1]

The government introduced a Reform Bill in 1831 partly for reasons of party advantage and to boost confidence in the survival of the new administration. But its primary and immediate aim was to avert revolution (Milton-Smith 1972; Cannon 1973: 253). Durham, Grey's son-in-law, argued that the French Revolution and the loss of the American colonies could both have been forestalled by timely concessions. Other influential Whigs felt that the best means of avoiding revolution in 1830–2 was to attach the middle classes more closely to the existing system and, by means of an alliance between aristocracy and plutocracy, prevent the discontented from going, in Macaulay's words, 'over to the side of revolution' and joining forces with the insurrectionary labouring classes. Such a development, claimed Macaulay, would mean 'the wreck of laws, the confusion of ranks, the spoliation of property and the dissolution of the social order'. Hence it was vital to 'save property divided against itself'.

What was new, compared with the threat from below mounted in 1815, 1817 and 1819, was that there now existed a vigorous middle-class Reform movement, anxious for the new industrial and commercial classes to be fully acknowledged by the landed elite and eager to get parliamentary seats for unrepresented towns like Manchester, Leeds and Birmingham. At the same time, they wished to procure legislation on free trade, the reform of the Church and the removal of Dissenters' grievances. Middle-class radicals had kept a low profile after 1815, but were now very vocal, not least through major provincial newspapers like the *Leeds Mercury* and *Manchester Guardian*. Fear of alienating the frustrated middle classes explains why they were constantly flattered by leading Whig politicians, as well as by Utilitarians like James Mill. Grey himself referred to 'the middle classes ... who form the real and efficient mass of public opinion and without whom the power of the gentry is nothing'.

The Whigs therefore aimed to broaden the basis of the political system without any major change in the structure of the electorate or letting the most important levers of power slip from aristocratic hands. No more than a pruning, purification and expansion of the existing electoral structure was intended. If seats were given to some new industrial boroughs, then they would also be given to counties. Aristocratic and gentry influence was intended to be increased rather than diminished (Gash 1953: 65–85), 1986: 57; Moore 1966, 1976: 137–242; Davis 1976). Once the middle classes had been permitted a subordinate share of power, it was anticipated that they would both side with the gentry and be seduced into adopting conservative attitudes and helping to keep the working classes in order. Moreover, 'the new voters would not be anxious to admit others to the electoral privileges which they had won' (Brock 1973: 145). Agitations which lacked middle-class leadership and money were unlikely, it was believed, to offer much danger in the future, while post-Reform parliaments would hardly display excessive concern for working-class radical interests. Given these attitudes and assumptions, the task of popular radicalism in attempting to force through universal suffrage was virtually an impossible one.

Grey's ministry was able to take office as the culmination of a series of major political changes since the resignation of Lord Liverpool in 1827. The short life of the Canning and Goderich ministries, the subsequent failure of Wellington to retain the support of the Canningites, and the fact that Wellington and Peel alienated the right-wing Ultra Tories by rushing Catholic Emancipation through a reluctant parliament, opened a pathway for the return of the Whigs. Repeal of the Test and Corporation Acts, as well as Catholic Emancipation, had brought about a significant change in the constitution, eroding the Anglican supremacy established by the Glorious Revolution of 1688 (Bentley: 1984: 57–72). Catholic Emancipation, according to John Cannon 'the battering ram that broke down the old unreformed system', led to the break up of the Tory alliance, providing the Whigs with their chance to regroup and grasp at power in the political and economic crisis which coincided with the death of George IV in 1830 (Cannon 1973: 191; O'Gorman 1982: 110; Hill 1985: 217–25).

If these developments owed little to popular agitation in England, they owed a great deal to mass pressure in Ireland, where O'Connell's Catholic Association had mounted an impressive campaign at the 1826 election, persuading Irish tenants to vote against their landlords and subsequently placing O'Connell himself head of the poll at the 1828 Clare by-election, though as a Roman Catholic he was ineligible to take his seat. Wellington and Peel were therefore obliged to take up Catholic Emancipation in order to avert civil war in Ireland, though they were well aware it would create deep divisions among the ruling elite. Meanwhile English radical leaders, both middle and working class, carefully noted how the tactics of the Catholic Association demonstrated the power of a centrally-organized mass movement, ostensibly peaceful, but with a barely-disguised threat of force if thwarted, to put parliament under successful 'pressure from without' (Royle and Walvin 1982: 140–1).

Severe economic distress in the autumn of 1829 brought widespread suffering to both industrial and agricultural districts, as the French Revolution of July 1830 helped to raise the political temperature. Radical Reform demonstrations now took place with increasing frequency. In January 1830 Thomas Attwood founded the influential Birmingham Political Union, followed by the emergence of Political Unions in London, as well as elsewhere in the provinces (Butler 1914: 56–64; Cannon 1973: 194–5; Brock 1973: 77–8). Through the winter of 1829–30 Cobbett toured the country, calling loudly for Reform in the columns of his *Weekly Political Register*. By this stage Wellington's government was no longer sufficiently strong to serve as a rallying-point for those anxious to preserve law, order and a degree of stability.

At the general election in the summer of 1830, necessitated by the death of George IV, a large number of new members was returned. Most of them were hostile to the ministry and pledged to parliamentary reform. Henry Hunt was elected at Preston, where virtual manhood suffrage existed and when *tricoleur* flags and banners inscribed 'Bread or Blood' and 'Liberty or Death' were paraded through the streets (Stevenson 1979: 219). There were serious riots at Bristol, Northampton, Norwich and Banbury, as well as at Preston itself.

In such a volatile situation, the Whig factions were swift to close ranks and reach agreement with Canningite and Ultra Tory groups. Outside parliament the spread of the Political Unions, especially the so-called 'low' Unions, caused considerable disquiet. At the same time, considerable alarm was aroused by the Swing Riots: the wave of arson, machine-breaking, food riots and threatening letters which swept across twenty counties in southern and eastern England during the second half of 1830 and the early months of 1831; riots which were economically motivated and had no connexion with the radical Reform movement (Rudé 1967; Hobsbawm and Rudé 1969: 89–91; Hammond and Hammond 1911: 176–241).

Industrial unrest failed to emerge on the same scale, although there were isolated Luddite outbreaks and a great spinners' strike in Manchester in 1829 which, although it failed, led 80,000 to join John Doherty's Operative Spinners' Union when a major strike broke out in the Oldham area (Kirby and Musson 1975: 85–114; Thompson 1968 edn: 875–6). Reform meetings and processions, attracting massive crowds, also helped to induce a sense of crisis. On 11 September 1830, Lady Georgiana Stuart-Wortley informed her mother: 'You have no idea how the wise and unwise of all parties croak, and no wonder; for the spirit of the lower classes at this moment is of a most alarming description.' The Tory Marquess of Angelsey wrote a few weeks later: 'I have a thorough conviction that nothing but a total change in the whole system of governing the country ... can save it from Revolution' (Brock 1973: 106; Angelsey 1963: 238).

Traditional Whig doctrines of government by consent and resistance to oppression made it difficult for Grey to adopt a deliberately repressive policy against political malcontents. He was made aware how strongly the tide was running in favour of Reform by the 3,000 Reform petitions received during the winter of 1830–1, while Durham ('Radical Jack') and the propaganda of James Mill and the Utilitarians pressed on him the importance of the provincial merchanting and manufacturing classes: 'those who have made wonderful advances in both property and intelligence'. At the same time, a substantial number of backbenchers in the Commons came to agree with ideologues like Macaulay that a measure of moderate Reform was a necessary antidote to a genuine threat of revolution (Hamburger 1963: 11–12; Cannon 1973: 245–6; O'Neill and Martin 1980).

In the event, it was to take over a year of frequent political crises and three separate Bills before the 1832 Reform Act received the royal assent. The Act conceded little or nothing to working-class radical aspirations. The new franchise qualifications remained firmly grounded in property ownership and in both county and borough constituencies were in all cases higher than the lowest of the existing ones. In the county seats the basic forty-shilling freeholder qualification was retained, with the addition of various prosperous tenants, copyholders and lease-holders. An extraordinary range of franchise qualifications in boroughs prior to 1832 was replaced by the occupation of property, as owner or tenant, worth an annual value of £10, plus a £10 lodger franchise (Seymour 1915: 35–8; Brock 1973: 137–42). About 300,000 were added to an existing electorate of around 500,000.

Before 1832 about one adult male in every thirty had possessed the franchise. After the Reform Act the proportion rose to one in seven (one in five in England). The £10 householder qualification, hedged by complex registration and tax-paying conditions, was designed as a crude means of further enfranchising those possessing sufficient property to be 'trusted' with votes. 'Respectable' was the key word which cropped up continually during debates over the Reform Bill. The franchise should not be conferred on those who might 'irresponsibly' abuse the privilege; namely those who lacked 'respectability' and a satisfactory degree of deference to the existing constitution and social order, as well as to a political system firmly based on the divine right of property. The Reform Act was therefore ostensibly designed to benefit what Brougham, speaking on the second reading in the Lords, termed 'those middle classes, who are also the genuine depositories of sober, rational, intelligent and honest English feeling' (Stewart 1986: 267; McCord 1967; Wright 1970: 34–5).

It is far from easy to assess the relationship between the new franchises and the class structure, given the anomalies which arose from regional variations in rental values and the problems of defining class in this period. While there is no doubt that ordinary agricultural labourers in the counties were completely excluded, in the boroughs the £10 householder voter varied in social status according to the prevailing level of property values. In high-rated London, Manchester and Sheffield, for example, the £10 qualification included a number of skilled working men; in remote Cornwall and parts of Wales even some shopkeepers failed to qualify.

On the whole, however, the new borough voters were middle class or *petit bourgeois*, most of whom possessed county votes before 1832 as freeholders. In Leeds, there were only 5,000 voters out of a population of 123,000 (Glen 1984: 28; Fraser 1970: 49). This figure very much confirmed the estimate of Edward Baines of the *Leeds Mercury*, who in 1831 undertook a canvass on Russell's behalf to establish that the £10 qualification would largely exclude the labouring classes and who reported reassuringly that: 'It appeared that in the parts [of Leeds] occupied chiefly by the working classes, not one householder in fifty would have a vote. In the street principally occupied by shops, almost every householder had a vote.'[2]

At the 1830 election, working men had formed a majority of the electorate in constituencies which in total returned 130 members to the Commons. It seems likely, therefore, that fewer working men possessed the vote after 1832 than before (Gash 1953: 86–101). Although steady inflation increased the number of artisan and skilled working-class voters during subsequent decades, the larger cities still had a very restricted working-class electorate in 1865. Coventry was unusual with 70 per cent of its electorate working-class; Leicester had 40 per cent, Nottingham 39, Manchester 27, Bristol 26, Newcastle 24, Sunderland 18, Oldham 14, Halifax 10 and Leeds a mere 7 per cent. By official calculations, working men then comprised 26 per cent of the electorate in England and Wales.[3] One barrier to the progress of popular radical objectives, therefore, was the restricted opportunity for working men to participate fully in mid-Victorian parliamentary elections.

Although Norman Gash and D. C. Moore have emphasized the essentially conservative nature of the Reform Act, there was an overwhelming tide of public opinion behind its passing. Many working-class radicals, while appreciating that it brought few direct benefits to them, regarded it as a welcome instalment of reform, on the 'half-a-loaf' principle. If the Whigs initially embarked on the introduction of a Reform Bill partly for reasons of party advantage, it is nevertheless implausible to argue that the whole crisis was both precipitated and resolved exclusively within parliamentary circles, with extra-parliamentary pressure on a massive scale relegated to a minor role. Maurice Cowling's interpretation of the passing of the 1867 Act can hardly be applied to the crisis of 1830–2 (Cowling 1967; Fraser 1970).

REVOLUTION AVERTED?

Historians writing in the Whig tradition, notably G. M. Trevelyan and J. R. M. Butler, believed that a revolutionary situation existed in 1831–2 and that an outbreak was avoided only by conceding Reform. More recent historians, like E. P. Thompson and Eric Hobsbawm, writing from the left, and Malcolm Thomis from the right, have taken much the same view (Thompson 1968 edn: 898–9; Hobsbawm 1962: 110–11; Thomis and Holt 1977: 93). Many of the ingredients of revolution were certainly present: economic distress, unrest among both industrial and agricultural workers, the influence of the July 1830 Revolution in Paris and signs of division and uncertainty, if not apocalyptic visions of disaster, among the ruling elite. There was also a well-organized radical movement, involving both the middle and the working classes, which embraced the Birmingham Political Union ('a General Political Union between the Lower and the Middle classes of the People') and, in the metropolis, the National Political Union (NPU) and the more radical and Owenite National Union of the Working Classes (NUWC), which emerged from the London co-operative movement. Undeniably wide support existed for the Reform Bill, whose opponents proved incapable of mounting a major agitation or of organizing anything like the impressive meetings, sustained by the carefully conceived ritual of banners, flags and massed singing, on Newhall Hill arranged by the Birmingham Political Union in October 1831 and May 1832, drawing crowds of over 100,000 (Read 1964: 91–2; Thompson 1968 edn: 935–6; Brock 1973: 295; Hobsbawm 1959: 150–4).

More significantly, the prolonged Reform crisis was regularly punctuated by violence. There were riots at the London demonstrations of April and October 1831, when windows of opponents of the Bill were smashed, including those of the Duke of Wellington and Bishop of London. During the general election of that year there were disturbances in several Scottish towns, as well as at Malmesbury, Boston, Banbury, Rye, Horsham and Whitehaven. The rejection of the second Bill by the Lords on 8 October 1831 was followed by rioting which some regarded as the commencement of a revolutionary outbreak. At Derby the houses of anti-Reformers were attacked and prisoners subsequently freed from the city gaol. Further disturbances were eventually put down by troops after two men had been killed. On 10 October rioters at Nottingham wrecked Colwick Hall and burned down (the unoccupied and largely undefended) Nottingham Castle, property of the Duke of Newcastle, a notorious borough-monger who had ejected pro-Reform tenants. Once military reinforcements arrived, the riots soon petered out and the Duke did not need to call on the 300 soldiers and 24 cannon defending Clumber, his actual residence (Hamburger 1963: 139–61; Thomis 1969: 225–36).

Minor disturbances at Leicester, Tiverton, Yeovil, Blandford, Sherborne, Exeter and Worcester paled before the great riots in Bristol in late October. Here the Bristol Political Union organized opposition to the visit of the Bishop of Bath and Wells, who had voted against the Reform Bill in the Lords, and to the arrival of the Recorder, a vehement anti-Reformer, to conduct the Assizes. When Lieutenant-Colonel Brereton led an inadequate force of ninety-three dragoons into the city, he was met by such a volume of stone-throwing opposition that he withdrew his troops to Newport in order to await reinforcements, leaving Bristol in the hands of a growing and increasingly drunken mob, who wrecked and looted both public buildings and private houses, inflicting damage amounting to £300,000. When the dragoons eventually re-entered the town, the rioters were easily overcome, though not before at least 12 had been killed and nearly 100 badly wounded. Thirty-one prisoners were sentenced to death, of whom four were actually executed. Brereton was later court-martialled and shot himself. His failure to act decisively and the reluctance of the magistrates to take a positive lead had caused the riot to get out of hand, an all too frequent occurrence before the introduction of professional policing (Hamburger 1963: 161–84; Thomis 1983).

During the 'Days of May' in 1832, designed to prevent Wellington's return at the head of an anti-Reform regressive ministry, there took place the celebrated 'run on gold', as well as rumours of collection of arms, of a revolutionary march on London, of the non-payment of taxes and of disaffection in the army. These aggravated an atmosphere made already tense by the 'tithe war' in Ireland and the spread of cholera in England. Non-political violence also caused alarm and social fear, as there occurred a renewed outbreak of rural arson and machine-breaking in late 1831, besides violent strikes in the mining areas of Northumberland, Durham, Staffordshire and Wales (Morris 1976: 14–25; Rudé 1967).

In his *James Mill and the Art of Revolution* (1963: 48–111), Joseph Hamburger argued that the threat of revolution in 1830–2 was more apparent than real, with Benthamite Radical intellectuals, assisted by Francis Place and Joseph Parkes, doing all they could to persuade the government that support for Reform in the country was so intense that revolution could only be averted by the strength of Political Union organizations and the demonstrable willingness of the Whig leaders to push the Reform Bill through. According to Hamburger, the strength of the Political Unions and of numbers attending meetings was consistently exaggerated by Place, Parkes and the Millite radicals. Their threat of stimulating and leading a genuinely national revolution in May 1832 was one which they were never called upon to carry out, for the Whigs came back into office after Wellington failed to form an administration. Moreover, there is little evidence that they made determined attempts to collect arms, to seduce the army into disloyalty, or to create a national revolutionary organization. As it turned out, the final agitation of May 1832 was largely confined to London and was chiefly financial in character, with relatively little violence. While Place's inspired slogan 'To stop the Duke go for gold' helped to drain the Bank of England of 40 per cent of its gold reserves, the provinces remained relatively calm, despite rumours of a 'march on London'.

Francis Place's constant emphasis on unanimity and class collaboration among Reformers hardly disguised a major flaw in his carefully cultivated image of imminent insurrection. Fissures within the Reform movement could neither be hidden nor brushed aside as insignificant, despite the elaborate steps taken to minimize the impact of discord. Hence the mass meetings, where conditions made it difficult for manhood suffrage radicals to pass hostile amendments. Place did all he could to exclude 'extremists', especially those adhering to the teachings of Hodgskin or Owen, from the Council of the NPU. Melbourne, the Home Secretary, was persuaded to ban demonstrations by the NUWC, thereby strengthening the influence of the NPU in London, so that by late 1831 it had twice as many members as the NUWC. The artisan ultra-radicals who met at the Blackfriars Rotunda and created the NUWC regarded Place, with his advocacy of orthodox political economy and his contacts with Benthamite circles, as a traitor to his class.

Even within the NUWC, however, attitudes towards the Reform Bill varied. Some took the view of Cobbett, Carlile and Gale Jones: that it ought to be supported as unlocking the door which might later be pushed open wide to admit universal suffrage and the ballot (Prothero 1981: 282). Others dismissed the Reform Bill as no more than a device whereby genuine radical reform would be indefinitely postponed by means of a firm alliance between the landed gentry and a well-organized and confident bourgeoisie against labouring men. A government informer reported that at one NUWC meeting: 'Gast, Osborne and Cleave were the principle [*sic*] speakers who in great abuse of the Government and the Reform Bill declared it to be nothing but a humbug to gull and would be of no use to the Working Classes without the Ballot and Universal Suffrage which was their just rights'.[4] Hetherington's *Poor Man's Guardian*, the main organ of the NUWC, consistently argued that leading supporters of the Reform Bill had no genuine desire 'to subvert, or even re-model our aristocratic institutions, but to consolidate them by a reinforcement of sub-aristocracy from the middle classes'.[5]

Men like Watson, Cleave and Lovett wanted universal suffrage, a free unstamped press and a rejection of the equation of political rights with property rights (Thompson 1968 edn: 892–3; Prothero 1981: 268–99; Thomas 1962). Yet the Rotunda radicals, mostly literate and highly politically aware artisans, proved unable to unite behind them the disorganized, heterogeneous mass of London's unskilled labourers, despite success in organizing processions and mass meetings. The formal membership of the main London radical associations together amounted to no more than 20,000, with a much lower active membership (Rowe 1977).

The divisions within London radicalism were mirrored in the provinces (Briggs 1952). Working-class radicals sought Reform both as a dramatic cure for economic distress and as a consequence of popular theories of political rights. By contrast, provincial merchant and manufacturing groups aimed at recognition of their status, as well as specific legislation and increased parliamentary representation for local interests, while remaining deeply suspicious of the 'extreme' aims of

Owenites, trade unionists and democrats. There were middle-class members of the Political Unions who saw themselves performing a dual role: to promote Reform and 'to protect life and property' from the depredations of 'the mob'. As Thompson neatly puts it: 'These middle-class incendiaries carried in their knapsacks a special constable's baton' (Thompson 1968 edn: 891).

Birmingham was exceptional in achieving relative class harmony during the Reform agitation, largely because of the city's small workshops and considerable social mobility, which tended to blur distinctions between masters and men. There was little labour-saving machinery to throw workers out of employment. Both middle and working class Reformers were therefore able to line up together behind the Birmingham Political Union and its high Tory leaders like Thomas Attwood, who embraced Reform as a means of protesting at government deflationary monetary policy since the restoration of the gold standard in 1819 and who proved able to keep a mass Reform movement firmly under middle-class control (Smith 1982: 35–6; Flick 1978: 17–26). The influence of the local branch of the NUWC was kept to a minimum. Leicester was similar, in that middle- and working-class radicals were able to act together for Reform against a common enemy: the old corrupt Corporation (Patterson 1954: 176–97).

Elsewhere it proved difficult to secure class co-operation. Towns like Manchester and Leeds contrasted sharply with Birmingham and Leicester. Manchester's cotton factories created a deep gulf between masters and men, resulting in keen class antagonism and the fragmentation of the local Reform movement. Prominent cotton masters were more concerned about the Corn Laws, *laissez-faire*, public economy and paying low wages than they were about Reform. The Manchester Political Union, which supported the Reform Bill, was composed chiefly of the lower middle-class 'shopocracy' rather than of working men, although it had little sympathy with the millowners. Strongly opposed to it was a 'low' working-class Political Union, containing large numbers of handloom weavers who were threatened by machinery, pledged to manhood suffrage and the ballot and to maintaining close links with the NUWC in London. The 'extreme' views of this working-class Union no doubt inhibited many of the lower middle classes from speaking out for Reform as firmly as their counterparts in Birmingham.

In Leeds there were even more complex divisions. Here the weavers felt menaced by the power-loom and intensely disliked Baines's 'Whig' Political Union. Some of them formed their own Union based on the full radical programme. Others joined the short-time committees of the Factory Movement, whose leaders opposed all versions of parliamentary reform (Read 1961: 119–24; Fraser 1980: 275–8). There was a similar pattern in other northern towns, including Bradford and Bolton. In a number of key provincial centres, therefore, fundamental ideological differences, reflected in the contrasting outlook of the illegal, unstamped *Poor Man's Guardian* and the sevenpenny 'respectable' *Manchester Guardian*, produced unbridgeable divisions between the middle- and working-class Reform movements. Admittedly, there were also divisions among middle-class Reformers, as indeed there were among the 'low' democratic Unions, for different sections of the middle classes varied in their enthusiasm for Reform. It may well be, however, that the widespread and deep-rooted middle-class fear of the 'threat from below' would have inhibited attempts to spark off a revolutionary outbreak and the Reform Bill failed in the spring of 1832, despite the forecasts of Place and the Benthamite radicals.

The major riots at Derby, Nottingham and Bristol stemmed more from local circumstances than forming sections of a centrally organized revolutionary movement. Not only did they, in their later stages, contain criminals and looters, but they were also easily suppressed. Only in Merthyr Tydfil in 1831 did popular radicalism and fierce community feeling fuse with economic discontent to such a degree that armed workers could repeatedly inflict defeats on regular and yeomanry troops (Williams 1978: 174). Throughout the Reform crisis, the government's determination to stand firm in the maintenance of law and order remained unshaken. A mass meeting planned by the NUWC for November 1831 was banned as treasonable by Melbourne, who nonetheless took elaborate military precautions in case the meeting went ahead. When the Birmingham Political Union proposed to form an armed 'National Guard', the government declared it illegal and the BPU promptly backed down. Only in May 1832, during the brief period when no government existed after Grey's resignation, was there any likelihood of revolution. Place concerted plans with the BPU for an armed rising, while Attwood provocatively argued that its members possessed the constitutional right to bear arms. Inflammatory language was employed at meetings all over the country as Reform petitions poured into the capital (Brock 1973: 268–310).

How far Wellington's failure to form a government and Grey's consequent return to office were influenced by the prospect of insurrection is problematic. One can only speculate on what might have happened had the bluff of Place and Parkes been called. Although there is some evidence of the sporadic collection and stockpiling of arms, the leadership and organization necessary for a successful rising appear to have been lacking. On the other hand, a simultaneous insurrection in various parts of the country might have stretched the forces of order to breaking-point, given that the government had only 11,000 troops available, 7,000 of whom would be required to defend the capital.

It may, however, be doubted whether the popular Unions, modelled on the NUWC and committed to manhood suffrage, would have been prepared to rise at the behest of Parkes and Place on behalf of a Bill which they saw as conferring benefits on the property-owning middle classes, so many of whom were reluctant to collaborate with working men, whose enfranchisement they no more desired than did land-owning Tories. It is significant that there was much less violence in 1832 than there had been in 1831, even in London. Neither was the NUWC anxious for an open confrontation with the authorities. It is true that many NUWC members obtained arms (usually wooden staves) and drilled under old soldiers of the line, while the *Poor Man's Guardian* reprinted extracts from Colonel Macerone's street-fighting manual *Defensive Instructions for the People*. Yet the NUWC in May 1832, thoroughly penetrated by government spies, decided to wait on events, rejecting formal plans for drilling its members and dismissing the proposal for a 'National Holiday', that is, a general strike, put by the headstrong and violent William Benbow (Prothero 1981: 292–9; Prothero 1971; Rowe 1977: 149–76). There were therefore serious disagreements on tactics within the NUWC and among its provincial supporters. Most supported Lovett on the need to arm in self-defence in case of determined government repression. Only a minority, including Benbow, favoured violence and confrontation with the authorities (Prothero 1981: 289–90; Large 1974: 116). On balance, then, it seems unlikely that the danger of revolution in London in May 1832 was as great as sometimes claimed.

For all their efforts to obtain parliamentary reform, working-class radicals had failed to obtain the vote for all adult males or to see any immediate prospect of the end of political privilege and heavy indirect taxation. In December 1831 the *Poor Man's Guardian* reported a Macclesfield radical declaring that 'It mattered not to him whether he was governed by a boroughmonger, or a whoremonger, or a churchmonger, if the system of monopoly and corruption was still to be upheld'. Defeat and betrayal in 1832 failed, however, to deflect working-class radicalism from its determination to obtain universal suffrage. Indeed, the gaining of the vote by the middle classes made the vocabulary of political radicalism more than ever the property of the working classes (Rule 1986: 289). The immediate origins of Chartism can therefore be found in the Reform crisis. But it was already clear that further attempts would have to face the increasing cohesion of the new middle-class voters, largely indifferent towards working-class aspirations, and a landed interest which still monopolized control of the resources of the state, remaining confident in its ability to survive any major challenge.

THE 'WAR OF THE UNSTAMPED'

During the remainder of the 1830s, in 'that era of hope, pain, suffering and fear', there was little in the way of solid achievement for working-class radical movements (Kitson Clark 1962: 31). The chief link between the popular agitation for Reform at the beginning of the decade and Chartism at its end was provided by the production and distribution of the unstamped illegal press between 1830 and 1836 in the face of mounting government persecution. It was the unstamped which nurtured the more widespread radicalism which had been created during the Reform crisis, as it cultivated a network of newsagents, coffee-house keepers and street vendors, maintaining essential contacts and a sense of participation in a common movement.

The 'taxes on knowledge' were increasingly opposed after 1830 by both working- and middle-class reformers. The 4d. gross stamp duty on newspapers was reduced to 1d. in 1836. An advertisement duty of 3s. 6d. was reduced to 1s. 6d. in 1833 and then persisted until 1855. Every edition of a pamphlet carried a 3s. duty. The press was also severely restricted by the law of libel: defamatory libel against individuals and, under the Blasphemous and Seditious Libels Act – one of the Six Acts of 1819 which remained law until 1869–70 – seditious libel against the political institutions of the country and blasphemous libel against the institutions of religion. Such restrictions had driven the cheap press virtually out of existence during the early 1820s, but the radical revival after 1830 brought the struggle for a cheap free press back to the forefront.

The 'war of the unstamped', headed by skilled and courageous publishers and journalists like Henry Hetherington, James Watson and John Cleave, involved a determined attempt to violate the press laws by publishing and distributing hundreds of illegal tracts and ephemeral newspapers. Between 1830 and 1836 over 550 illegal journals were issued, priced between 1d. and 3d., leading to at least 1,130 cases before the London magistrates alone, involving 737 vendors, many of them young boys, and prison sentences of between seven days and three months (Hollis 1970: 171–3).

Illegal unstamped papers like the *Poor Man's Guardian, Destructive* and *Voice of the West Riding* roused intense hostility from both the ruling elite and conservative middle class and clerical groups, not least because of their assaults on the competitive economic system and individual property rights. Clergymen, local magistrates and 'loyal associations' especially disliked the 'infidel' strain in popular radicalism, grounded in eighteenth-century deism and nurtured by Paine and Carlile. Although only Carlile and Watson were prominent critics of Christian doctrine *per se*, many radical journalists were hostile to the established Church in particular on various grounds. Among these were the Church's role as the spiritual and intellectual arm of the aristocratic conservative state, evidenced by the fact that in 1831 twenty-one bishops voted against the Reform Bill in the House of Lords, with only two in favour and six abstaining. No less irritating was its imposition of widely resented tithes and church rates, as well as the willingness of clergy to act as much-hated magistrates (Royle 1971: 4, 6–8; Wiener 1969: 230–2; Hollis 1970: 203–11).

Not surprisingly, the radical unstamped papers soon found themselves in competition with religious papers and the *Penny Magazine*, issued by the Society for the Diffusion of Useful Knowledge in the hope of creating a stable, God-fearing and deferential workforce, anxious to eschew rick-burning, strikes and questioning the rights of property. Such papers, although themselves unstamped and therefore technically illegal, were never prosecuted, given their belief that people should primarily be educated for their station and duties in life (Hollis 1970: 6–7, 67, 138–9; Wiener 1969: 34–8; Harrison 1961: 39–40; Stewart 1986: 192–3).

Although the working-class unstamped agitation received valuable support from a middle-class campaign against the taxes on knowledge, orchestrated at parliamentary level by Francis Place and Joseph Hume, middle-class radicals aimed merely to change the law. Working-class radicals were out to destroy it. Journalists like Bronterre O'Brien argued that every man had a right to cheap knowledge, and to knowledge that had not been laundered by middle-class hands. Whatever was taught by the middle classes was bound to be in the interests of capitalists and middlemen rather than the workers. According to O'Brien:

> Some simpletons talk of knowledge as rendering the working classes more obedient and dutiful – better servants, better subjects, and so on, which means making them more subservient slaves, and more conducive to the wealth and gratification of idlers of all descriptions. But such knowledge is trash; the only knowledge which is of any service to the working people is that which makes them more dissatisfied, and makes them worse slaves.[6]

Knowledge was power, and therefore essential for an organized working-class movement. The kind of knowledge provided by the radical unstamped would, it was widely assumed, lead to the end of crime and class conflict with the creation of a more just society. There were many who, like William Lovett, placed enormous and rather exaggerated faith in the power of the printed word.

Issuing and distributing the unstamped papers formed a vast working-class movement in its own right, offering political activists an outlet for their energies and providing destitute workers with a chance to earn their living as street-vendors. Although it was possible for an unstamped paper to run at a profit, few in fact did so. A circulation of 3,000 or so was needed to break even and only a handful of papers was able to reach 10,000, even if readership enormously exceeded sales. Even so, by 1836 the predominantly radical unstamped papers had a combined circulation far in excess of that of the 'respectable' stamped press (Hollis 1970: 119). Government repression, intensified in 1835–6, proved unable to quell the unstamped; too many people in both London and the provinces were willing to risk imprisonment, having relatively little to lose on near-starvation incomes. The accompanying protest meetings and petitions eventually created a more favourable public climate, so that by 1836 it was proving difficult to obtain witnesses to testify against illegal street hawkers. In London and Manchester, crowds attacked the hated new police when they attempted to arrest those concerned with selling the 'pauper press' (Wiener 1969: 200–8).

The unstamped press did not, however, speak with a single voice, but rather expressed the contradictions inherent in working-class radicalism during this period; radicalism which may often have been as much a matter of temperament as it was of intellectual adherence to a single creed (White 1965: 14). As Patricia Hollis has argued, there were two radical rhetorics rather than one. The old rhetoric, shaped in the years prior to 1819, focused its attacks on aristocracy, priestcraft, monopolies, rents, pensions and taxes – the whole structure of 'Old Corruption'. Occasionally, Spencean notions of land nationalization and Owenite critiques of competition and exploitation were invoked. But a second radical rhetoric, more attuned to an industrializing society, was developed by Hetherington, William Carpenter and, above all, Bronterre O'Brien. Based on the ideas of Thompson, Hodgskin and the new 'people's science' of radical political economy, this nascent socialist critique involved emphasis on the labour theory of value, on theories of working-class under-consumption and the need for higher wages and full employment. Assaults on capitalism were underpinned by persistent contrasts between 'productive' and 'unproductive' labour (Hollis 1970: 203–58).

Despite this more sophisticated analysis of industrial society, O'Brien and Hetherington placed their final emphasis on political, rather than industrial, action. Universal suffrage was the key to the door of a new society, where primogeniture, entail, Corn Laws, tithes, monopolies, taxes on knowledge, the press gang, assessed taxes and the duties on salt, soap and malt would all be abolished. Much emphasis was placed on the need to abolish flogging in the army, a popular radical demand since the 1790s (Steiner 1983; Dinwiddy 1982). The way would then be open for the appearance of a new society: an industrial, highly-mechanized society of high wages, full employment and profit-sharing (Plummer 1971: 52–6). In the meantime, working men could assist the gestation of the new society by supporting the unstamped, demanding the vote and a National Convention, joining in processions and demonstrations, engaging in exclusive dealing and abstaining from dutiable commodities like alcohol, tea, coffee and tobacco.

Yet the 'new' analysis of O'Brien, Hetherington and their colleagues did not succeed in displacing the old radical reasoning, more appropriate to a pre-industrial society, for another two generations. It remained common popular belief that monarchy, aristocracy and landed property were the result of usurpations in history, when property had been unjustly and inequitably expropriated from the public domain. Laws passed in parliament by the heirs of such usurpers were not, therefore, binding on an unrepresented majority. A graduated property tax ought to be introduced, as well as ten-hour factory legislation and the repeal of the New Poor Law. The collectivization of private property and the use of revolutionary violence were hinted at, rather than openly advocated. There was also much emphasis on Owenite co-operative production and exchange. Hetherington, Watson and Cleave, for example, were all enthusiasts for the co-operative programmes put forward in the *Crisis* and the *Pioneer* (Wiener 1969: 222–8).

When in March 1836 the government reduced the newspaper duty to a penny, with a corresponding reduction in paper duties, the unstamped agitation came to an end. This compromise, which still left substantial taxes on the press, themselves the subject of a renewed campaign in the 1850s, provided an important stimulus to the stamped press, which increased its circulation by 50 per cent during the following two years. The *Daily Telegraph* could now appear as a penny daily. Once again, as in 1832, the working class felt betrayed. Unstamped papers had either to accept the stamp – and the *Northern Star* was to become an outstandingly successful stamped working-class radical newspaper – or go out of business. As it was, the increasing costs of newspaper production and the greater prominence assumed by advertising in the economics of the press, made it increasingly difficult for newspapers to be established without considerable capital (Curran 1978: 67–72).

In spite of its ultimate failure to remove all taxes on knowledge, the war of the unstamped was of major importance in the development of popular radicalism. The pauper press played a key role in diffusing information about political movements, in relaying local grievances to a national audience, in sponsoring radical organizations as well as raising money for trade unions and strike activity. If O'Brien and Hetherington failed to displace the old radical analysis of the economic and social system, then at least some elements of their analysis of profits and power, as opposed to priestcraft and pensions, became accepted doctrine.

Above all, as a movement in its own right, the unstamped agitation provided jobs and training in journalism and distribution for scores of working-class activists. Areas of Britain most deeply involved in distributing the unstamped press were to be those most active in Chartism. Feargus O'Connor and Henry Vincent were the only prominent Chartist journalists who had not been trained and nurtured by the unstamped. It was no accident that the London Working Men's Association, founded in June 1836, was the direct successor of the April 1836 Association of Working Men to Procure a Cheap and Honest Press (Hollis 1970: 259–94).

THE FACTORY MOVEMENT

Another major ingredient in the working-class radicalism of the 1830s was the Factory Movement, with its demand for the ten-hour day for children and women in textile mills, a movement which received strong support in the columns of the unstamped. This agitation underwent a long period of gestation, for concern about deteriorating conditions in child employment had developed during the eighteenth century. Early legislative efforts, however, depended largely on benevolent individuals. Sir Robert Peel the Elder's Health and Morals of Apprentices Act of 1802, restricting pauper apprentices in the cotton industry to twelve hours daily labour, was largely unenforced. So was Peel's 1819 Act to limit 'free' child labour in cotton mills to twelve hours. However this Act, prompted by proposals put forward by Robert Owen in 1815, was accompanied by considerable popular pressure from the well-organized Lancashire cotton spinners, in liaison with some enlightened cotton masters, Anglican clergy and medical men (Ward 1970: 65).

A further burst of agitation during the 1820s by the cotton spinners led only to J. C. Hobhouse obtaining minor improvements to existing legislation in 1825 and 1829, as the Lancashire cotton operatives became disillusioned with the lack of enforcement of existing legislation and demoralized by the collapse of strikes against wage reductions. But the Factory Movement, it is now clear, began in Lancashire, rather than with Oastler's Yorkshire agitation in 1830, and it was the militant Cotton Spinners' Union which first created the rudiments of a popular organization and gained support from the radical press (Kirby and Musson 1975: 346–406; Glen 1984: 70–2).

The widespread employment of female and child labour long predated the steam-powered factory. Domestic and workshop manufacture in the eighteenth century was based on intensive exploitation. Nobody thought it desirable to protect children from the tyranny of their parents; on the contrary, parents were expected to accustom their offspring to early 'habits of industry'. As Maxine Berg has pointed out: 'Small was sometimes beautiful, but more often it was dependent, oppressive and exploitative' (Berg 1985: 19–20). Again, it is important to recall the relatively limited extent of the factory system in the early nineteenth-century economy, as it developed alongside a massive expansion of outwork processes and small-scale enterprises. A vast amount of capitalist enterprise was organized on the basis of hand technology rather than steam power and on fearsomely back-breaking physical labour. The outworkers, 'insecure, exploited, undefended, often unnoticed', remained for decades more numerous than the factory operatives (Musson 1976; Samuel 1977; Levine 1985; Hopkins 1982; Bythell 1978: 254). There is a good deal of evidence for an overall deterioration of working conditions, especially for children. According to John Rule:

> to a greater and more systematic extent than pre-existing modes of production, the factory system separated child labour from the family economy and placed it in a more intolerable total environment. Long, regimented hours, more formal discipline and the danger of the mangling of tired limbs from unguarded machinery, all imply differences in both the form and pace of child labour (Rule 1986: 142).

Steam-powered factories not only had an adverse effect on the health of their younger employees, but also posed a threat to the livelihoods of thousands of handworkers in the domestic system in the cotton, woollen and worsted textile districts. Not surprisingly, Lancashire, Yorkshire and the Glasgow area formed the heartland of the Factory Movement. In 1833 there were 100,000 power looms in the cotton industry and 213,000 handloom weavers. By 1850 the latter had been reduced to 40,000. Worsted mills proliferated during the 1830s as hand-spinning disappeared and handloom weavers were squeezed by the growth in the number of power looms from 2,800 in 1836 to 19,000 in 1845. The handloom weavers had largely disappeared by the end of the 1850s. Only in woollens did weaving remain a predominantly manual and domestic industry before mid-century (Bythell 1969: 54–7; Crouzet 1982: 216–17). Hence the Factory Movement of the early 1830s focused on present fears and future trends rather than reflecting the actual structure of the textile industry. In 1835, for example, there were only 204 worsted mills, employing 17,800 workers, with a mere smattering of woollen mills (Jenkins and Ponting 1982: 31).

The Factory Movement, which first made a major impact at national level late in 1830, when Richard Oastler, a Tory land steward from Huddersfield, sent his celebrated letter to the *Leeds Mercury* on 'Yorkshire Slavery', was a strange and complex agitation (Driver 1946: 39–42). Most of its founders were Tories and Anglicans from northern industrial towns, committed to a romantic and paternalistic model of society, which, if necessary, might be promoted by state intervention. They were as deeply hostile to parliamentary reform and workers' organizations as they were to Dissenters, orthodox political economy and *nouveaux riches* manufacturers. Many of those who financed the movement were themselves well-established factory owners and members of Tory urban elites facing a challenge locally from Dissenting entrepreneurs. They were supported by courageous pioneers of social medicine concerned about epidemics and deformity among factory children, by literary figures like Coleridge, Southey and Wordsworth, and by many landowners and squires. Attitudes towards factory legislation were complicated, for agrarian interests, industrial interests, Tories, Whigs and Radicals were all divided on the issue. Even the classical economists failed to speak with one voice, most of them favouring the regulation of child labour, though not that of adults, whilst at the same time opposing the ten-hour day (Ward 1970: 58–62; O'Brien 1975: 277–8).

Oastler, who possessed considerable histrionic oratorical and journalistic gifts, was soon drawn into the already existing working-class agitation for the restriction of the hours of child labour in textile factories, becoming head of a network of 'short-time committees' in the northern textile districts which demanded the ten-hour day. The Factory Movement, which reached its peak simultaneously with the Reform agitation at a time of severe economic recession, held considerable appeal for those domestic workers in textiles who had formed proud and prosperous labour elites, but who now faced the prospect of declining living standards, inferior working conditions and redundancy in the face of new machinery. This was especially true of the handloom weavers, croppers and combers in the West Riding of Yorkshire.

Although much of the evidence, even that given before government inquiries, has to be treated with some caution, there is little doubt that children, particularly pauper children without family protection, were cruelly treated in many textile mills, as well as working long hours in unhealthy conditions at a time of intense competition. There were certainly many middle-class supporters of factory legislation who were primarily motivated by moral outrage and humanitarian sentiments, shaped by Christian sensibilities. On the other hand, there were also those who were in it for very unsentimental motives of political power and social status. The mass of working-class supporters tended to regard the Ten Hour Movement basically as a struggle over the length and control of the working day, rather than as a moral crusade on behalf of little children. A survey of 1833–4 suggested that about half the children in cotton factories were engaged, supervised and paid by adult operatives, often the children's parents.

The ten-hour day had become normal in much eighteenth-century industry, but hours in mechanized textiles inexorably lengthened during the first three decades of the nineteenth century. To restrict the hours of factory children opened the prospect of slowing down the introduction and competitiveness of steam-powered factories and (assuming that a reduction in children's hours by law would mean a reduction of adult hours in practice) of gaining wage increases by working fewer hours for the same pay (Hunt 1981: 11; Henriques 1979: 67, 86–7; Berg 1980: 233). Factory operatives, understandably less anxious than workers in domestic industry to restrict the spread of machinery, hoped that a ten-hour limitation would increase the use of machinery, and with it the demand for labour, thus resulting in higher wages and more employment.

During the early 1830s the Factory Movement amounted to an impressive mass agitation in the textile districts of England and Scotland in support of the Ten Hours Bill. Central committees and delegate conferences were organized by Oastler and financed by rich manufacturers like John Fielden of Todmorden, Joseph Brotherton of Salford and John Wood and William Walker of Bradford. Pamphlets, petitions and tracts were issued by the thousand, as 'missionaries' were despatched throughout the textile areas to highlight the horrors of child labour in the mills. Impressive mass demonstrations were held, including the 'pilgrimage' to York on Easter Monday 1832 and the July 1833 giant rally at Wibsey Low Moor, near Bradford (Ward 1962: 104–5). Thousands of workers proved willing to ignore the hostility of the Movement's leaders towards their political aspirations, besides putting on one side popular hostility towards the Church and turning a blind eye to the darker side of paternalism: its insistence on a harsh penal code, savage game laws, low wages and poor living conditions for rural labourers, as well as its desire to exercise close supervision of the conduct and morals of the lower orders (Roberts 1979: 109–28, 143, 204).

Apart from a combination of humanitarian feeling and economic self-interest, workers were also motivated by anger at the exclusiveness of the Dissenting Liberal manufacturers who supported the Reform Bill but opposed universal suffrage, while welcoming the erosion of the old 'moral economy' and legislation regulating wages, working conditions and the labour supply. Nevertheless, the alliance between Anglican Tories and working-class radicals was always something of a marriage of convenience, given that many working-class supporters of the Factory Movement retained their membership of Political Unions and were unwilling to go so far as to offer automatic support to Tory election candidates (Royle and Walvin 1982: 154–5).

In the event, Oastler and his movement had little success with the Whig government, while Peel and the Conservative leaders kept the agitation at arm's length. When Michael Sadler moved a Ten Hours Bill in March 1832 he was obliged to accept the appointment of a Select Committee to take evidence from the operatives. Meanwhile the factory masters organized a vigorous lobby to resist further legislation, arguing that shorter working hours could result only in a victory for foreign competition, leading to lower wages and unemployment (Ward 1962: 56–63). The dissolution of 1832 led to Sadler's defeat at Leeds and his replacement by the young Evangelical Lord Ashley as parliamentary spokesman for the Ten Hours campaign. A Royal Commission was appointed, whose recommendations formed the basis of the Factory Act of 1833 which banned the employment of under-nines in most textile mills, limited children aged nine to thirteen to an eight-hour day and 'young persons' of thirteen to eighteen to a twelve-hour day. Thus the ten-hour day was rejected and Ashley out-manoeuvred. The hope of working-class supporters of the campaign that adult hours would in practice be limited was dashed by the tactic of working children in shifts to permit an adult day of up to sixteen hours. Although an inspectorate was established, it took some years before the Act was effectively enforced (Henriques 1979: 99–105).

From 1834 the Factory Movement had a chequered history, never again reaching the scale of the early 1830s. The 'Society for National Regeneration', based in Manchester and headed by Robert Owen and John Fielden, aimed at 'an eight-hour day for twelve hours pay', but folded with the collapse of the Owenite general unions in 1834. Factory Movement leaders like Oastler and the Rev. G. S. Bull became increasingly involved in resistance to the New Poor Law of 1834. Further campaigns during the 1840s, conducted in a somewhat lower key, although still involving conflict with self-interested millowners, eventually led to the Act of 1847, although relays of child workers persisted until the 10½ hour Act of 1850. A fixed working day for children came only with Palmerston's 1853 Act and a genuine Ten Hour Act only in 1874, which coincided with the beginning of a really substantial decline in child labour.

TRADE UNIONISM AND THE TOLPUDDLE MARTYRS

During the early 1830s, working-class radicalism pressed forward on several fronts: the political, the ideological and the economic. Much organized working-class radical pressure was provided by the trade societies, for the years 1829–34 witnessed an unprecedented burst of trade union activity. Attempts were made to establish more district and general unions of skilled workers and to embrace radical social and political theories. John Doherty and the Lancashire cotton spinners led the way by vainly attempting to create a general federation of cotton spinners for England, Scotland and Ireland in the wake of failed strikes. Doherty's National Association for the Protection of Labour sounded grand, but amounted to very little. In the *Crisis* of October 1833, a year of rapid trade-union growth at a time of good harvests and full employment, Robert Owen announced the establishment of a body which the trade societies transformed into the Grand National Consolidated Trades Union in February 1834.

The GNCTU aroused considerable fear and hostility among employers, although its actual membership and scope were subsequently exaggerated by the Webbs in their pioneering *History of Trade Unionism* and by G. D. H. Cole in his *Attempts at General Union* (1953). In fact the GNCTU proved a spectacular failure, lasting only a year before collapsing because of internal divisions and employer opposition. It had only 16,000 paid-up members and was essentially London-based, failing to attract the four major unions: Builders, Potters, Spinners and Clothiers (Oliver 1964). Most of the societies of skilled men in the provinces confined themselves to traditional sectional 'bread and butter' issues of wages, hours and working conditions, unwilling to subordinate themselves to Owen, whose contact with working-class leaders had been negligible before 1832 and who, dealing in broad generalities, had little real insight into trade union activities and ambitions.

The fact that Owenite experiments involving labour exchanges, where notes denoting 'labour value' would become a medium of exchange, came to little, was a further factor prompting the majority of skilled societies to steer clear of Owen and grandiose attempts to create a national network of strike relief funds. The swift collapse of the attempts at general union was not, in fact, so great a setback as once supposed. A considerable number of trade societies were able to survive and remain active, even in the less favourable economic climate of the later 1830s (Fraser 1970: 95–114; Musson 1972: 29–35; Finlayson 1969: 80–1; Rule 1986: 298–304).

By contrast, most attempts at formal unionism among unskilled workers were short-lived, given the abundance of unqualified labour seeking work and its consequent lack of scarcity value. Unskilled unionism also faced formidable problems of organization, communication, funds and leadership (Hunt 1981: 196–7). Trade unions remained, therefore, largely confined to skilled workers. Unskilled unionism also faced intransigent opposition from employers. When, in late 1833, a group of farm labourers at Tolpuddle in Dorset, paid only seven shillings a week and determined to resist a reduction to six, established a Friendly Society of Agricultural Labourers after making contact with London and Leeds trade unionists, and later with the GNCTU, it met with a savage response both from the local magistracy and the Whig government, still smarting from the Swing riots of 1830.

James Frampton, a vindictive local squire and magistrate, had six men arrested and, with considerable guidance and assistance from Home Secretary Melbourne and the government law officers, tried at Dorchester Assizes in March 1834. After a travesty of a trial, where the grand jury of local squires was chaired by Melbourne's brother-in-law, and the petty jury was composed of tame farmers, the six men were convicted of the extraordinary offence of administering an oath not to reveal a combination which administered such oaths. They were sentenced by a biased judge to seven years transportation for an initiation ceremony which they did not realize constituted a criminal offence, a conviction made possible by prosecution under laws against sedition passed in 1797 and 1799 (Marlow 1972: 59–79).

Evidence is steadily accumulating that Tolpuddle was only the most prominent example of quite widespread rural trade unionism during the early 1830s, which helps to explain why Frampton and his fellow landowners and clerical magistrates were determined to prevent the spread of organization among agricultural workers (Rule 1986: 362). As he wrote to Melbourne:

> the event of this trial has been looked forward to with the greatest anxiety by all Classes in this County: the farmers feeling that on it depended whether they should in future have any controul over their Labourers; and the Labourers only waiting to join the Union as soon as they were satisfied they could do so with impunity. The conviction and the prompt execution of the sentence of transportation has given the greatest satisfaction to all the Higher Classes, and will, I have no doubt, have a very great effect among the Labourers.[7]

Meanwhile Melbourne was writing to Lord Lyttleton complaining about 'the obstinate fidelity with which the lower classes cling to one another', adding 'at the same time I trust that the convictions which have lately taken place in Dorchester will have some great effect in proving to them the illegality of their combinations' (Ziegler 1976: 160).

As the convicted men were sent through the dreaded hulks and on their way to New South Wales and Tasmania with suspicious haste, their case was taken up by the trade societies, the press (both stamped and unstamped) and by Radical MPs like Joseph Hume, Thomas Wakley and Daniel O'Connell. A procession of at least 30,000 radicals and trade unionists through the capital on 21 April 1834, ostensibly in protest at the sentence, but also as a symbolic display of resentment at government and employer hostility, caused Melbourne to have sworn in 5,000 special constables, besides having troops ready in case of violence (Citrine 1934: 63–6). After a flood of petitions and a series of parliamentary motions, with Melbourne replaced by the more flexible Russell at the Home Office in 1835, a full pardon was granted to the six 'Tolpuddle Martyrs' exactly two years after sentence.

It was a famous victory for both working-class and middle-class radical movements, yet something of a Pyrrhic one, in that agricultural trade unionism failed to develop before the 1870s on any scale. But it is satisfying to record that James Hammett, the most silent and obdurate of the six, who did not set foot back in England until five years and four months after sentence, insisted on living in Tolpuddle under the noses of the Frampton family until his death in 1891.

THE ANTI-POOR LAW AGITATION

An enormous amount of working-class radical energy and indignation was poured into the Anti-Poor Law Movement, which rose to a crescendo in the manufacturing areas of Lancashire and the West

Riding of Yorkshire in 1837–8 before merging with the Chartist agitation. It was to a considerable degree an extension of the Factory Movement, in that it involved much the same organization and personnel. Impetus for the reform of the poor law in 1834 stemmed from what many men of property regarded as unacceptably burdensome poor rates, which fell disproportionately heavily on the agrarian community. Between 1803 and 1833 poor rates in England and Wales rose by 62 per cent, though population growth meant that the increase in *per capita* expenditure was relatively slight. The Swing Riots of 1830 also helped undermine the old poor law and further encouraged an increasingly punitive attitude towards the poor (Digby 1982: 9–11; Apfel and Dunckley 1985).

Like the Factory Act of 1833, the 1834 Poor Law Amendment Act was based on the report of a Royal Commission dominated by Utilitarians and orthodox political economists. A central board of three Poor Law Commissioners, aided by Assistant Commissioners, was created to recast the poor relief system in line with the recommendations of the Royal Commission. The Board was encouraged to eradicate idleness, corruption and parochial maladministration, while assuming that much poverty was a result of individual moral failings. There was to be less aid in the future. Hitherto independent parishes were to be grouped into Poor Law Unions, governed by elected Boards of Guardians. The Commissioners aimed to guide these local boards in implementing improved methods of relief, especially the gradual withdrawal of 'outdoor relief' in the form of payments in cash or kind, and its replacement by 'indoor relief' in a well-regulated workhouse.

Although the Act met relatively little opposition in parliament, it was widely unpopular in the localities, even in areas where there was no organized protest movement. Samuel Kydd, a young shoemaker in the 1830s, later wrote: 'The passing of the New Poor Law Amendment Act did more to sour the hearts of the labouring population, than did the privations consequent on all the actual poverty of the land.' It caused working men to 'dislike the country of their birth, to brood over their wrongs, to cherish feelings of revenge, and to hate the rich of the land' (Thompson 1984: 30). In southern and eastern England, the incidence of rural protest against the 1834 Act was greater than was once realized, although there was a lack of leaders to weld together a coherent movement from a scattered rural population. In many urban areas there was relatively little agitation; for example on Tyneside, where the late 1830s were relatively and unusually prosperous, as well as in Manchester, Doncaster, Nottingham, Derby and Leicester (Digby 1976: 152; McCord 1979: 90–1; Ashforth 1976: 131).

When in late 1836 the Commissioners began to implement the New Poor Law north of the Trent, they met determined resistance in the textile towns which had formed the backbone of the Factory Agitation and where the short-time committees were promptly transformed into anti-Poor Law organizations. Magistrates and poor-law officials in these towns had assumed that the new system was specifically devised for the rural south, with little relevance to northern industrial areas. No workhouse could accommodate the thousands of able-bodied men suddenly thrown out of work by a downward swing of the trade cycle. It would be more economical, as well as more humane, to relieve unemployed factory operatives and textile outworkers by a dole of a few shillings a week (Rose 1966, 1970: 83). Not only did administrators of the old poor law in the northern textile districts intensely dislike the centralizing features of the 1834 Act and the power of the Poor Law Commissioners, but they also prided themselves on already having introduced reform in the industrial parishes by establishing select vestries and employing salaried officials. *Per capita* costs were significantly lower than in the 'pauperized' south. Hence there was much resentment of the threat of interference from London. As Joseph Ellison, a Dewsbury guardian, informed a Select Committee in 1837: 'The general feeling is this "What a pity that a system which has worked so well and has produced so much good, should now be broken up!"' (Rose 1971: 112). Meanwhile large numbers of working men and women feared mass incarceration in poor-law 'Bastilles' under a punitive and cruel regime.

Some of the methods adopted by Oastler, Ferrand, Fielden and other leaders of the Anti-Poor Law movement were those they had developed during the Factory Agitation: petitions, press and pamphlet campaigns, and protest meetings culminating in massive demonstrations like that at Peep Green (Hartshead Moor) in the heart of the West Riding textile area on Whit Tuesday 1837. Unlike the earlier agitation, however, there was also considerable violence. Assistant Commissioner Alfred Power, already much disliked for his role as a Factory Commissioner in 1833, was burned in effigy at Huddersfield, had to escape from an angry crowd at Bury, had his greatcoat torn off his back at Keighley and went in fear of his life at Bradford (Edsall 1971: 53–115). An angry mob stormed the meeting place of the Guardians at Huddersfield, preventing the election of a clerk and delaying the implementation of the Act for over a year.

Power himself reported to his superiors the Bradford violence, where a running battle in the streets between a crowd of about 5,000 and 500 troops and special constables was only finally quelled by substantial military reinforcements and a state of virtual martial law. Power described how the Court House, where the Guardians and magistrates were to meet, was defended by cavalry against a huge hostile crowd, which showered the building with stones. The Guardians and magistrates were smuggled out, but the clerk, Mr Wagstaff, was trapped:

> Mr. Wagstaff was detained in the building and beset by the mob for some hours, who, on the military retiring, demolished the windows on every side. . . . About five o'clock Mr Wagstaff was rescued from his perilous

situation by a detachment of the cavalry, attended by the magistrates . . . on returning through the streets to the Talbot Inn, the crowd closed upon the party in such a manner as to make it necessary to charge them, when several shots were fired, and some persons cut down. . . . Many persons have been seriously hurt, both by sabre and gun-shot wounds.[8]

Similar violence, in which a good many women participated, took place in 1838 at Dewsbury and Todmorden.

In Power's words, the Anti-Poor Law agitation involved 'a considerable number of respectable and influential persons', including Anglican clergymen like the Rev. Patrick Brontë of Haworth, who argued that the New Poor Law undermined traditional Christian responsibility to care for the poor, as well as squires and magistrates who regarded the Poor Law Commissioners as usurpers of the power of parliament, threatening to interfere with the hallowed practices of local administration and the ability of local bodies to manage their own affairs and their own finances. Lesser officials, like parish overseers and members of select vestries, feared loss of status, jobs and lucrative contracts.

The working classes, alarmed by the multitude of (often exaggerated) horror stories of ill-treatment and starvation in the new workhouses, feared confinement in conditions more severe than those of penal servitude. In the eyes of popular radical leaders, the New Poor Law was yet another example of Whig betrayal, to be ranked alongside the Reform Act of 1832, the Factory Act of 1833, the persecution of the unstamped press and the sentences inflicted on the Tolpuddle labourers in 1834 and the Glasgow cotton spinners in 1837. According to Bronterre O'Brien, writing in the *Northern Star* on 24 February 1838: 'The New Poor Law was passed . . . to place the whole of the labouring population at the utter mercy and disposal of the monied or property owning classes' (Rose 1970: 81).

As a mass agitation, the Anti-Poor Law movement did not last long. It was to some extent a victim of its own success, for the new Law was applied only in very diluted form in Yorkshire and Lancashire before mid-century. It proved impossible for the Poor Law Commissioners to browbeat recalcitrant Guardians without holding the purse-strings. The notorious 'workhouse test' was therefore never enforced, while outdoor relief continued as before, administered by much the same personnel. No workhouse was erected in the West Riding during the 1840s; the very geography of the new Poor Law Unions remained unsettled before the 1860s. Much the same was true of north-east Lancashire (Ashforth 1976: 133; Boyson 1960). In Fielden's Todmorden, the existing workhouse was closed and no replacement opened. The New Poor Law was therefore successfully resisted for some considerable time.

By 1839, moreover, the Tory–Radical alliance was beginning to come apart, as working men were increasingly attracted by a renewal of the campaign for manhood suffrage and by the commencement of the struggle for the People's Charter. They therefore increasingly resented the paternalistic attitudes of the Anti-Poor Law leaders, who were as hostile to democracy as they were to utilitarian bureaucracy and regarded Chartism as an attempt to subvert 'the good old Constitution'. Popular radicals and Church-and-King Tories were poles apart on such issues as the Corn Laws and church rates, let alone extension of the franchise. There were also a number of rank-and-file resisters of the New Poor Law who by late 1838 had become alienated by the violent tactics of the movement.

Although the majority of working-class supporters of the Anti-Poor Law movement were diverted into Chartism for a decade, popular hatred of the Poor Law persisted in radical political programmes until after the First World War. While there was no starvation in the workhouse, which generally provided a better standard of diet and physical accommodation than found in most labourers' cottages, the depersonalization of the individual under the workhouse regime, the wearing of uniforms, the splitting up of families and a monotonous and regimented existence amounted to formidable psychological terrorism. In some areas, like County Durham, an initially benign regime became much harsher during adverse economic conditions in the 1840s (McCord 1969; Dunkley 1974).

Few people looked forward to the prospect of being deprived of sexual intercourse, tobacco and fermented liquors; to being silent at meals in frequently crowded conditions behind high walls, without being free to go out or to receive visitors. Horror of the workhouse and the final indignity of a pauper's funeral remained deeply ingrained in working-class consciousness until the twentieth century (Digby 1982: 16–17; Henriques 1968; Henriques 1979: 49; Laslett 1971: 213).

By the summer of 1838 a powerful working-class radical movement was in existence, representing a revival and extension of that which had flourished after 1815 before fading during the 1820s. Working-class radicals in the later 1830s were angry and frustrated at the policies of the Whig government: the failure of the vast majority of working men to gain votes in 1832, the administration's outmanoeuvring of the Ten-Hour campaign by the Factory Act of 1833, the passing of the detested New Poor Law of 1834, the treatment of the Dorset labourers and Glasgow cotton spinners, as well as persecution of trade unionism generally. Such anger and frustration had led to the creation of more extensive and securely based working-class radical organizations: the short-time committees, the Anti-Poor Law networks, the spread of trade societies and the elaborate infrastructure of the unstamped press.

When a major economic depression loomed in 1838–9, these organizations reverted to the common denominator uniting them: the belief that only a campaign for manhood suffrage, leading to significant working-class influence on, if not control of, the central organs of the state, could effect a substantial improvement in the dignity, status and material living standards of labouring men and their families. There is a sense, therefore, in which study of popular radicalism from the late eighteenth century is essentially a study of the pre-history of the Chartist movement.

NOTES AND REFERENCES

1. T. B. Macaulay, *Speeches, Parliamentary and Miscellaneous*, 1853, i: 12–14.
2. Edward Baines to Lord John Russell, 7 November 1831. E. Baines junior, *Life of Edward Baines*, 2nd edn. 1859, pp. 129–31.
3. Parliamentary Papers, 1866, lviii, *Borough Electors (Working Classes) Return*: 47ff.
4. H.O. 64/11. 6 August 1831.
5. *Poor Man's Guardian*, 72, 27 October 1832.
6. *Destructive*, 7 June 1834.
7. James Frampton to Viscount Melbourne, 29 March 1834. Melbourne Papers, British Library Add. Mss, 41567, f.125.
8. Alfred Power to Poor Law Commissioners, 21 November 1837 (copy), Harewood Papers (Lord Lieutenancy), Leeds City Archives.

Chapter 6

THE CHARTIST CHALLENGE 1838–48

INTERPRETATION

During the decade 1838–48 popular radicalism was dominated by Chartism, a mass working-class movement making a determined bid for political power. Chartism marked the climax of the radical technique since 1815 of applying pressure on the government by means of a constitutional campaign, embracing mass-platform agitation and mass petitioning, to achieve a radical political programme which originated in the third quarter of the eighteenth century (Belchem 1981). At the same time, it proved the apogée of the underground conspiratorial tradition reaching back to the Despard Plot. The two traditions were encapsulated in the Chartist slogan 'Peaceably if we can: forcibly if we must' and were to provide a constant source of disagreement and friction among both leaders and followers.

Historians still have difficulty in providing a satisfactory interpretation of Chartism. When, in the final years of the nineteenth century, a new generation of working men took the initiative in recreating independent working-class politics, intellectuals and academics associated with the revival saw Chartism as providing them with a legitimizing tradition. For the next half-century Chartist historiography was dominated by *The Chartist Movement* (1918), a Fabian interpretation by Mark Hovell, whereby the Chartists were viewed as precursors of mid-century working-class Liberalism. He depicted Chartism as beginning with the drawing up of the People's Charter by a group of rational, self-educated, non-violent and wholly admirable artisans. Unfortunately their sterling work was appropriated by the vain, demagogic O'Connor, who took their programme to the illiterate and semi-barbaric population of the northern industrial districts, whose violence alienated middle-class sympathy and prevented parliament from accepting the Chartist petition, thus depriving the movement of any chance of success.

Marxist writers in the twentieth century have tended to follow the contemporary arguments of Engels in his *The Condition of the Working Class in England*, written when he was only twenty-four and published in 1845. For Engels, Chartism was the first genuinely proletarian political movement, attempting to 'put a proletarian law in the place of the legal fabric of the bourgeoisie ... in Chartism it is the whole working class which arises against the bourgeoisie and attacks, first of all, the legalistic rampart with which the bourgeoisie has surrounded itself'. It was the strikes and demonstrations of 1842 which, according to Engels, marked 'the decisive separation of the proletariat from the bourgeoisie', as the bourgeoisie turned their backs on physical force. From 1843 and the failure of the Complete Suffrage Union, 'Chartism was purely a working-man's cause, freed from all bourgeois elements ... a class movement' (Engels 1969 edn: 254, 259–61).

Both the above interpretations have, however, suffered at the hands of recent scholarship. Hovell's dichotomy between London as the source of ideas concocted by intelligent skilled artisans, and the provinces as the source of unfocused energy and mindless, self-defeating violence, has been effectively undermined (Thompson 1977). In industrial Lancashire, for example, there existed in the decade before the Charter a sophisticated and powerful political and industrial organization, involving trade unionism, attempts at general unions, campaigns for the suffrage and factory reform, as well as resistance to the New Poor Law and to coercion in Ireland. It is now clear that, whereas Chartism became a mass movement in the northern industrial districts in 1838 and 1839, in London it became so only after 1840 among the artisan trades which made up the bulk of the metropolitan labour force (Kirby and Musson 1975; Goodway 1970). Nor were the artisans all moderate, rational and non-violent, in the mould of, say, William Lovett, given that many were involved in riots and conspiracies, including the Newport Rising.

Engels has fared rather better, especially in perceiving the essential aims of the movement and its basically working-class character. But he depicted the proletariat as more monolithic and united than it actually was, and neglected the connections which many Chartists maintained with both middle-class organizations and bourgeois ideology, especially after 1842. Chartists never became 'sharply separated from the radical petty-bourgeoisie', for the simple reason that many of its local activists were members of that very social stratum, so much despised by Engels. Preoccupied with an increasingly exploited industrial proletariat and seeing Chartism as an embryonic socialist movement, which it certainly was not, Engels failed to stress the prominence in Chartism of the artisan tradition and how Chartism may be seen as marking the climax of an increasingly politicized artisan ideology. Hence he neglected the traditional elements in Chartism. For example, the wide appeal of O'Connor's Land Plan lay partly in the prominent role independent cultivation played in the radical tradition from the Levellers to Cobbett. The six points of the Charter were themselves mere restatements of an eighty-year-old radical agenda (Engels 1969 edn: 255; Price 1986: 57).

In 1959 the publication of *Chartist Studies*, edited by Asa Briggs, inaugurated something of a new orthodoxy. Briggs stressed the localized orientation of Chartism, a movement lacking inner coherence and organizational identity, being essentially a cluster of movements sheltering under the Chartist banner and drawing its support from obsolescent handloom weavers, skilled artisans and factory operatives. These groups, uneasily bound together by the vibrant personality of Feargus O'Connor and the agency of the *Northern Star*, lacked a common economic base to provide unity. Political energies were seriously divided between those whose main goal was manhood suffrage and those more concerned with factory legislation, Poor Law reform, trade union and co-operative programmes, newspaper stamp repeal and a host of lesser campaigns (Briggs 1959: 1–28; Judge 1975).

Emphasis on the diverse and episodic character of Chartism stimulated a valuable series of detailed local and thematic studies, though often at the price of undervaluing Chartism as a national political movement greater than the sum of its parts and of exaggerating local irrationality and spontaneous protest. The view of Chartism as essentially a national political movement and, following Engels, the world's first national labour movement, was reasserted by Edward Thompson in 1963 when he portrayed the Chartists as natural heirs of a new working-class identity and consciousness forged in the popular radical movement from 1792 and tempered by the exclusion of the propertyless from the franchise in 1832 (Thompson 1968 edn: 909). More recent research has tended to reinforce the nature of Chartism as a considered rational agitation; primarily a political reaction to political events (Royle and Walvin 1982: 161). Distinguished by their commitment to political radicalism, Chartists can no longer be dismissively categorized as mere 'hunger politicians'.

In his penetrating speculative essay 'Rethinking Chartism', Gareth Stedman Jones has pointed out how a good deal of recent research on the local roots and occupational peculiarities of Chartism has tended to obscure the extent to which it was a national movement with primarily political aims. This is not, of course, to deny that thousands of rank-and-file supporters were deeply affected by the vagaries of the trade cycle and the introduction of machinery, as well as by the atrocious living conditions and environmental pollution in expanding and largely unregulated industrial towns. Many of those drawn into Chartism by unemployment and hunger during the economic recessions of 1837–42 and 1847–8 may have regarded the six points of the Charter as a kind of ritual incantation, recited as a solution to their desperate situation; as a means of restoring the pre-industrial 'moral economy' and traditional artisan status. It may be that the intense political awareness of Chartist leaders and spokesmen at both national and local level was only imperfectly reflected among the mass of supporters of the movement and that the vigorously pursued programme of Chartist political education had its limits (Stedman Jones 1983: 98–9; Royle 1980: 6–7).

It was to the relatively untutored rank-and-file that J. R. Stephens, the Tory Methodist minister and Anti-Poor Law demagogue, appealed in his speech at the great Chartist meeting on Kersal Moor, Manchester, in September 1838:

> This question of Universal Suffrage was a knife and fork question after all; this question was a bread and cheese question, notwithstanding all that had been said against it; and if any man should ask him what he meant by Universal Suffrage, he would answer that every working man in the land had the right to have a good coat to his back, a comfortable abode in which to shelter himself and his family, a good dinner upon his table, and no more work than was necessary for keeping him in health, and as much wages for that work as would keep him in plenty, and afford him the enjoyment of all the blessings of life which a respectable man could desire.[1]

None the less, it is erroneous to read back into Chartism the economic and social programme of later socialism and depict the six points as the cosmetic surface of a basically economic movement, an interpretation adopted by earlier historians like Mark Hovell and G. D. H. Cole. Political ideology and organization have at least an equal claim with economic and social structures to constitute the prime category of historical explanation. In much contemporary radical ideology, the significant class division was between the represented and the unrepresented. Hostility towards the middle classes stemmed not so much from their role as capitalists and employers, despite the efforts of Bronterre O'Brien and other advocates of radical alternative political economy, as from their participation since 1832 in a corrupt and unrepresentative political system. It was by means of this political system that the labouring classes – the real producers of wealth – were deprived of the fruits of their labour, most of which ended up in the pockets of the 'parasitic idle classes' who controlled parliament and taxation. Hence political rather than economic power remained the fundamental source of exploitation.

For Chartist leaders and the radical press, economic inequality derived from political inequality, not *vice versa*. The cardinal sin of the middle classes was their 'betrayal' of the working classes between 1830 and 1832 and their subsequent support of a government which had repressed trade unions, resisted the Ten Hours Bill, passed the New Poor Law and meted out harsh punishment to the Swing rioters, the Dorset labourers, the Glasgow cotton spinners, the Canadian rebels and those involved in the production and distribution of the unstamped press. There still persisted bitter resentment at a tax system which absorbed up to a half of a labourer's income, with 50 per cent of the revenue going to service the national debt and thus redistribute wealth up the social scale. As Robert Lowery noted in his autobiography: 'The prominent topics of the new press which had sprung up was class legislation, the unequal pressure of taxation on the working classes as shown in the taxes on leather, soap, tea, coffee, sugar and corn' (Harrison and Hollis 1979: 101). Only political power could shift the unequal fiscal burden, as well as providing an outlet for the growing artisan critique of industrial capitalism.

The increasing politicization of the working classes was facilitated by the operation of the electoral system itself. Between 1830 and the initial drafting of the People's Charter in 1837 there was considerable and unprecedented participation by working-class non-electors at five general elections, especially contested elections in industrial boroughs (Wright 1969b). The network of booksellers, newsagents, publishers and street vendors developed during 'the war of the unstamped' could be switched with little difficulty in 1837–8 to agitating for universal suffrage. So could the grass roots organization created in the northern industrial areas under the auspices of the Factory Movement and the agitation against the New Poor Law. The thousands of labouring men and women who had been involved in these movements brought to Chartism something of the moral, quasi-religious fervour of these campaigns, which provided a contrast to the rather more abstract concentration on political rights favoured by many Chartists elsewhere, especially in the metropolis. It is therefore hardly surprising that the cotton districts of Lancashire and the textile areas of the West Riding of Yorkshire were to prove the real heartland of Chartist militancy.

CHARTIST CLIMAX 1839–40

The Chartist movement did not follow a pattern of unilinear growth, but rather rose to a clear peak on three occasions; 1839–40, 1842 and 1848, each involving a mass petition to parliament and some disorder. The first occasion attracted by far the most widespread and impressive degree of support. In June 1836 the London Working Men's Association (LWMA) was founded, initially for metropolitan artisans, with Hetherington as treasurer and Lovett secretary. Honorary members from the provinces, as well as higher-class radicals like Fielden, Oastler, O'Connor and a couple of sympathetic radical MPs were also admitted. A petition was drafted in January 1837 containing the six points of the 'People's Charter': universal manhood suffrage, the ballot, annual parliaments, constituencies of equal size, payment of MPs and the abolition of the property qualification for members of the Commons. These were endorsed at a series of public meetings and by

May a petition had been signed by 3,000, whereupon the Charter in its final form was drawn up by a joint committee of six Radical MPs and six working men. The draft Bill, published a year later as 'The People's Charter', was composed by Lovett and Francis Place (Rowe 1967). Chartism therefore emerged from a tradition of articulate, politically-conscious, metropolitan artisan associations, with assistance from a small group of middle-class radicals.

Meanwhile Thomas Attwood revived the Birmingham Political Union in 1837, initially to campaign for the householder franchise, but soon supporting universal suffrage. Both the LWMA and BPU despatched 'missionaries' to various parts of the country to drum up support for the Charter. Radical associations committed to manhood suffrage had in fact already appeared in Scotland and northern England some of them at the instigation of Feargus O'Connor, who toured the north in 1835 after losing his Irish parliamentary seat and embarking on a new career as a leader of English working-class protest. Already prominent in the London unstamped agitation, O'Connor realized the difficulty of unifying London radicalism under single leadership. The huge size of the capital city, its pronounced localism and the existence of four hundred different trades prevented any strong sense of community (Goodway 1982: 223; Thompson 1968 edn: 23). But in northern industrial towns, often dominated by a single industry, O'Connor met with a more unified communal response to his ambitions and organizational plans.

During his three-week northern tour in December 1835, O'Connor founded manhood suffrage radical associations in Manchester, Stockport, Oldham, Rochdale, Leeds, Halifax, Huddersfield, Barnsley, Keighley, Hull and Sheffield. His attacks on the New Poor Law and support for the unstamped press, a Ten-Hour Bill and the release of the Tolpuddle labourers struck a sympathetic note with northern audiences, who accepted the desirability of national organization culminating in a 'National Convention'. Assuming the mantle of Henry Hunt as the leading radical gentleman of the platform, O'Connor soon became a popular hero, gaining the support of key local radical leaders like Lawrence Pitkethley of Huddersfield, Peter Bussey of Bradford and John Vallance of Barnsley. His reputation was consolidated by the formation of an alliance with Oastler and Stephens, his denunciation of the Whigs and the energy he invested in subsequent visits to the north, where he laboured to create a well-organized movement capable of sustained agitation (Read and Glasgow 1961: 44–5; Epstein 1982: 32–53; Thompson 1984: 32–3).

If O'Connor was an extraordinarily gifted demagogue, he was an equally effective organizer. During the winter of 1836–7 he broadened his base from London–Lancashire–Yorkshire to Nottingham, Newcastle and Scotland. O'Connor was a firm opponent of any alliance with the Whigs or middle-class radicals; hence his breach with Lovett and the

LWMA over the latter's continued co-operation with middle-class reformers and its lack of enthusiastic support for the convicted Glasgow cotton spinners. By mid-1838 O'Connor was in a position to exercise considerable hegemony over northern popular radicalism, having established the *Northern Star* in Leeds in November 1837 and gathered northern radical associations and Working Men's Associations into his Leeds-based Great Northern Union in April 1838. According to Francis Place, it was at this time that 'Feargus O'Connor became the Apostle of the North, the constant dominant leader, and at length ... in his own conceit, the master of the Radicals'.[2] In the absence of any national organization, O'Connor's constant touring helped to create a sense of inter-regional coherence. When other London radicals went north as 'missionaries', they discovered that the ground had already been well-prepared. It was O'Connor, more than anyone, who linked together traditional artisan radicalism and the more spontaneous mass movement of working-class protest emerging in the industrial districts.

Relative unity in the provinces contrasted with rivalries and divisions within London Chartism. In March 1838 Harney and some colleagues expressed their opposition to the LWMA's continuing connexion with Daniel O'Connell and middle-class radicals by seceding and joining Spenceans and Owenites in forming the East London Democratic Association to cater for the more depressed London trades like the Spitalfields silk weavers (Bennett 1982; Schoyen 1958: 23–6; Prothero 1969). By the summer of 1838 Chartism was a national movement. Although its main centres lay in the cotton districts of south Lancashire and the industrial areas of the West Riding, Birmingham and the East Midlands, Chartism was emerging rapidly in Scotland, while Henry Vincent's missionary tours founded associations in Wales and the West Country (Ward 1973: 96–9). In September came the first major outdoor meeting in the north on Kersal Moor, Manchester, when a large crowd was persuaded that a parliament elected by manhood suffrage would provide an all-embracing cure for their ills. Such regional meetings were held to enable the election of delegates to a National convention, scheduled to assemble in London early in 1839. Initially conceived for the purpose of organizing the national petition and seeing it through parliament, there were those who came to want the Convention to take on the role of a 'People's Parliament' or 'anti-parliament'.

During the winter of 1838–9 Chartist groups in numerous localities concentrated on gaining signatures to the petition. There was also a good deal of arming and drilling, which continued throughout 1839. In the cotton town of Ashton-under-Lyne, local millowners reported arming 'by great numbers', while the constables witnessed hundreds being drilled. Cutlasses and pikes were on open sale at shops in Stalybridge and in the market-places of Hyde and Rochdale. Similarly, in the West Riding there was evidence of the manufacture of pikes and purchase of muskets. According to the Bradford magistrates, 'the general belief is that a large number of the adherents of the Chartists are under Arms' (Sykes 1985; Thompson 1971: 206–17). In both Lancashire and the West Riding there were local leaders who supported a policy of mass arming, seen as a 'defensive' and 'constitutional' response by an exploited people at the mercy of a corrupt and unrepresentative government.

Bradford Chartists were among those most resolutely committed to physical force. At a meeting to establish a branch of the Great Northern Union in September 1838, addressed by O'Connor and attended by nearly 3,000, Joseph Brook, a woolcomber whose brother was to serve three years in Northallerton prison for his part in the 1840 'rising', declared:

> Should our petition be rejected, our demands resisted, what of that? The day of reckoning will come, and that quickly. Let us be prepared for this day, the day when we shall have to fight for our rights. I have been for three years acquainted with the use of the firelock, and when the day does come, I shall not flinch from my duty (loud and tremendous cheers). I wish that our rights might be obtained without bloodshed, though I greatly doubt it, and if the day of blood is ordained to come, then all I can say is that the sooner it come the better (continued cheers).[3]

At the West Riding meeting held on Peep Green on 15 October to elect delegates to the Convention, Peter Bussey, leader of the 6,000-strong Bradford contingent and himself elected a delegate, urged the crowd to obtain firearms, while a subsequent meeting of the Bradford Northern Union passed a resolution 'recommending the people to possess themselves of arms' (Peacock 1969: 19–20).

The fifty or so members of the National Convention met in London in February 1839, some representing several 'constituencies'. A quarter of the delegates were from the capital itself, with 20 from the industrial north, 8 from Scotland, 5 from Birmingham, 3 from the East Midlands and 2 from Wales. About half were working men, the others being mainly radical gentry and small employers. Divisions soon appeared over major issues. Should the Convention simply regard itself as an association, confined to managing the petition? Or should it become a 'People's Parliament', an overt and provocative rival to the House of Commons? There was also a failure to give a clear lead on such matters as organizing missionaries or collecting the 'national rent', although it was decided to oppose the middle-class Anti-Corn Law League.

The really crucial issue was whether, if the petition were rejected, physical force and insurrection should be contemplated, as was urged by militants like Bussey, G. J. Harney, Richard Marsden and Dr John Taylor, who assumed that the government would impose massive and violent repression after the rejection of the petition. Harney, who looked to French models of revolution, argued that troops could either be won over, or defeated in street fighting. In a speech at Derby, waving his red cap of liberty, he declared: 'Believe me there is no argument like the sword – and a musket is unanswerable'.[4] As the language of such militants became more extreme, so many of the more moderate delegates, including those from Birmingham, left the Convention and returned home (Parssinen 1973b; Ward 1973: 113–19; Kemnitz 1978).

In the meantime the government banned torchlight meetings and made it clear that violent rhetoric, arming and drilling, marching to fife and drum, would all be firmly resisted by the forces of law and order. John Frost, the tailor and draper who had been Mayor of Newport, was removed from the bench of magistrates for his colourful language and defence of Harney's views when he was chairman of the Convention. Henry Vincent was arrested and eventually imprisoned for attending illegal meetings. Six thousand troops were stationed in the Northern District under General Napier (Mather 1959a). When the Melbourne government resigned in May, the national petition – three miles long and containing 1,280,000 signatures – could not be presented to parliament. So the Convention, with its thirty-five surviving delegates, moved to Birmingham, where it proceeded to discuss a series of 'ulterior measures' to be adopted if the petition were eventually unsuccessful.

Chief among these were the withdrawal of bank deposits (in emulation of the threatened 'run on gold' of May 1832), abstention from excisable goods and liquor, and exclusive dealing, whereby pressure would be exerted on shopkeepers and tradesmen to contribute to Chartist funds (the 'national rent') at the risk of loss of custom. This latter tactic had been developed to a fine art by non-electors in industrial constituencies like Halifax. Most discussion took place on whether to launch a 'sacred month': a general strike advocated in a pamphlet published in 1832 by William Benbow, a militant shoemaker from Middleton who had helped organize the March of the Blanketeers. In the spring of 1839 he toured the north, calling on supporters to purchase muskets and prepare for the 'National Holiday' (Prothero 1974; Ruter 1936; Judge 1975).

At this stage the Home Office sharpened its offensive. A detachment of the much-hated Metropolitan Police, which acted as a national riot squad during the first decade of its existence, was sent to put down rioting Chartists at Llanidloes in Montgomeryshire in May. Severe punishments were handed out to some of those arrested (Thompson 1971: 17, 26, 222–5). After further arrests, the Convention was adjourned, with rank-and-file opinion tested at mass meetings in Lancashire, Yorkshire and Tyneside. Three days after the Convention reassembled in Birmingham on 1 July a crowd gathered illegally in the Bull Ring, clashing with troops and Metropolitan Police. Extreme 'physical force' demagogues like Dr John Taylor and Peter McDouall were seized, followed by William Lovett and John Collins when they criticized the authorities' handling of the affair (Hovell 1918: 156; Behagg 1982: 79–81). The remnants of the Convention, decimated by further arrests, moved back to London, where the petition was finally presented in the House of Commons by Thomas Attwood and John Fielden on 12 July, before being rejected by 235 votes to 46.

It was now time for the 'ulterior measures', but the Chartist movement was already in considerable disarray. In his pamphlet, Benbow had stressed that 'Before a month's holiday can take place, universal preparations must be made for it ... Every man must prepare for it, and assist his neighbour in preparing for it.'[5] The 'sacred month', to commence on 12 August, was endorsed in the Convention by only thirteen votes to six, with five abstentions. Letters from the localities pointed out that the necessary degree of preparation had not been undertaken. On 24 July, therefore, largely at O'Connor's instigation, the decision was reversed; it being left to the localities to decide for themselves whether to launch a general strike in their region. Thus the leadership drew back from a nationwide confrontation with the authorities involving widespread violence (Gammage 1854: 154; Epstein 1982: 174–5; King 1981: 12–14). The Convention itself was prorogued on 6 August, being finally dissolved in September by a rump of twenty-three delegates.

With national leadership in abeyance, it was now a matter of local initiatives, especially with the resurgence of the conspiratorial tradition of direct action and armed force. London's failure to rally to the Chartist cause in 1838–9 had dealt a fatal blow to the movement's chances of success (Goodway 1982: xiv). The bluff of the physical force Chartists was now being called. Secret meetings took place in the early autumn apparently concerned with planning a national rising, the lead to be taken by South Wales, Scotland and the West Riding. Only in South Wales, however, did a genuine rising take place.

On the night of 3–4 November 1839, seven thousand miners and ironworkers from the South Wales coalfield marched in three massive processions towards Newport, Monmouthshire. They were an organized force, bearing loaded guns, swords and pikes, and their rising, now the subject of definitive studies by David Jones and Ivor Wilks, proved to be the most serious clash between government and people in modern industrial Britain and the last genuine insurrection of British workers (Wilks 1984; Jones 1985). By the time the marchers belatedly reached Newport, their numbers had already been depleted by a torrential storm and all hope of surprise had been lost. The insurrectionists were led down the main street of Newport by John Frost, William Jones, a travelling actor and watchmaker, and Zephaniah Williams, mineral agent and infidel landlord of the Royal Oak, Blaina. The immediate aim of the insurgents was the release of Henry Vincent from Newport Gaol; yet there is evidence to suggest that they were also bent on launching a massive uprising and creating a people's republic in the Welsh valleys, which, hopefully, might spread across Britain.

When they reached the Westgate Hotel in the town centre, about thirty troops concealed inside the building opened fire. After a battle lasting only half-an-hour, the Chartists were put to flight, leaving behind at least twenty-two dead and scores wounded. Triumphant magistrates and employers proceeded to inflict severe retribution on Chartists, radicals of any description and friendly innkeepers. Over 250 men were arraigned in what turned out to be the last mass treason trial in British history. A Special Commission at Monmouth sentenced to death Frost, Williams and Jones. For reasons which are still not entirely clear, the death penalty was commuted to transportation for life to Australia.

Earlier historians were rather dismissive of the Newport Rising, depicting it as a small-scale and relatively innocuous affair, or as the work of *agents provocateurs* in the pay of the Whig government, or merely 'intended as a monster demonstration' (Williams 1939; Williams 1959: 241). Although Frost's exact role remains mysterious, it is now clear that the Welsh Chartists intended to launch a mass rising in south-east Wales, to link up with militant Chartist groups in various parts of England. The Newport rising emerged from a rapidly expanding industrial society, strictly demarcated on class lines, centred upon the ironworks and coalmines at the heads of the south-east Welsh valleys. The vast mining workforce not only revealed a remarkable capacity for self-help and self-reliance, manifest in an impressive range of institutions, but also a sophisticated political ideology, a network of secret organizations, and clear political objectives. The Newport rising was a product of this radical political culture, rather than being simply a spontaneous inchoate protest of the hungry and downtrodden. It also had ramifications outside Wales. From Nottingham, Carlisle, Birmingham, East London, Trowbridge and the West Riding came reports of radicals who were prepared to take up arms in the aftermath of Newport. While languishing in Monmouth Gaol, Frost anticipated a general rebellion about Christmas. Had he been executed, it is likely that Britain would have experienced unprecedented popular violence (Jones 1985: 213).

Further risings were planned in the wake of Newport, but attempts at insurrection took place only in Sheffield, Dewsbury and Bradford in January 1840. These towns had avoided the violent confrontation of July and August, which had led to Lancashire Chartism being crippled by a wave of arrests and the presence of large military and police forces (Sykes 1985: 233–4). Sheffield possessed a coherent and confident working-class movement, confronted by a weak and anomic bourgeoisie (Smith 1982: xi). Its vigorous tradition of political radicalism reached back to 1792 and in the later 1830s Chartism took a firm hold on the cutlers and edge-tool makers organized in the Sheffield Working Men's Association. By the summer of 1839, as elsewhere, divisions had appeared between the advocates of 'physical force' and 'moral force', with the former in the majority. After the rejection of the Chartist petition, there was a considerable amount of exclusive dealing in

Sheffield, as well as among the increasingly proletarianized Barnsley linen weavers, many of them militant Irishmen.

On 12 August a token one-day 'National Holiday' led to a mass meeting in Paradise Square, eventually cleared by dragoons. Samuel Holberry, a distillery worker, ex-soldier and General Baptist, emerged as leader of the militant Chartists. Moderates lay low after a series of meetings in defiance of the authorities led to clashes with troops and police, followed by numerous arrests. During the autumn of 1839, Sheffield Chartism went through a quasi-religious phase in a town where plebeian Nonconformity was endemic, with emotional torchlight camp meetings on Hood Hill, Attercliffe Common and Loxley Chase. At the same time, plans for insurrection were being hatched. There were south Yorkshire representatives at the secret committee held in London in October to co-ordinate preparations, while close contact was maintained with Peter Bussey and the Bradford militants. It seems likely that Sheffield and Barnsley Chartists knew of the planned Welsh rising well in advance.

Anger at the fate of John Frost pushed the hard core of Sheffield militants along the road to insurrection. At a meeting in Paradise Square on 11 November, the crowd was urged to obtain muskets. Holberry visited Dewsbury and various parts of South Yorkshire and the West Midlands to co-ordinate plans for a regional insurrection. It was finally decided to act on the night of 11–12 January 1840, when Sheffield, Rotherham and the outlying villages would rise simultaneously. Dewsbury would move independently, and Barnsley when news came of success at Sheffield. Holberry planned to create diversions in Rotherham and on the outskirts of Sheffield to lure the military from the town centre before proceeding to fortify the Town Hall and Tontine Inn. His followers, Irish immigrants and miners from nearby coalfields, rather than the cutlers, were equipped with guns, daggers, 'fireballs', bombs, pikes, hand-grenades and bayonets, as well as spiked iron 'cats' for throwing at the feet of charging cavalry horses. But the plan was never carried out, being betrayed to the magistrates and Lord Howard by the landlord of the Station Inn, Rotherham, who attended the final meetings before the projected rising. Holberry and his close associates were arrested before they could act. Consequently, only fifty or so men marched into the town centre before being put to flight by troops and police. At York Assizes, Holberry was sentenced to four years imprisonment (Pollard 1959: 44–47; Baxter 1976: 135–52; Salt 1967: 4–20).

Although Dewsbury failed to rise after the Sheffield *débâcle*, Bradford went ahead. The evidence concerning the background to the Bradford 'rising' of 26–27 January 1840 is fragmentary and elusive. It appears, however, that Peter Bussey had discussed the possibility of a national rising with Frost and others during the last days of the Convention and had chaired a meeting in West Yorkshire on 30

September which planned a simultaneous rising in South Wales and the north of England. In October 1839 a delegate from Bradford visited South Wales and tried to persuade Frost to postpone the Welsh rising, as the Yorkshire Chartists were ill prepared. When Frost insisted on carrying out his plans, it was promised that Bradford would rise once Newport was captured. As the time for the Welsh insurrection approached, Bussey got cold feet, went into hiding and left Bradford Chartists leaderless, although arms had been collected, bullets cast, and an insurrectionary network set up among the West Riding industrial towns and villages.

In Bradford, as in other places, there was much anger at the death sentences passed on Frost, Williams and Jones in December, and there was persistent talk of a rising to prevent their being hanged. Robert Peddie, a wild, quasi-Byronic Scots stay-maker arrived in Leeds after being in touch with the ultra-revolutionary Dr John Taylor and insurrectionists in Newcastle. Keen to replace Bussey and lead the West Riding in revolt, he was welcomed by Bradford militants as he concocted a scheme to take over the town at night, plunder the shops and banks, and then, with assistance from other West Riding towns, seize the local ironworks (a major manufacturer of armaments) before moving on to rouse further insurrections at Dewsbury, Sheffield and the East Midlands prior to marching on the capital. Like that at Sheffield, however, the Bradford rising was doomed by the presence of a spy at the heart of the plot. When Peddie and about forty armed men moved to seize control of the town centre after midnight on 27 January 1840, the authorities were ready. Messages calling up contingents from Halifax and Dewsbury had been entrusted to the spy, who naturally failed to deliver them. The Bradford insurgents were therefore speedily rounded up and sent to York for trial, where Peddie received three years hard labour and nine others lesser sentences (Jones 1985: 206; Thompson 1971: 280–6; Peacock 1969: 23–46).

By the spring of 1840 the Home Office, magistracy and military had systematically battered Chartism to defeat by mass arrests. Most of the national leaders, scores of local activists and hundreds of the rank-and-file were tried and imprisoned. Between June 1839 and June 1840 at least 543 Chartists were incarcerated, with sentences ranging from a few weeks to a few years. Lovett and Collins, for example, got twelve months; O'Brien and O'Connor eighteen months (Godfrey 1979). The first and most dramatic stage of Chartism was over, with its head well and truly lopped off. Never again was the movement able to recapture the excited atmosphere and sense of liberation and exhilaration created by the widespread belief in the possibility of success that existed in 1839, when there were over 500 centres of organized Chartism in England alone.

Chartist confidence was, however, based on mistaken assumptions. It was believed that a decisive confrontation between a mobilized, united people and an unrepresentative government would lead to precipitate acts of repression. Such acts would alienate public opinion and spark off an explosion of protest sufficient to overwhelm the forces of reaction. As in 1831–2, the government would be unable to resist overwhelming numbers. But things failed to work out as expected. Extreme Chartist rhetoric alienated moderate working men and potential middle-class radical allies. And it quickly became apparent that 'the people' were not united. Once the Chartists adopted defensive tactics, with leaders constantly warning against 'premature outbreaks', the initiative was handed to the authorities. Before the spring and summer of 1839, the Whig government was careful not to adopt a policy of uncompromising repression, thus allowing middle-class reformers and moderates time to become more anxious about Chartist violence than government repression.

The Chartists were left with a simple choice between defeat and insurrection, for there was no chance of the 'ulterior measures' and 'National Holiday' proving effective. Even at its peak in 1839, Chartism was geographically patchy, being heavily concentrated in towns dominated by a single industry. In some major boroughs with diversified economies, for example Bristol, Chartism attracted only a small minority of workers (Cannon 1964: 14–15). Vast tracts of agricultural England played no part in the agitation. The hardening of middle-class opposition in 1838–9 dealt a further blow to Chartist assumptions concerning a people united against a small parasitic class who used an unrepresentative parliament to pass 'unjust' laws. And to the surprise and chagrin of the Chartists, the authorities proved determined, competent and flexible. By the end of 1839 it was manifestly clear that there was no chance of defeating the state by force and that troops had no compunction about firing on Chartists if ordered to do so.

THE NATIONAL CHARTER ASSOCIATION

Defeat and mass arrests in 1839–40 left Chartism in considerable disarray. Nevertheless, there still existed a widespread desire in industrial areas to promote the People's Charter and 'a fair day's wage for a fair day's labour', despite disagreements about tactics and rivalries between Chartist leaders. As early as the summer of 1840 there was something of a revival as new organizations were created. In April, Hetherington's Metropolitan Charter Union was established in London. Three months later, very much at the prompting of O'Connor in his letters to the *Northern Star* from gaol, twenty-three delegates met in Manchester and founded the National Charter Association, which was to remain the major national organization for the next decade and has a claim to be the first independent political party of the working class (Epstein 1982: 220–35; Jones 1975: 70–6).

Under the Corresponding Societies Act, local branches of a national political organization were illegal, so the NCA was obliged to be a central body, with localities represented on a general council several hundred strong. During 1841 the NCA claimed 50,000 members from 401 localities, as it arranged lecturing circuits and co-ordinated the hard core of Chartist support. It was very much O'Connor's organization, which itself led to rival associations headed by men who could not stomach the super-confident Irish demagogue. Lovett, recently released from prison, launched a scheme for a National Association, while the Scots localities steered clear of the NCA until 1843. O'Connor himself, the 'Lion of Freedom' in the words of Thomas Cooper's popular song, was released from York Castle in August 1841, to resume his role as Chartism's most charismatic and dynamic leader, as he embarked on a triumphant tour of the country, welcomed everywhere by those he affectionately called his 'children'. Clad in symbolic working-class fustian, he rode in splendid coaches surrounded by flags and banners, amid cheering crowds (Read and Glasgow 1961: 96–7; Pickering 1986).

At a meeting in Birmingham in September, Dr Peter McDouall proposed that another national petition be launched and a Convention organized. This Convention, which eventually met in April 1842, was more efficiently organized than that of 1839; delegates being limited to twenty-four from English constituencies and twenty-five from Scotland and Wales. This time they were elected by paid-up members of the NCA rather than by mass meetings. The petition, better organized than three years previously, was claimed to contain over 3 million signatures, over two-and-a-half times the number on that of 1839. But T. S. Duncombe's motion that the petitioners be heard at the bar of the House of Commons was rejected by a derisory 287 votes to 46 on 1 May 1842, a rejection which created much bitterness in the Chartist localities.

A month later, Chartist anger was further inflamed by the death in York Castle of Samuel Holberry at the age of twenty-seven. His public funeral in Sheffield attracted 50,000 to follow the coffin and hear Harney's oration (Ward 1973: 160–2; Thompson 1984: 280–1). By this time the industrial districts were being afflicted by the worst economic recession of the century, forcing Chartists to reconsider their tactics against a background of short-time working, unemployment, wage cuts and considerable hunger and suffering. In Bolton, for example, over 60 per cent of mill workers were unemployed in 1842, with an even higher percentage among building workers. Hundreds of families in industrial towns were reduced to a diet of oatmeal porridge or potatoes and salt (Rule 1986: 39; Kitson Clark 1953).

THE 1842 STRIKES

In July and August 1842 many of the industrial areas of the north and Midlands were swept by a great wave of strikes and riots involving up to half a million workers. The extent of Chartist involvement created as much controversy at the time as it has among historians since. Large-scale unrest began in July, with a major strike of Staffordshire coal miners against wage cuts and truck payments. Considerable violence occurred when coalowners defended their pits with special constables, yeomanry and regular troops. By September, fifteen English and Welsh shires and eight Scots counties had been affected, although the main impact was felt in the Black Country, the Potteries and the textile areas of Lancashire, Cheshire and Yorkshire, areas where the population was already predominantly urban (Mather 1974: 115–16; Rose 1957; Philips 1974: 153–5).

Chartist leaders seem to have been largely taken unawares by the strikes. Some, like certain members of the government, suspected a cunning plot, hatched by the Anti-Corn Law League. The strike movement spread quickly to the cotton districts when manufacturers in Ashton-under-Lyne and Stalybridge reduced wages by 25 per cent. Processions of striking workers had brought Ashton to a standstill by 5 August; three days later a meeting in Stalybridge resolved to turn out all local factories and those of Dukinfield and Newton. Next day crowds marched on Manchester and, after assuring the authorities they intended to act peaceably, were allowed to enter the town and attempt to persuade the Manchester trades to join in the strike. In the event there was much disorder after police and military moved in to try to arrest turnouts and prevent further processions and mass picketing. During the following week, over 100 cotton factories, as well as numerous dyeworks and machine shops, involving in all about 50,000 workers, stood idle.

A conference of eighty trades delegates, assembled at the Carpenters' Hall and assuming direction of the strikes, appealed for law and order and endorsed the Charter. There were no violent speeches like those of 1839, with the strikers proving remarkably restrained and disciplined, given the vast numbers involved. The technique had been borrowed from the Staffordshire miners of raking out boiler fires and drawing boiler plugs: hence the term 'Plug Riots'. There was relatively little looting and pillaging, apart from bread, although there was large-scale theft when the Stockport Workhouse was attacked. On the other hand there was considerable violence; at Preston the military opened fire, killing four strikers, while troops defending the Adelphi Works at Salford seriously wounded five turnouts. With the notable exception of the Newport Rising, the extent of violence in 1842 was greater than in 1839, despite the absence of organized arming and drilling (Jenkins 1980: 64–90; Rudé 1964: 186).

Almost simultaneous with events in south Lancashire were the strikes which broke out on Tyneside and in lowland Scotland. The Lancashire and Cheshire strikes themselves spread to the West Riding, as the cotton workers marched over the Pennines to stop mills in Skipton and the Halifax–Huddersfield area. Worsted operatives from Bradford marched west to assist in the stoppage of Halifax mills and forced their way through a barrier of troops on 14 August. On the way back from escorting prisoners arrested at Halifax to Elland railway station, the soldiers had to run a gauntlet of 'thousands of people gathered at Salterhebble and Elland Wood, armed with staves'. One soldier died from his injuries, whilst numerous strikers and Chartists were seriously wounded as troops fought against a hail of stones and bricks. At Huddersfield, the magistrates described the leaders of the Plug Rioters as 'all strangers, evidently in humble life – sensible, shrewd, determined, peaceable ... the burden of their speeches was to destroy no property, to hurt no human being, but determinedly to persist in ceasing from labour and to induce others to do the same until every man should obtain "a fair day's wage for a fair day's work".' Mills and pits in Bradford and its surrounding textile and mining villages were stopped over three days by remarkably well-organized processions of turnouts, despite clashes with cavalry.

By the last week in August, however, the strikes and turnouts were beginning to peter out, as the participants trickled back to work and the authorities continued methodically to round up those involved in disorder. O'Connor himself recommended an end to the strikes in the columns of the *Northern Star*, after a trades delegates conference on 20 August called for a return to work. Only the south-east Lancashire cotton operatives held out through September, confining their demands to restoration of wage cuts, without insisting on the Charter (Wilson 1887: 199–201; Thompson 1984: 292; Reynolds 1983: 109–11; Peel 1880: 338–9).

Although the general strike and Plug Riots of 1842 lasted only two months and began and ended with demands for wage increases, there was substantial Chartist involvement from the very start. Staffordshire miners in July passed resolutions that 'nothing but the People's Charter can give us the power to have a fair day's wage for a fair day's work'. By coincidence, the executive of the NCA met in Manchester on 16 August to unveil a statue to Henry Hunt on the anniversary of Peterloo and were very much taken unawares by the mass turnouts, even though individual members of the NCA were closely involved in the Staffordshire strikes, as well as those in Cheshire and Lancashire. Both Harney and William Hill, editor of the *Northern Star*, opposed McDouall's motion that the NCA offer official support, although the majority followed O'Connor in seizing the opportunity for Chartists to display their solidarity with trades delegates.

However, by no means all those who demanded wage increases also supported the Charter, despite a two-thirds vote of the Manchester trades delegates to endorse Chartism. Workers in Stockport, Maccles-field, Stalybridge, Mossley, Leeds and Bury preferred to restrict the issue to one of wages. Even the Oldham cotton spinners decided against supporting the Charter, although Hyde, Glossop and Royston workers took a contrary view. Such differing attitudes appear to have owed as much to location as to occupation, although there was a general tendency for the more skilled and prosperous trades, less vulnerable to competition, to remain aloof from political agitation, as did the Sheffield cutlery trades in both 1839 and 1842 (Jenkins 1980: 6; Gammage 1854: 218–19; Mather 1974: 132–5; Reids 1979; Smith 1982: 84).

There is, in fact, a great deal of evidence concerning close Chartist involvement in the 1842 outbreaks and little to suggest that most operatives repudiated Chartist political action as Donald Read has claimed (Read 1959: 56). There was a strong Chartist presence in Staffordshire; membership of the NCA in Bilston, for example, increased from 150 in 1840 to over 1,000 by early 1842. Local Chartist leaders played a crucial role in organizing strikes of miners and pottery workers. Most of the chairmen and principal speakers at the mass open-air meetings in Ashton, Stalybridge and Manchester were Chartist activists. Richard Pilling, a power-loom weaver, had been a leader of Stockport Chartism in 1839. As a member of the south Lancashire delegate conference in 1842, he spoke at meetings, drew up instructions, led the marches of Ashton turnouts to Oldham and toured the Lancashire cotton towns in order to co-ordinate strike activity and Chartist demonstrations. In 1842 the *Northern Star* reported 200 meetings in south Lancashire at which the Charter was advocated. Admittedly, there is nothing to suggest that the 1842 strikes were the result of a preconceived Chartist plan. In many places, Chartists clearly jumped on a moving bandwaggon and remained uncertain whether they were supporting a movement with the prime aim of obtaining the Charter or that of procuring the redress of trade grievances.

There is, however, no doubt that local Chartists exercised strong influence on the tactics that were pursued and the manner in which various discontents became focussed on mass confrontation with employers over a wide area. This was especially so in Yorkshire, where trade unions were weaker and less widespread than across the Pennines. Even the trades delegates in Manchester, responsible for much of the organization and direction of the strikes, adopted a resolution for all trades to cease work until 'the Charter becomes the law of the land', thus helping to give the strikes a strong political flavour. It was their success in gaining the support of the trades in many areas, if by no means all, that made Chartist activity in July and August so effective (Barnsby 1977: 157; Mather 1974: 121–8; Jenkins 1980: 102–27; Thompson 1984: 214–16).

The easing of tension and the end of the strikes in September was partly the result of improving economic conditions. The 1842 harvest was a good one and trade was already reviving. Consequently many employers, including those in Ashton, agreed to cancel wage reductions. Another important factor was the policy of the government. As in 1839–40 it struck hard at rioters. Sir James Graham, Home Secretary in Peel's government, anticipated disorder and was determined to quell it forcibly: 'to prevent the forced cessation of labour by intimidation'. Writing to Croker on 20 August, he argued that the strikes amounted to 'a social insurrection of a very formidable character and well organized with forethought and ability'. Colonel Beckett at Leeds was told 'You must whip these fellows without loss of time; if once they get ahead we shall find them troublesome' (Mather 1959a: 156; Mather 1959b: 387; Ward 1967: 191). Graham was constantly complaining about what he regarded as excessive laxity on the part of local magistrates and military commanders. Not surprisingly, therefore, arrests began in August, soon after the NCA had endorsed the strikes. In October a Special Commission in Staffordshire tried 274 cases, imprisoning 154 and transporting 5 men for life (Philips 1974: 157).

In the north-west, over 1,500 strikers were brought to trial for attacking Stockport workhouse and stealing bread and meal. Four men were transported for life, 1 for 15 years, 5 for 10 years and 3 for 7 years, while 54 were imprisoned. The Liverpool Special Commission was no less savage. Here 115 were imprisoned and 11 transported, mostly for stealing bread. Chartist leaders were treated more leniently than the poor rank-and-file. O'Connor was arrested in September for sedition and conspiracy, but when he and 58 others appeared at Lancaster Assizes the following March they were released on a faulty indictment. By this time there was little need for harsh treatment, as the strikes were over and unrest had been damped down. Besides, Peel's government was wary of alienating public sympathy by pushing repression too far and creating voluble martyrs capable of answering back.

There was to be no further major disorder until 1848. Even at the height of the 1842 strikes there was little risk of the state's monopoly of power being seriously challenged. Withdrawal of labour by the industrial working class was incapable of undermining the government in less time than it would take for starvation to force the operatives back to work, especially when violence was officially repudiated by the strike leaders. Divisions among the workers of Lancashire and Cheshire on whether their aims were primarily political or industrial diminished the chances of political success. Again, as in 1839–40, swift action by the government to restore order helped ensure that the strikes remained relatively short-lived. There was no way that the state could effectively be challenged so long as the police could bring large numbers of men before courts which continued to function. Yet the 1842 strikes were not completely unfruitful. By contrast with the General Strike of 1926, wage cuts were restored, and in some places increased to the rates of 1840. In the cotton districts, trade unionism emerged on a more organized and confident basis.

KNOWLEDGE CHARTISM AND MUNICIPAL CHARTISM

After 1842 Chartist leadership continued to disintegrate. At the local level, Chartist activists were deprived of a mass following. Although Chartism was never to be the same again, as many localities abandoned the movement for good, it refused to wither away and was to reveal surprising powers of revival in 1848. Different leaders went their various ways. Lovett placed the emphasis on gaining the Charter by educating the labouring classes. Henry Vincent and Robert Lowery took up temperance Chartism (Large 1974: 112–15; Harrison 1973). Christian Chartism appealed to many in Scotland and Birmingham. O'Connor increasingly devoted his attention to the land question. Other diversions took the form of increased trade union activity, Owenite socialism, support for the Anti-Corn Law League and for European republicanism. In May 1846 the *Manchester Guardian* reported that the former Chartist stronghold of Mossley had become a centre of the Anti-Corn Law agitation, with its Chartist Assembly Room closed and its floorboards used for pig-styes (Read 1959: 60).

Lovett's 'New Move' to 'Knowledge Chartism' was thought out by him and John Collins in Warwick Gaol and published in 1840 as *Chartism: A new Organization for the People*. They argued that there was no means of gaining the Charter so effective 'As a peaceful combination of the millions, founding their hopes on the might and influence of *intellectual* and *moral* progress ... The reflecting portion of our brethren are beginning to perceive the great necessity for this intellectual and moral preparation'.[6] The book was very much a re-hash of the educational arguments of the NUWC and LWMA, and was immediately denounced by O'Connor as placing Chartism's success only in the distant future. Local supporters of the New Move were denounced as heretics in the columns of the *Northern Star*. With the support of Hetherington and Watson, Lovett ran the National Association Hall and Sunday Schools as a centre for Chartist educational schemes until 1857, but at the price of distancing himself from mainstream Chartism.

Both Vincent and Lowery, former extreme agitators, now shared Lovett's view that links should be forged with middle-class radicalism, especially by means of the temperance movement.

Although O'Connor, far from temperate himself, was not opposed to temperance as such, he firmly opposed any moves detracting from pure 'O'Connorite' Chartism. Religious Chartism he dismissed as little more than an irrelevance, despite the twenty Chartist churches in Scotland by 1841. Other Chartists, like Henry Hetherington of London, Lawrence Pitkethly of Huddersfield and Isaac Ironside of Sheffield, returned to their Owenite roots and preached moral regeneration. George Julian Harney, 'the Marat of Chartism', had developed a loyal Chartist following in Sheffield before becoming assistant editor of the *Northern Star*. He now placed the emphasis on encouraging republicanism in Europe, as he made contact with Engels and foreign exiles in London. These refugees joined with Owenites and moderate 'Knowledge Chartists' of the Lovett school to form the People's International League. Harney himself assisted in the creation of the Fraternal Democrats in 1845, which attracted English republicans like the young Ernest Jones, as well as Polish and German exiles, including both Marx and Engels (Harrison and Hollis 1967; Wilson 1959: 273–7; Royle 1974: 135–7, 182; Schoyen 1958: 122–45).

In some areas, most notably in Leeds and Sheffield, Chartists aimed at gaining influence in local government by exploiting the relatively wide ratepayer franchise. In Leeds, Chartism flourished as a municipal movement aiming to appoint Chartists to borough offices. This strategy was master-minded by Joshua Hobson, the Owenite printer and publisher of the *Northern Star*. From 1842, when their full list of nineteen candidates was elected, Chartists controlled the vestry meetings and through them the election of improvement commissioners. In the same year the Chartist list of churchwardens was carried *en bloc*, with seven Chartists elected, a performance repeated in 1843, 1844 and 1845. Chartists also became members of the Board of Surveyors for Highways and of the Poor Law Guardians. In 1843 two Chartists, including Hobson himself, were elected for the working-class Holbeck and Hunslet wards.

Enlarged to four in 1844, the Chartist caucus on Leeds Borough Council constantly promoted candidates in working-class districts. In all, some twenty-five Chartists contested elections between 1843 and 1853, with eighteen gaining seats. Within the Council chamber the Chartists never numbered more than seven or eight out of sixty-four and could therefore be of little more than nuisance value. All township offices required being rated at £30–£40: hence Chartists elected were mostly shopkeepers and small tradesmen rather than genuine proletarians. They adhered to no distinctively Chartist municipal programme, normally voting with the 'Advanced Liberals' and disagreeing among themselves over projects requiring substantial expenditure. Only the question of extending police powers invoked immediate united Chartist opposition (Harrison 1958; Harrison 1959: 86–8; Fraser 1976: 35–6, 93–4, 257–61).

In Sheffield, with its egalitarian political tradition, Isaac Ironside, an eccentric but politically-skilled accountant, was the key figure in municipal Chartism. By means of a system of ward committees, he created a more impressive caucus than that of Leeds. By November 1848 there were twenty-two Chartists on the Council, which found itself obliged to discuss topics like the Charter and national secular education, as well as to take radical initiatives on poor relief and public health. Chartists fused with Radicals to form the Sheffield Democratic Society, challenging the informal management of Liberal politics by means of a system of ward and township democratic self-government, based on a formidable apparatus of committees and delegates and capable of 'experiments in anarchism' in a town where there was powerful resistance to centralizing authority at all levels above the workplace, pub and chapel. But Ironside was never able to harness the power of the trade societies or the more plebeian and politically passive Primitive Methodist Chapels (Pollard 1959: 48–9; Salt 1972; Fraser 1979b: 140–3; Smith 1982: 83–91). Over the Pennines in Rochdale, Chartists and Radicals took control of the Board of Guardians from 1844, ensuring that few of the basic principles of the New Poor Law were applied before the 1870s (Garrard 1983: 118–19).

The failure of the confrontational tactics of 1839 and 1842, as well as the sobering effects of mass imprisonment, meant that Chartism between 1842 and 1847 was no longer a mass movement. Relative economic prosperity no doubt helped to dampen the enthusiasm of the rank-and-file. 'New Moves' like educational, temperance, religious and municipal Chartism represented attempts by activists to find alternative strategies, although they failed to attract mass support. More impressive was trade union activity, which concentrated on purely economic aims. Skilled and prosperous workers, organized in strong trade societies, had always tended to maintain a certain distance from Chartism and political activity. With a few exceptions, those drawn into the Chartist campaigns were more often than not members of the relatively depressed small-scale handicraft trades, like tailors, shoemakers, carpenters and domestic textile workers, rather than engineers, printers, ironfounders and potters. Improving trade after 1842 led to the establishment or revival of national unions among miners, cotton spinners, printers, potters, glass makers, tailors and curriers. Some unions, however, proved merely temporary. For example the Miners' Association, founded in 1842, enrolled up to 100,000 members from most British coalfields. But after conducting an unsuccessful strike in 1844 which involved brutal evictions from tied housing, it folded under the impact of the depression of 1847–8; a depression which also undermined a new attempt at general union in the form of the National

Association of United Trades, created in 1845 (Musson 1972: 46–8; Prothero 1971; Challenor and Ripley 1968; Jenkin 1971: 89).

FAILURE OF RADICAL CLASS CO-OPERATION

There were those on the moderate wing of Chartism who, after the *débâcle* of 1839, let alone 1842, argued that the only future for working-class radicalism lay in collaboration with middle-class radical organizations. The chief attempt to cement such an alliance during the 1840s was that of the Complete Suffrage Union, founded in Birmingham in January 1842 by Joseph Sturge, a Quaker corn merchant and free trader. Behind him were middle-class radical Dissenters who aimed at religious equality, free trade and a wider suffrage, while at the same time distrusting the militant followers of O'Connor. By April 1842 there were over fifty Complete Suffrage Associations, with the CSU staging a rival parliamentary petition to that of the NCA. O'Connor himself, suspecting a plot by the Anti-Corn Law League to wean popular radicalism from the pure milk of the Charter to supporting repeal of the Corn Laws, was quick to denounce the CSU, noting how it attracted such anti-O'Connorites as Vincent, Lowery, Lovett and Collins.

Eventually the CSU was obliged to adopt the Charter in all but name, although its petition, like that of the NCA, was rejected at Westminster. After conducting a vitriolic campaign against the CSU, O'Connor performed a brazen *volte-face* in July 1842, advocating class collaboration in the *Northern Star*. Having come to see the tactical advantages of a brief alliance with middle-class radicals, he was willing to support Sturge against the Tory-Radical John Walter of *The Times* at the August 1842 Nottingham by-election, thus abandoning the support for the Tories he had advocated at the 1841 general election.

By the autumn, however, O'Connor had once more reversed his attitude as he poured scorn on the CSU as 'a League job', partly because his prevarication during the Plug Riots had left him open to criticism from Chartist hard-liners, while the Chartist leaders who supported the CSU represented a threat to his own dominance. At a CSU conference in Birmingham in December, packed with Chartists in defiance of a prior agreement, the middle-class contingent insisted on the adoption of a 'New Bill of Rights' for universal suffrage, rather than employ the emotive word 'Charter'. Even Lovett was unwilling to swallow the rejection of a term which represented so much more than mere semantics, joining O'Connor in moving a successful resolution to substitute 'the Charter' for 'the Bill' and provoking an immediate secession by the majority of middle-class CSU delegates. Thus the brief experiment in class collaboration terminated, as O'Connor tightened his grip on the NCA and converted the thinning ranks of militant Chartism into his own personal following (Wilson 1974: 84–93; Ward 1973: 158–60, 165–7; Epstein 1982: 287–93).

Collaboration between Chartists and middle-class radicals of the Anti-Corn Law League proved equally difficult. Working-class opinion on the repeal campaign was divided. Some accepted the League's argument that repeal would reduce bread prices, promote exports and improve working-class living conditions. Others suspected that lower food prices were advocated by employers as a means of reducing their costs by proceeding to justify wage-cuts in the wake of repeal, and therefore insisted that repeal would benefit the common people only if accompanied by legislation to control wages and working conditions. In any case, argued trade union and Chartist leaders, the Charter should take priority, whatever the attractions of repeal. O'Connor despised the Manchester radicalism behind the League as a similar attempt to dilute Chartism as that of Birmingham and the CSU. Until the depression of 1842, relations between the League and the Chartists were marked by distrust and hostility, with Chartists frequently invading and disrupting League meetings, sometimes employing considerable violence. After 1842 relations began to improve, as many moderate Chartists were won round to the cause of repeal. O'Connor himself was converted during a debate with Cobden in 1844, while repeal in 1846 was generally welcomed (McCord 1958: 51–3, 96–103, 111–16; Brown 1959: 342–71).

O'CONNOR'S LAND PLAN

Between 1842 and 1848 the Land Plan provided a major outlet for frustrated Chartists, as well as an opportunity for further scorn and ridicule from their opponents. The Land Plan has to be seen in the context of a multiplicity of experiments in home colonization and community-building during the 1830s and 1840s, particularly by Owenites and other socialists (Hardy 1979: 20–105). Its basic aim was the resettlement of industrial workers on the land as small independent producers, thus helping to solve the problem of surplus industrial labour and low wages. Like Owenism, the Land Plan offered a means of restoring artisan independence and self-reliance. The Chartist Co-operative Land Society was launched in 1845 with NCA backing, soon attracting much support from *Northern Star* readers during the depression of 1847–8, especially since there was an exciting lottery element in the ballot for which subscribers could become tenants on the estates, of which the Company ultimately purchased five. Over £100,000 was collected from some 70,000 subscribers, although only 250 were actually settled on the two-acre allotments.

The Land Plan was partly intended as a means of holding Chartism together in the difficult conditions of the late 1840s, but the Company and its associated Land Bank were plagued by legal difficulties, never having been registered either as a joint-stock company or as a friendly society, or even as a lottery. Such legal problems were mainly a consequence of deliberately obstructionist policies by the government and the courts. The appointment of a parliamentary Select Committee of Inquiry undermined confidence in the scheme and, amidst a legal tangle made no better by O'Connor's syphilitic mental illness, the Company finally dissolved in 1851 (MacAskill 1959: 304–41; Hadfield 1970; Read and Glasgow 1961: 108–17; Yeo 1982: 368–73).

ENGLAND'S 1848

The final phase of Chartist mass political agitation began against a background of harvest failures, commercial crises and a wave of revolutions on the Continent. Chartists were much encouraged by the return of O'Connor as Member for Nottingham at the 1847 general election, by Ernest Jones obtaining 279 votes at Halifax out of an electorate of just over a thousand, by the February 1848 Revolution in Paris and the overthrow of the July Monarchy, and by the activities of the Irish Confederation creating the possibility of a united radical movement on both sides of the Irish Sea.

Once again, the onset of economic distress made mass meetings feasible. In March 1848 a middle-class radical meeting in London was taken over by Chartists and, after dispersal by the police, resulted in window-smashing crowds rampaging through the capital for three days. Riots by gangs of unemployed culminated in looting and the killing of five people by troops in Glasgow. In Manchester the Union workhouse and a police station were attacked. These riots, conducted by non-Chartists, were unfortunate in that they associated Chartism with disorder, looting and criminality in the eyes of the propertied classes. Mass meetings, often under the *tricoleur*, were organized by Chartists across the country to rally support for a further petition and for the Irish Confederates (Ward 1973: 197–200; Belchem 1982: 277–9).

During this final upsurge of Chartist energy forty-nine delegates were elected to a third National Convention, which began its proceedings in London on 4 April 1848 and planned a peaceful mass demonstration on Kennington Common on 10 April, to be followed by a procession to present the petition to parliament. If the petition were again rejected, then a 'National Assembly' would be elected to call upon the Queen to dissolve parliament and accept only a government prepared to implement the Charter. By this stage there was considerable fear amounting to panic among London property-owners, apprehensive lest the Kennington Common rally provoke a revolution along the lines of that in Paris in February. The government swiftly took precautions, banning the projected procession from the Common to Westminster, putting the Duke of Wellington in charge of the capital's garrison and defences, and swearing in thousands of special constables.

On 10 April a crowd whose size has been variously estimated, but was at least between 50,000 and 100,000, met on Kennington Common. After O'Connor had addressed it and told how the procession over the Thames bridges had been banned, most of the crowd dispersed peaceably, having no intention of confrontation with the authorities, at least not before rejection of the petition. The latter was conveyed to parliament in three cabs and the crisis was over. London was not Paris. The relief of those possessing substantial property was expressed in the ridicule they poured on the Kennington Common 'fiasco' and the Chartist leaders (Gammage 1854: 301–18). O'Connor had claimed 5,700,000 signatures on the petition, but Commons clerks calculated only 1,975,467 genuine ones, excluding multiples in the same hand, obscene entries and pseudonyms like 'Victoria Rex', 'Punch', 'Flatnose' and so on. The suggestion that these were genuine signatures of people who wished to disguise their identities for fear of victimization can remain only speculative (Royle 1980: 43).

Despite the events of 10 April, the Convention was undaunted, as it continued to sit and organize more mass meetings preparatory to the summoning of a National Assembly. Both O'Connor and Harney opposed the Assembly, which became dominated by the young aristocratic republican, Ernest Jones (Saville 1952: 30). It soon became evident that it lacked mass support and was therefore quickly dissolved. But Chartism did not wither away in April and May 1848, for the spring and summer saw a great deal of activity, many arrests and trials, and several riots, against a background of imminent insurrection in Ireland. There had been a contingent of thousands of Irishmen at Kennington Common, while conspiratorial plans for a rising in London continued through June and July. In his journal for 3 June, Greville noted that 'the Government are now getting seriously uneasy about the Chartist manifestations in various parts of the country, especially in London, and at the repeated assemblies and marchings of great bodies of men' (Thompson 1984: 326). In fact the government had already embarked on a policy of firm repression. John Mitchel, the Irish confederate leader, received fourteen years transportation in May, with Smith O'Brien similarly sentenced in August after an abortive rising in County Tipperary (Lyons 1973: 104–10).

So far as the government was concerned, the Bradford district of the West Riding of Yorkshire, 'perhaps the most outstanding centre of physical force in England in the spring of 1848', was a potential revolutionary flashpoint (Mather 1965: 17). Thousands of hand combers were being thrown out of work by machinery and an inflated labour supply, while 10 per cent of the population of Bradford Poor Law Union were on poor relief. The town's large and militant Chartist following was by this time about 50 per cent Irish, with its leaders, including the notorious George White, commuting across the Irish Sea with suspicious regularity. A local Tory county magistrate informed the Home Secretary of the violent speeches made at Chartist meetings: 'urging the people to arm and be prepared to use physical force ... A Man in this Place is constantly employed in making pikes & there is reason to apprehend that the Chartists would rise if there should be an outbreak in Ireland or anywhere in England'.[7]

After arming, drilling and marching through the town in quasi-military formation, Bradford Chartists created a 'no-go' area in the densely packed streets on the south side of the town centre, from which they were able to defy magistrates, police and special constables for at least a fortnight. Only when the Home Secretary prodded a rather reluctant Liberal borough magistracy was the military in the locality reinforced and then sent in on 29 May to quell, not without difficulty, what had become a virtual Chartist mini-republic (Wright 1986a: 37–58).

At the same time, London was still in a state of tension, as workers marched silently through the streets, with clashes ensuing after police broke up meetings in the East End on 4 June. The provisional executive of the National Assembly had called a day of protest for 12 June, prompting the government to arrest the main speakers at London meetings, including Ernest Jones, who was gaoled for two years. Groups of revolutionaries in the capital, many of them Irish divided into brigades and divisions, planned an outbreak for 15 August, but these groups failed to rally sufficient support and were quickly infiltrated by government spies. On the day of the projected rising, police found it easy to round up the would-be insurrectionaries.

The 1848 Revolution in Britain came to an end with numerous arrests of the active leaders of physical force Chartism. Although fewer Chartists were arrested and sentenced than in 1839–40 or 1842, nearly 300 served at least a year in prison (Large 1974; Gammage 1854: 333–418; Thompson 1984: 309–28). In the country generally, Chartism made relatively little impact in 1848. By this time many Chartist communities had lost faith in the efficacy of political change, turning instead to movements with more limited and realizeable aims: co-operative societies, friendly societies, Land Plan branches and Owenite redemption societies. Such groups, relying on self-help, carried little risk of confrontation with the authorities and gaol sentences.

Chartism lingered on for a further decade, displaying surprising vigour in some areas; for example, Halifax. As a mass movement, however, it clearly came to an end in the summer of 1848 (Jones 1975: 169–81; Tiller 1982: 311–44). From 1839, and increasingly in its declining years, Chartism was seriously weakened by internecine quarrels, which persisted in the autobiographies and reminiscences of participants like Lowery, Lovett and Gammage, who were its first historians. Contemporary writers from the ranks of the establishment proved willing, once the threat of insurrection had passed, to treat Chartism with patronizing forgiveness. For novelists like Elizabeth Gaskell and Charles Kingsley, the Chartists were child-like, ignorant men and women who had been deluded by 'frothy agitators', above all O'Connor. Yet it was acknowledged that they had performed the useful service of drawing attention to the widespread hunger and atrocious living conditions experienced by so many working people during the late 1830s and the 1840s and the need for sanitation, religious education and police forces in the manufacturing districts.

During the 1850s and 1860s Chartism tended to be held in contempt – a troublesome disease which had been successfully cured. Most former Chartists were forced into embarrassed silence, while working-class radicals continued to be regarded with suspicion, given their continued hostility to both the police and the Poor Law. By the early 1880s, however, the apparent political docility of so many working men, surrounded by the warm moral glow of Gladstonian Liberalism, led to Chartism ceasing to be a largely unmentionable subject for the propertied classes less open-minded than the novelists. Old Chartists were encouraged to publish their memoirs in Liberal newspapers, with their contribution to the age of improvement now being more widely appreciated, provided, of course, that they studiously repudiated their youthful errors.

CHARTIST CULTURE

Engels noted in 1845: 'I have often heard working-men, whose fustian jackets scarcely held together, speak upon geological, astronomical and other subjects, with more knowledge than most "cultivated" bourgeois in Germany possess' (Engels 1969 edn: 266). Chartist branches at the local level, like those of the Owenites, provided a substantial menu of recreational, educational and religious activities which amounted to an alternative culture, within which members could move freely during their leisure hours. For many people, therefore, Chartism was more than a political campaign; it was a living experience, based upon a democratic radical culture, where the emphasis was placed on mutuality, self-respect and a profound sense of independence.

While there was no specific Chartist religious outlook, the movement was permeated by religious sentiment and rhetoric. Great camp meetings, drawing on the Primitive Methodist model, were held on the moors of Lancashire and Yorkshire in the late 1830s and 1840s, with brass bands and quasi-religious processions, the proceedings being opened with a hymn and a prayer. In some districts, Chartists founded their own chapels, or formed congregations around a radical preacher (Jones 1975: 49–57). Funerals were conducted, babies named (often after Chartist leaders) and celebrations held to commemorate the Chartist 'saints', for example the birthdays of Tom Paine and Henry Hunt. Unlike the Owenites, few Chartists rejected Christianity, preferring to regard Jesus Christ as 'the first Chartist'. Most, however, were anti-clerical, with particularly hostile feelings towards the Church of England, regarded as a morally bankrupt aristocratic institution, too closely interwoven with government, magistracy and military. 'More pigs and fewer parsons' appeared regularly on Chartist banners, as it had on those of radicals for half a century (Yeo 1981; Mather 1980: 271–302).

A good deal of Chartist community feeling was channelled into education, especially after 1842, with both Sunday and day schools founded to provide knowledge for working-class children and to enhance a sense of independence and community solidarity. In Chartist and Owenite assembly rooms and halls, adults fostered rationality, conviviality and communal harmony through lecture programmes, education classes, vocal and instrumental music, dances, *soirées* and theatrical productions. Elaborate processions were organized, with flags, banners, caps of liberty, scarves, sashes and rosettes.

These images of radicalism and symbolic forms of political practice had been part of the standard repertoire of opposition and contestation since the time of the French Revolution (Hunt 1984: 52–119; Pickering 1986). Poetry had particular appeal for Chartists, especially imitations of the verse of Shelley and Byron (Kovalev 1971: 57–73). All these activities amounted to a positive and creative effort to construct an alternative society and culture able to resist and to compete with that of the middle classes. It proved difficult for much of this Chartist and Owenite cultural activity to survive beyond mid-century. Lovett's New Move had a weakening effect by its acceptance of the assumptions of middle-class ideology that working-class culture was something to be reformed through individual self-improvement, while in the 1840s it became increasingly difficult to maintain coherent opposition to the values of middle-class political economy and social policy (Price 1986: 61). Nevertheless, the concept of the working classes creating a culture through their own collective efforts, promoting active participation and control in both social and economic affairs, persisted in the co-operative movement and bequeathed an important legacy to the late nineteenth-century socialist revival (Peel 1880: 317–18; Epstein 1982: 221–68).

ANALYSIS

Recent research has resulted in substantial reinterpretation of the Chartist movement. One major contribution has been Epstein's reassessment of the role of Feargus O'Connor (Epstein 1982b). Most Chartist leaders had little good to say about 'The Lion of Freedom', who was admittedly often arrogant and brutal to colleagues, as well as being excessively fond of the girls and the brandy bottle. Gammage, the first Chartist historian, depicted O'Connor as a conceited flatterer of the people who refused to brook any rivals; Lovett had old scores to settle in his 1876 autobiography. Neither did O'Connor's style and aims appeal to early Fabian and Marxist writers. According to the Fabian, Julius West, he 'had most of the qualities of a great demagogue and all the defects of the low-grade politician' (Gammage 1854: 247; West 1920: 84). Yet O'Connor clearly possessed advantages which set him above other leaders of working-class movements of his generation. His mastery of the press and platform, as well as his ability to respond to working-class expectations, gave him an astonishing hold over vast numbers of the Chartist rank-and-file. It was O'Connor, more than anyone, who constructed a mass radical party of the unrepresented working classes, distinct from the Whigs or Tory Radicals, right from his first visit to the north of England in 1835.

During the next three years his following built up to a point where it stretched from Aberdeen to Brighton. O'Connor was a master of the deployment of the radical 'platform', developed from the days of Henry Hunt and the immediate post-war agitation. This ritualized exercise depended on a strategy of intimidation by vaguely defined menace and sheer numbers in order to remedy the grievances of the people. It was more a matter of miming insurrection than of provoking genuine violence, for it was assumed that violence would emanate from the authorities, giving the people the right and duty to resist, by force of arms if need be. For O'Connor, it was an elaborate and skilful game of bluff, since he had no intention of encouraging real violence. He backed away from it at the time of the arrest of Stephens, again when the government banned torchlight processions, and by retreating from his earlier advocacy of the 'sacred month' during the aftermath of the rejection of the 1839 petition. Nobody was transported for anything which O'Connor provoked, even if his brand of confrontation ultimately proved politically sterile.

In terms of radical organization, O'Connor was a distinct innovator, arguing for a permanent form of party organization, with a paid executive and salaried lecturers financed by profits from the *Northern Star* – a standard feature of modern labour movements. Moreover, if O'Connor was instrumental in dividing the Chartist leadership and driving his most obvious rivals from the movement, it is equally true that he, more than anyone, was responsible for holding the movement together after the trauma of 1839–40 by means of the NCA and the Land Plan. There was a tendency for other Chartist leaders to use O'Connor as a scapegoat for the failure of the movement and their own shortcomings. There seems no reason to suppose that the 'moral force' New Move strategy of education and self-improvement advocated by Lovett and his supporters would have had any greater chance of success than the tactics of O'Connor, who so accurately reflected the emotions and frustrations of the Chartist rank-and-file. Without O'Connor, it seems unlikely that Chartism as a mass movement would ever have made the impact it did (Thompson 1984: 96–101).

Although Chartism was a national movement, it was clearly much more prominent in some areas than others, with its main English centres being the textile areas of Cheshire, Lancashire and Yorkshire, followed by the north-east, the Midlands and London. In Scotland, Chartism attracted most support from the central valley and the east-coast lowlands, especially from the Glasgow area. In London, mass support for Chartism came only in the 1840s, for the small-unit workshop structure of London industry, with over 400 trades situated in a broad and flexible economy, made it difficult to combine the myriad pockets of radicalism, with their numerous divisions and rivalries, into a broad and unified movement in a city of London's size.

The London artisan radical tradition was based on club life, trade societies, taverns and friendly societies, lacking the crusading spirit of the Factory and Anti-Poor Law campaigns. By May 1839, London had provided only 19,000 signatures for the National Petition, compared with 100,000 from the West Riding. Meetings were thinly attended, while Londoners would not turn out on the streets and the enthusiasm of the London trades could not match that of the northern manufacturing districts, much to the disgust of northern delegates at the 1839 Convention. Nevertheless, London Chartism was to gain in strength during the following decade, with mass support for O'Connor and the NCA; by 1848 it posed a genuine threat to the government (Goodway 1982: 38–96; Jones 1975: 9[map]).

The textile areas of Lancashire, Cheshire and Yorkshire were undoubtedly those of most intense Chartist activity and loyalty, areas where a long tradition of political radicalism had been deepened and intensified by the Factory and Poor Law struggles and by the decline of hand workers in cotton and worsteds. Within these districts, Chartism was stronger in industrial villages and middle-size towns like Ashton, Stalybridge, Stockport, Oldham, Bolton, Halifax, Bradford and Barnsley than it was in major provincial centres like Manchester and Leeds. Similarly in the West Country, Chartism in Bristol was never more than lukewarm, whereas before 1842 it was vigorous in textile towns like Bath, Trowbridge and Bradford-on-Avon. In the north-east there was an early burst of extreme Chartism, stimulated by Harney from London and Dr John Taylor from Ayrshire, but no lasting basis for deep-rooted loyalty after 1840 when mining unions predominated. In Coventry, Chartism was little more than a branch of Owenite socialism and faded completely after 1842 (Searby 1964).

Chartism attracted relatively little support from strongholds of Wesleyan, as opposed to Primitive, Methodism. In the Cornish mining districts, for example, Methodist and temperance leaders combined to exclude Chartist influence (Rule 1971). By contrast, Chartism in Wales was able to draw upon a powerful radical tradition, involving Welsh Nonconformity, the Rebecca riots and the speedy and brutal industrialization of the south Welsh valleys. In Ireland, Chartism was much weaker and made relatively little impact, given the opposition of O'Connell and his supporters (Briggs 1959; Cole 1941: 5–8; Sykes 1982; Royle 1980: 62–7; Cannon 1964; Rowe 1977).

Beneath the regional and local diversity of Chartism, however, there lay a very real sense of unity in a national movement, especially during the peak years 1839–42. The Chartist localities were bound together by the constant touring of national leaders, by an army of itinerant lecturers, by organizations like the network of National Associations and the National Charter Association. Central to both Chartist organization and propaganda was the Chartist press, which performed the vital service of keeping Chartists informed of developments in other localities and regions. A plethora of newspapers and journals, drawing on the tradition of the unstamped and mostly short-lived, represented regional and sectional Chartist opinion. By far the most important was the *Northern Star*, founded in Leeds in 1837 as a Factory and Anti-Poor Law journal, but after its acquisition by O'Connor becoming a national vehicle for O'Connorite Chartism. A number of Chartist prisoners confessed that they had joined the movement through reading or hearing 'the Star'. Not only was it a commercial success, with a peak circulation of 50,000 at the height of the 1839 agitation, providing valuable funds for the movement, but the distribution of the newspaper also became a political campaign in its own right. Paid agents for the *Star* became local Chartist organizers and *vice versa*. Although, as a 4½ pence stamped newspaper, the *Northern Star* was expensive, readership exceeded circulation by a factor of between twenty and fifty, for the *Star* was frequently purchased for group reading in pubs, coffee houses and the workplace. It was a general newspaper whose quality puts to shame the present-day popular press.

O'Connor owned the paper and used it as an outlet for his extremely skilled journalism, yet he allowed his editors considerable freedom, while opponents of O'Connorite Chartism were given access to the *Star's* columns. With its reports of Chartist meetings in every conceivable locality, its dispensation of exhortation, advice and information, its advertising of patent cures for venereal disease, the *Northern Star* was very much the people's paper, unique in the history of the press. The slow decline in its circulation to 12,500 weekly in 1842, 6,000 in 1844, and under 5,000 in 1850–1 after a leap to 12,000 in 1848, mirrored the fortunes of the Chartist movement (Epstein 1976; Thompson 1984: 37–56; Jones 1975: 94–102).

In recent years there has been a good deal of research on the Chartist rank-and-file, based on sources like the handful of Chartist auto-biographies, the occupations and addresses of about 1,000 Chartists gleaned from Chartist journals, NCA local committee lists printed in the *Northern Star*, surviving lists of members of the Land Plan and records of some 500 men arrested and imprisoned for political offences. Although these sources cover only a small minority amounting to a few thousand, and are heavily weighted towards the more active and militant, a much clearer picture of the sociology of Chartism can now be drawn (Jones 1975: 24–32, 134–7; Thompson 1984: 91–233; Royle 1980: 75–9). The backgrounds of the national leaders vary. O'Connor, O'Brien and Ernest Jones were gentlemen with higher education and legal training. Most of the leaders, however, were of artisan origin, with no more than elementary education. Hetherington, Watson and Vincent were printers, Lovett a cabinet-maker. Cooper a shoemaker. Harney, a cabin-boy turned pot-boy and vendor of the unstamped, came from a lower rung of the social ladder.

One can only speculate on the total number of Chartist adherents. National and local leaders, the hard core of activists in the localities, the followers who drifted in and out of Chartism with the ebb and flow of popular enthusiasm and were willing to sign the three Chartist petitions, read the *Northern Star* and give O'Connor their loyalty, were, taken together, certainly a minority of the adult population. Chartism was heavily regionalized, weak in large cities and failed to touch the 21.7 per cent of the working population in agriculture in 1841, involving over 2 million workers. It was, however, a sizeable minority. Royle suggests that, judging from the number of signatures on the petitions, Chartism at its peak in 1839–42 involved 2 to 3 million people out of a total adult population in 1841 of 10 million. Much the same figure is reached if each copy of the *Northern Star* at its highest point of circulation in the summer of 1839 was read or heard by fifty people. Chartism therefore involved far more than the 813,000 or so propertied men who possessed the parliamentary franchise.

All the sources confirm the fact that, despite the presence of shopkeepers, traders and small employers, Chartism was over-whelmingly a working-class movement, led by males but including a significant female membership, especially in areas where Owenism and the Anti-Poor Law Movement were prominent (Jones 1983; Taylor 1983: 264–72; Thompson 1984: 120–51). Apart from agricultural workers, admittedly the largest single occupational group, virtually all trades were involved in Chartism: 'modern' occupations like textile factory operatives and metal workers, as well as 'obsolescent' hand workers in the domestic textile industry. While the evidence is too patchy to permit an accurate occupational analysis of the whole movement, it appears that, in any Chartist locality, the bulk of support came from the dominant trade of that district. Only one membership list for a Chartist locality has survived, that of the NCA from 1840 to 1866 in the worsted textile township of Great Horton in the borough of Bradford, which had formed a vigorous branch of the Great Northern Union in 1838, mounted an ambitious programme of educational classes from the winter of 1841–2, and was to remain a centre of Owenism, co-operation and radical Liberalism until the 1870s. The 111 men who joined the NCA in Great Horton between November 1840 and July 1842 included 49 weavers, 36 wool combers, 4 masons, 4 coalminers, 3 dyers, 2 warehousemen and 1 pit labourer, tailor, schoolmaster, engine tenter, whitesmith, corn miller, gardener, sawyer, shoemaker, mechanic, turner and joiner.[8]

Textiles, employing over a million workers in 1851, was Britain's largest industry and second occupational group after agriculture. Textile workers naturally formed the largest group in the Chartist rank-and-file, with handloom weavers forming the majority among textile occupations. Both hand weavers and hand combers were suffering deteriorating living standards during the 1840s, able to find no easy route to growth sectors of the economy. Both groups, moreover, possessed a long history of independent culture and political radicalism. Yet there were also considerable numbers of factory workers, less literate than the hand workers, more under the eye of their masters and with fewer opportunities to take time off work for political activities. Even so, they formed a key element in cotton towns like Stalybridge, Stockport and Ashton-under-Lyne (Sykes 1982: 152–93).

Shoemakers were also a prominent group, whose irregular hours, control of the pace of work and lack of noise in the workplace promoted reading and political discussion. In London Chartism, shoemakers were outnumbered only by masons (Goodway 1982: 16). Tailors, like shoemakers, were members of a craft which, though unmechanized, was under severe pressure from dilution. Wage-cuts and declining standards of workmanship in an overcrowded market, were also prominent in Chartism. Blacksmiths, metalworkers and wood workers were other groups which helped to swell the Chartist ranks, while printers formed something of an aristocracy of labour, given their disproportionate representation among the leadership (Thompson 1984: 91–116, 173–229; Mather 1980: 17–21).

Recent research has also indicated a strong Irish presence in Chartism, especially in the industrial districts of northern England, as well as in London. Prominent Irishmen included such national leaders as O'Connor and O'Brien, and local leaders like George White. Tensions between English and Irish workmen certainly existed before the mass immigration of the late 1840s, but have been exaggerated. Irish immigrants were rarely confined to separate ghettoes during the Chartist period. Although there were numerous clashes between Chartists and Irish followers of O'Connell, there were many Irishmen for whom class consciousness eclipsed ethnic and denominational awareness. Not only did Irishmen form a significant proportion of the trade societies, like those of the shoemakers and tailors, but they also furnished a substantial number of Chartist activists. Those involved in the Bradford rising of 1848, it will be recalled, were predominantly Irish. In the same year there was a strong Irish presence in the plots hatched in London (O'Higgins 1961; Thompson, D. 1982: 120–51; Treble 1973: 33–70; Goodway 1982: 61–7).

Chartism was not, then, merely a reactive protest on the part of deprived and depressed members of the proto-industrial workforce. The groups of artisans and operatives in domestic industry, many of them creations of the industry itself, remained an important sector of the workforce during the 1830s and 1840s. Of course, it is undeniable that many of the Chartist rank-and-file were strongly motivated by economic considerations, above all by declining living standards in the depressions of 1838–42 and 1847–8. In Carlisle, for example, as Robert Lowery noted in his autobiography, the condition of the handloom weavers was so desperate that Chartism for them was necessarily 'a knife and fork question' (Harrison and Hollis 1979: 113–14, 137–8). There were similar groups elsewhere. For prosperous artisans, however, the driving force was as much their tradition of economic independence and political radicalism as a fear of loss of economic status. Militant Chartism was often more a product of the structure and history of local communities than of economic deprivation automatically causing political radicalism. Militant Chartism in many localities depended on the presence of men who had been involved in radical movements since the Napoleonic Wars; men who were able to command allegiance to a communal and occupational sense of dignity and independence in a language which drew both on the Bible and on seventeenth- and eighteenth-century radical and millenial movements, as well as Owenite socialism. Even so, only detailed local knowledge can explain, for example, why Merthyr Tydfil, scene of a mass rising under the red flag in 1831, was committed to moral force by November 1839 and failed to participate in the march on Newport; or why Huddersfield, where in November 1831 an assembly of 20,000 people burned a bishop in effigy and where in 1837 thousands attacked the New Poor Law for over a year, was relatively quiet during the Chartist decade (Thompson 1970).

As a political movement, Chartism clearly failed. None of the six points was achieved before 1871. Numerous local studies demonstrate that Chartist enthusiasm never again reached the level of 1839–40, while in many localities the movement petered out in 1842. The revival of 1848 created little tremor outside London and Bradford. Once it became clear during the summer of 1839 that the government was not going to play into the hands of the Chartists by embarking on immediate vicious repression and was willing for the Convention to meet and the petition to be presented to parliament, then the bluff of the Chartist leaders was called. The only way to succeed, as the government moved to arrest national leaders and local activists, was by large-scale armed revolution, But there existed neither the will nor the capacity for this to occur. The fact that about thirty troops in the Westgate Hotel in Newport could put a force of thousands of armed workers to bloody rout, revealed the military incompetence of even the most militant and insurrectionary Chartists. There is little wonder, therefore, that Newport largely discredited the strategy of physical force. Chartists were never able to prevent magistrates courts, assizes and special commissions from functioning. Communal solidarity was rarely sufficiently firm to prevent the Crown obtaining witnesses and persuading some of those arrested to turn Queen's evidence. The army and the police experienced no great difficulty in containing Chartism when called upon to do so.

London Chartism, for example, impressively militant and united in 1842 and even more so in 1848, was successfully held in check by the efficiency of the Metropolitan Police, who speedily developed effective methods of crowd control and dispersal. The post-Chartist century witnessed the creation of an illusory image of the benign and friendly policeman. David Goodway, however, has shown how the clashes between crowds and police in the metropolis during the 1840s have a distinctly modern ring, with accusations of police brutality, the rough handling of innocent bystanders, and crowds pelting the police with missiles snatched from roadworks. Very unfriendly policemen showed no compunction in smashing skulls with their truncheons or riding down crowds by mounted charges. In August 1842 it was the police who brutally moved in when angry demonstrators tried to prevent troops entraining at Euston to put down provincial riots. It was the police who preserved calm in the capital on 10 April 1848 and dealt with the serious riot of 12 June and a number of insurrectionary conspiracies (Goodway 1982: 99–146). Chartism, as Dorothy Thompson has pertinently pointed out, 'needed the small communities, the slack religious and moral supervision, the unpoliced street and meeting place'.

After 1840 England was increasingly policed. The control which local communities had been able to exercise over old-style constables, shopkeepers, schoolteachers and (in many places) Poor Law Guardians, made little impression on well-organized police forces who were, in the last analysis, agents of the will of the central government (Thompson 1984: 338; Emsley 1983: 68–75; Mather 1980: 25–6). Once the government, supported by the vast majority of the propertied classes, had made it clear that it would not be intimidated by the techniques of the mass platform and mass petitioning, then the only realistic way forward was by means of weighty disciplined pressure exerted by organized trade union and labour movements seeking to improve living standards and working conditions. Such a strategy necessarily aimed at piecemeal and long-term success, at the price of both political rights and the immediate and overwhelming victory sought by Chartists and doomed by the impossibility of mass revolution.

That the Chartist movement was distinctly weaker and less extensive after 1842 can partly be explained by the scale of arrests and the severe legal restrictions imposed on Chartist organizations. For the Chartists faced the most confident and securely-based structure of authority in Europe. The rival policies of Chartist leaders, internecine quarrels and the attraction of rival groups and organizations also played a major part in the fragmentation of the movement. A further factor was Peel's administration of 1841–6 which to a considerable degree undermined radical and Chartist rhetoric by adopting a high moral tone, distancing itself from 'Old Corruption' and passing measures which made it increasingly difficult to argue that beneficial reforms could never emerge from an unreconstituted political system. A government which passed a Mines Act, a Joint-Stock Company Act and a Bank Charter Act, as well as helping to stimulate economic prosperity through its budgetary policies, proved difficult to reconcile with the Chartist slogan of 'class legislation', even though the unrepresentative House of Commons, aristocratic constitution and privileged position of the Church survived substantially intact. Hence it became implausible for Chartist journalists and leaders to argue that wages and working conditions were primarily determined by a government resolved on the imposition of centralized despotism and the defence of partial and sinister interests (Stedman Jones 1983: 171–8).

Chartism can certainly no longer be regarded as basically a massive hunger protest, a mere Pavlovian response to the exigencies of the trade cycle and bewildering economic and social change. At a general level, there exists no simple or necessary direct correlation between economic deprivation and political extremism. The thousands who read the *Northern Star* and attended Chartist meetings were themselves evidence that the movement cannot be reduced to a 'knife and fork' question, but amounted rather to an enormous wave of popular protest, constantly threatening insurrection. At its very centre, Chartism contained a widespread desire by working people to exercise a significant degree of control over their working and living conditions, as well as over the education of their children. Craft workers resented the threat which the new capitalism and intensified competition posed to their status, independence and control over the work process. Chartism also offered factory workers a powerful critique of the new system of mechanized factory production, a critique eloquently expressed by Richard Pilling, a former handloom weaver forced into the factory by economic necessity. Speaking from personal experience, Pilling detailed the evils of the system: over-production, cut-throat competition, excessive hours of labour, constant wage reductions, victimization of labour activists, the employment of juvenile labour and the break-up of the family, the indifference of many factory masters to the suffering of their employees and their implacable hostility to Chartism or any challenge to orthodox political economy (Mather 1980: 189–92).

The dynamism and inspiration behind the Chartist challenge, behind its anti-aristocratic and anti-capitalistic outlook, was fuelled by deep and powerful feelings of anger at the unfairness of existing society and by a widespread desire to create an alternative society where workers would be adequately rewarded and recognized, even if there was considerable imprecision and disagreement concerning the exact nature of such a radically different society and a coherent anti-capitalistic philosophy was not fully developed (Ward 1973: 143–67, 220–4). Many Chartists continued to exhibit a pre-capitalist mentality, assuming that people had a right to a decent livelihood and that the private interests of the owners of capital ought not to be allowed to over-ride community interests and values.

Chartism attracted those who were conscious of the birthright of the free-born Englishman. 'Am I a Man?' was a question repeatedly posed in Chartist speeches and literature. To adopt Sir Isaiah Berlin's celebrated definition of 'negative liberty', Chartists desired to be somebodys not nobodys; to be doers, deciding rather than being decided for; to be self-directed and not merely acted upon by external nature or by other people, as if they were simply things, or animals, or slaves, incapable of playing a human role or of conceiving goods and policies of their own and realizing them. Like most human beings, they not only wished to have their rights acknowledged, but also to be respected as persons and treated with due consideration. While bread was very important for Chartists, the Chartist movement was concerned with more than bread; for it was also about human rights and individual and collective dignity and self-respect (Berlin 1969: 131; Ignatieff 1984: 13).

NOTES AND REFERENCES

1.   *Northern Star*, 29 September 1838.
2.   Francis Place, 'Historical Narrative, 1838', British Library, Add. Mss, 27, 820.
3.   *Bradford Observer*, 13 September 1838.
4.   *The Operative*, 10 February 1839.
5.   William Benbow, *Grand National Holiday and Congress of the Productive Classes &c*, 1832, p. 10.
6.   William Lovett and John Collins, *Chartism: A new Organization for the People*, 1840, p. 8.
7.   Colonel J. P. Tempest to Sir George Grey, 3 May 1848, PRO, HO 41/19.
8.   Bradford Central Library, Membership Book of the Great Horton Chartist Association. Case no. 1. Deed box 4.

Chapter 7

THE MID-VICTORIAN CONSENSUS 1850–80

Historians of nineteenth-century England have frequently made a sharp distinction between the first half of the century and the three decades after 1850. While the earlier period has been characterized by such phrases as 'the years of distress and discontent' or 'the bleak age', the years after the Great Exhibition of 1851 have been depicted as a time of 'the balance of interests', 'the age of equipoise' and 'the boom decades' – a 'golden age before the depression of 1873'. According to one eminent historian, 'the years before 1850 supplied a contrast to the secure opulence and peace of what came after ... it might be said that to a dangerous night and stormy morning had succeeded an afternoon which was sunlit and serene' (Kitson Clark 1962: 32–3).

The sources of that relative serenity have been the cause of much debate among historians and not only because the years between 1850 and 1880 were until recently the most under-researched in nineteenth-century labour history. Historians disagree on how far working men were seduced into acceptance of bourgeois values and aspirations towards middle-class lifestyles. If such a seduction did take place, to a greater or lesser degree, then how much was owed to mid-Victorian economic prosperity, assuming that such prosperity directly benefited the mass of the working population? After the collapse of the Chartist political challenge, a good deal of skilled working-class organizational initiative was channelled into trade union activities. Here again there has been dispute over the role of the so-called 'New Model' unions and the extent to which they encouraged a policy of collaboration with the capitalist system, involving increased loss of control over the work process and willingness to function as an agency of capitalistic hegemonic control over their respective workforces. Another major theme within the mid-Victorian consensus is the success of the trade unions in consolidating and extending their legal position by 1875; an outstanding single-issue campaign which formed one clear exception to the otherwise smooth convergence between working-class politics and a mellowed popular Liberalism, a process assisted by the emphasis which mid-Victorian working-class labour activists placed on sectionalism and localism, as well as the individual values of independence and respectability.

Much historical debate in recent years has centred on the concept of the 'labour aristocracy': the existence of a privileged elite of skilled, regularly employed and highly paid craftsmen aiming at respectability and status and therefore willing to adopt bourgeois values and protect themselves against social and economic degradation, whilst gaining a satisfactory degree of independence and respectability, by distancing themselves from the vast undermass of depraved, sweated outworkers and casual labourers. The existence of such a labour aristocracy, the argument runs, sowed a deep and fundamental division within the ranks of the working class and explains not only the absence of widespread revolutionary feeling, but also the lack of any serious challenge to the legitimacy of property ownership and capitalist productive relations. On the other hand, sceptical historians have attacked the thesis of the labour aristocracy as confused, lacking in clarity and inadequate as a cause of the phenomena it seeks to explain.

Another major issue of the mid-Victorian years dealt with in this chapter is the failure of a working-class political party to emerge, within a context of a distinct absence of working-class political movements on a national scale at a time when working-class voters, admittedly very few in many constituencies, remained open to the forces of influence and deference exerted by the Liberals and Conservatives. Such relative political apathy is best illustrated by the difficulty experienced in launching a mass campaign for further extension of the suffrage in the 1850s and 1860s, despite an alliance in many places between working-class political activists and those middle-class Radicals on the 'advanced' wing of the Liberal Party. So far as the actual passing of the Reform Bill in 1867 is concerned, there has been considerable debate on just how much significance should be attached to the effects of the agitation outside parliament in pushing the Bill through, as opposed to the complex party political manoeuvres within the House of Commons. Finally, research is only just beginning on the post-1867 popular electorate and how the two major parties were able to exert traditional influence on an expanded scale in order to invoke loyalty from the enlarged working-class electorate and organize the popular vote until the 1890s without serious opposition.

FROM CONFLICT TO CONSENSUS

If the years around 1850 have been seen as marking a watershed in Victorian history in general, there have also been those who, from the

Webbs onwards, have seen mid-century as marking a turning-point in the history of labour and working-class radicalism, when there took place an obvious break in the structure and ideology of the labour movement, especially in its trade-union aspect (Webbs 1911: 162, 185). Although it is acknowledged that class conflict did not suddenly evaporate with the rapid decline of Chartism after 1848, working-class radical energies increasingly became focussed on the more limited objectives of the co-operative movement, friendly societies, trade unions, and schemes for adult education and improvement. Industrial capitalism, no longer the subject of fundamental criticism, let alone rejection, came to be accepted as a system to be modified and reformed from within, rather than challenged from a quasi-socialist standpoint. At a number of levels, class consciousness became transformed into class collaboration and reformism, features which distinguished the mid-Victorian period (Stedman Jones 1983: 35–6, 69–75). So far as working-class political activity was concerned, the major development between Kennington Common in 1848 and the Hyde Park Riots of 1866 was the emergence of a popular Liberal party, in which middle-class and working-class Radicals co-operated in an alliance secure on the political level but extremely shaky as far as industrial relations were concerned (Vincent 1966: 57–66).

There has been considerable speculation about the reasons for this alleged swift transition from the militant popular radicalism of the 1830s and 1840s to the relative quiescence of the 'age of equipoise'. Traditional interpretations have emphasized how mid-Victorian economic prosperity and rising living standards blunted the edge of popular radical attitudes, while working-class radicals themselves were progressively seduced by middle-class ideology and the cult of respectability. In 1858 Engels despaired that 'the English proletariat is actually becoming more and more bourgeois, so that this most bourgeois of all nations is apparently aiming ultimately at the possession of a bourgeois aristocracy and a bourgeois proletariat *as well as* a bourgeoisie.'

However, this picture of progressive and passive working-class *embourgeoisement* has been considerably modified in the light of recent scholarship. It is, for example, no longer possible to argue that the demise of Chartism was primarily a result of improved living standards among the mass of the population during the later 1840s and the 1850s. Assumptions have too often been substituted for research on the mid-Victorian period, permitting Hobsbawm, among others, to refer to 'the upswing of the "golden years" of the Victorians' from the late 1840s to 1873. One may readily concede the enormous boost which railway building, the development of capital goods industries and the vast expansion of overseas markets gave to the mid-Victorian economy. But it does appear that the Victorians prospered much more in the 1860s than in the 1850s; in other words long after Chartism had lost mass support. Moreover, increases in both money and real wages were unevenly distributed, as wage earners fared much less well than the expanding middle-income groups. Among wage earners themselves, disproportionate gains were made by skilled and regularly-employed men like adult male cotton spinners, building workers, engineers, ship builders, miners, printers and flint glass workers (Burgess 1980: 16; Gray 1981: 20–29). During a period when the wage differential between skilled and unskilled workers widened beyond 2:1, unskilled and casual workers, subject to substantial cyclical unemployment, gained little if anything.

Despite the difficulty of making allowances for widespread regional and occupational income variations, as well as for unemployment and irregularity of earnings, it seems undeniable that, in terms of real income, mid-Victorian prosperity was limited, both in time and extent. As Church has argued:

> It is to be found only towards the end of the period, and even then largely among the middle classes and skilled operatives ... For whatever reasons, the course of real wages for the mass of the population does not appear to have risen substantially before the mid-1860s, and to portray this as an era of mid-Victorian tranquility when prosperity was the anodyne ignores both the chronology and trend in real wages (Church 1975: 73–4; Hunt 1973: 27–35).

In the Lancashire cotton industry, for example, there was a distinct increase in both money and real wages between 1850 and 1875, but such overall figures conceal increasing wage differentials, a sharp rise in the number of low-paid jobs and the fact that the most substantial and lasting advances took place, not in the 1850s but between the end of the cotton famine and 1874. On Merseyside and in the Black Country workers derived little material benefit from 'the new era of prosperity that now dawned' (Chambers 1961: 163; Foster 1974: 204; Kirk 1985: 102–03; Barnsby 1971; McCabe 1974).

Poverty and gnawing economic insecurity continued to haunt the majority of working-class families. Geoffrey Best concludes that there might well have been, during the 1850s and 1860s, at least as much corrosive poverty as Booth and Rowntree discovered persisting in the 1890s; in other words affecting about 30 per cent of the population. Hence the mid-Victorian years were substantially no less hungry than the 1830s and 1840s (Best 1971: 124). As Foster noted in his study of Oldham, Northampton and South Shields, in spite of the more secure employment and improved earnings during the third quarter of the century, few working-class families in these three towns were able to escape economic insecurity and periodic bouts of poverty during illness, old age and when women left paid employment to start a family. It has been claimed that in mid-Victorian Preston only about one in seven of all working-class families were permanently free from poverty. In the Black Country, although about a quarter of the workers possessed a minimum standard of comfort, 20 per cent existed more or less permanently below the minimum level necessary to maintain basic physical efficiency, while 53 per cent lived above subsistence level but below the minimum standard of comfort. In Manchester and Salford at least a quarter of working-class families were living in primary poverty during the mid-1860s. There is, therefore, considerable evidence to suggest that poverty continued to plague the lives of a majority of workers throughout the second half of the nineteenth century (Foster 1974: 96; Anderson 1971: 31–2; Barnsby 1971; Kirk 1985: 105).

Furthermore, there appears to have been little improvement in the health, housing and sanitation of the urban working class before the 1870s (Smith 1979: 197–203, 223–6; Hunt 1981: 94–5). Public health was a local responsibility, with most legislation merely permissive. Progress was restricted by a plethora of local and often conflicting elected and appointed organizations and by the expense of obtaining private acts of parliament, as well as by conflicts between the 'improvers' and those 'economists' reluctant to spend ratepayers' money. As late as 1870 London still lacked a constant supply of running water, while the capital's annual death rate increased from 21 per 1,000 in 1850 to 24.1 in 1870. Urban overcrowding was exacerbated by rapid growth and by the demolition of much city-centre housing to make way for warehouses, banks, offices, railway lines and stations. Rather than destroying slums, such clearances merely moved them a mile or two into conditions of even more intense over-crowding. The working classes needed to live near their place of work, yet the space available for working-class housing near city centres shrank annually. The older working-class areas of Manchester and Salford, for example, were dominated by cramped, ill-ventilated, back-to-back housing, open cesspools and totally inadequate sanitation, resulting in unusually high death rates. In Bradford, the fastest-growing industrial town of the first half of the century, the problem of overcrowded slums was never seriously tackled (Stedman Jones 1971: 159–78; Kirk 1985: 108–14; B. Thompson 1982: 148–9).

THE TRADE UNION STRUGGLE FOR RECOGNITION

If it is all too easy to exaggerate mid-Victorian prosperity and rising living standards, it nevertheless remains true that 1850 marks something of a watershed in the evolution of working-class radicalism. Owenite and Chartist inspired mass movements, which had posed a direct challenge to limited political representation and unfettered industrial capitalism, faded away. Henceforth the Victorian labour movement advanced in more piecemeal fashion on a limited occupational front.

Only relatively small minorities of workers were able to maintain stable organizations. It was largely the more skilled, better paid and strategically placed workers, profiting from the mid-Victorian boom and exercising a degree of control over the work process and occupational recruitment, who were able to impose collective bargaining procedure and achieve a negotiated consensus with employers, which involved a balance in production relations between capital and labour (Burgess 1980: 22–3; Price 1986: 71–2). Between 1850 and 1880 the most impressive achievement of the British labour movement was the way in which trade unions managed to change the attitude of employers from one of deep suspicion to one of somewhat grudging acceptance and co-operation. The unions not only increased their membership from under 250,000 in 1851 to some 750,000 by 1888 (equivalent to 10 per cent of the adult male workforce), but also became more adept at presenting an image of themselves acceptable to the traditionally hostile upper and middle classes. During the first half of the century trade unions had appeared mysterious, secretive and subversive institutions, with middle-class observers largely excluded from the workplace and the linked public houses where secrecy, ritual, oath-taking and folk violence made trade unions exceptionally opaque institutions for outsiders (Behagg 1982: 154–74). From the 1860s the workplace became less inaccessible as trade unions accepted a more open role in the running of industry. As Joyce has commented, the acceptance of the legal right to combine 'was long preceded at the local level by a practical and *de facto* acknowledgement, at first grudging and then more open-minded, that the unions were essential for the successful running of the [textile] industry' (Joyce 1980: 71). Given the failure of autonomous regulation to alter substantially either the nature or pace of structural economic change, there were obvious advantages in achieving 'official' recognition in a workplace relationship between masters and employees.

Trade union growth occurred at an uneven rate. During the economic boom of the early 1870s, for example, when unemployment was relatively low, union membership doubled to over a million. But the depression later in the decade led to the collapse of numerous smaller trade societies. Trade union strength was heavily concentrated among skilled occupations, whose members had benefited most from the economic changes of the 1850s and 1860s in the more industrialized parts of Britain, especially in the large urban centres (Gray 1981: 64). Among the leading craft unions was the Amalgamated Society of Engineers (1851) which, despite its failure to ban overtime and piecework in the strike and lockout of 1852, had 21,000 members by 1860 and 44,000 by 1875. Although there were several other engineering unions, it has to be borne in mind that the majority of skilled and semi-skilled workers remained non-unionized as late as 1880.

If the ASE was the largest union, it was closely rivalled by the Amalgamated Society of Carpenters and Joiners, the largest of the building trade unions. Its secretary, Robert Applegarth, became the most prominent unionist of his generation, doing more than anyone to surmount the crisis confronting trade unionism in the late 1860s, when the legal position of union funds, public acceptance of unions and prospects of further legislative advance all seemed imperilled (Briggs 1954: 176–204; Hunt 1981: 252). The foundation of the ASCJ lay in the prolonged and bitter dispute in the London building trade in 1860 over an unsuccessful demand for a nine-hour day. As with the engineering industry, there were numerous other building unions, with the majority of workers in the trade still unorganized. The engineering and building craftsmen, together with the miners, cotton operatives and ship builders, were to account for two-thirds of trade unionists on the eve of the 'new unionism' in 1888.

'New Model' unions like the ASE and ASCJ have been seen as marking an intermediary stage of consolidation and collaboration between the pre-1850 'revolutionary' period and the mass unionism of the late nineteenth century (Turner 1962: 169). 'New Model' characteristics have been taken to include size, efficiency, concentration of power in the hands of full-time officials at head office, acceptance of orthodox liberal economic doctrine, emphasis on inoffensive friendly society activities, amicable relations with employers and avoidance of the strike weapon. The skilled trade unionists have been depicted as willing agents of hegemonic control by capitalist employers: 'In the major industries, the privileged minority of "labour aristocratic" trade unionists usually performed managerial functions that in mediating conflict between labour and capital saved the employers considerable expense and trouble' (Burgess 1980: 27).

Their political ambitions have been described as largely confined to trade union affairs and pursued through the Liberal and Tory parties, with little inclination for independent working-class representation. Such unions, it has been claimed, were essentially exclusive and elitist, more concerned with safeguarding their craft status and privileges than with improving the lot of the mass of unskilled workers. Indeed, initial unionization among the unskilled was directed more against the craftsmen and their restrictive practices than against capitalist employers. Trade union development in this period has therefore been depicted as concerning conflict between workers's sectional interests as much as being devoted to any general struggle between capital and labour (Turner 1962: 260).

However, the above interpretation of the role of the New Model Unions remains open to considerable qualification. In the first place, the model was not really new, since craft exclusiveness, political quiescence and conciliatory attitudes towards employers were characteristic of some skilled unions before 1850. And union membership after the mid century extended far beyond the New Model Unions, whose leaders carefully projected a misleadingly reassuring image in order to gain public approval during the 1860s. In practice, the strike weapon was never abandoned, since New Model Unions frequently despatched funds to support strikes called by other unions (Musson 1962; Fraser 1974: 69). Of course it remains true that the New Model Unions were cautious about embarking on strike action, since an unsuccessful strike could quickly lead to the collapse of the union involved. Boycotting employers and imposing a work-to-rule were frequently adopted alternative tactics, without ever renouncing strikes as the ultimate weapon. If employers mounted a determined assault on craft job-control, as in the engineering conflict of 1852, then they were vigorously resisted. In the Lancashire cotton industry there were numerous local disputes, as well as major strikes in 1853–4, 1861 and 1867 (Musson 1972: 52–3; Dutton and King 1982: Kirk 1985: 247–66).

The New Model leaders did not, in fact, completely accept orthodox economic doctrine. While they studiously emphasized the undesirability of strikes, they were well aware that monopoly and restriction lay at the very heart of craft unionism, fitting ill with contemporary economic thought (Clements 1961). Neither were the New Model Unions as centralized as they appeared, since local branches acted independently in such crucial areas as wage demands, negotiations with employers, hours of work and apprenticeship regulations. Furthermore, tension always existed between London-based leaders and provincial districts and branches (Murphy 1978). The sectionalism and exclusiveness of the New Model Unions was quickly abandoned for the sake of labour solidarity in major disputes like the engineering lockout of 1852, the Preston cotton strike of 1853–4 and the London building strike of 1859–60, when substantial funds were contributed by other unions.

The prominent role played by the New Model Unions during the 1867–75 crisis over the legal position of trade unions has tended to divert attention from the large number of small unions, often composed of skilled and semi-skilled men not organized on New Model lines. At the same time there were some unskilled unions capable of militant action, for example the dockers, gas workers and builders' labourers during the prosperous early 1870s. Preoccupation with the New Model Unions can also lead to neglect of the trades councils, usually established at a time of industrial conflict in order to campaign for reform of the law of contract and laws affecting trade unions and to facilitate mutual aid among all organized workers in a particular town, as well as assisting small unions during trade disputes. By 1875 trades councils existed in every major town, acting as spokesmen for local working-class interests and organizations at the same time as they encouraged unionization among the unskilled and the unorganized (Hunt 1981: 259–64; Lovell 1969: 59–76; Clinton 1974; Musson 1972: 56–7).

Working-class political activity during the second half of the nineteenth century, less radical and widespread than before 1850, was dominated by the trade unions, which reached the peak of their prominence in the ten-year crisis over their legal position, a crisis which, by 1875, had been resolved in the unions' favour. Although trade unions in Britain were in a stronger position than those in Continental Europe, their activities during the 1850s and 1860s were restricted by four major legal disabilities. Firstly, while trade unions were no longer regarded as criminal conspiracies after the repeal of the Combination Laws in 1824, intimidation, molestation, obstruction and threats all remained criminal offences, rendering strike action legally precarious. Secondly, unions lacked redress against embezzling officials. The *Hornby* v. *Close* decision of the court of Queen's Bench in 1867, when the Bradford branch of the Boilermakers' Society failed to recover £24 from its treasurer, established that trade unions were not entitled to protection under the 1855 Friendly Societies Act, even if they had taken the precaution to register as friendly societies. Thirdly, the right to strike was circumscribed by the Master and Servant Law, under which both employers and workmen could take action for breach of contract of employment. Workers held to be in breach of contract were charged in criminal courts and faced imprisonment; employers were liable only to civil action for payment of damages or arrears (Simon 1954). A final grievance was the law governing accidents at work, whereby employers could escape liability for injuries to workers caused by the action of another employee. Besides being anxious to change the law in their favour on these issues, trade unions also sought legislation on other aspects of safety at work, on the length of the working day, on education, and on payment in truck, as well as demanding further extension of the franchise in order to exert a more positive voice in the legislative process.

Agitation on these issues intensified after the London building dispute of 1859–60, which not only led to the formation of the ASCJ and the London Trades Council, but also deepened a sense of solidarity among trade unionists and invoked renewed demands for universal manhood suffrage. It was the crisis of the 1860s which brought to prominence a small group of London-based salaried officials whom the Webbs termed 'the Junta', portraying them as 'what may almost be described as a cabinet of the Trade Union Movement' (Webbs 1911: 215; Pelling 1963: 66–7). This group of five men, which assumed the title of 'Conference of Amalgamated Trades' and met secretly once a week, aided by a small group of radical lawyers and literary men, consisted of Robert Applegarth, secretary of the ASCJ, William Allan, secretary of the ASE, Daniel Guile, secretary of the Friendly Society of Ironfounders, Edwin Coulson, secretary of the Operative Bricklayers' Union and George Odger, a skilled shoemaker. The Junta acted as an adroit political lobby, focusing on political and legal issues. Its members were the main influence behind the formation of the Manhood Suffrage and Vote by Ballot Association in 1862 and of the Reform League in 1864. The latter was very much a by-product of English popular enthusiasm for Italian liberty, originating in a committee set up by the Junta to welcome Garibaldi to London, when a crowd of 30,000 gathered to greet the hero of the *Risorgimento* before dispersing peaceably.[1] The Reform League was firmly committed to manhood suffrage and the ballot, as opposed to the household suffrage advocated by many 'Advanced Liberals', though with no real intention of seeking the enfranchisement of casual labourers.

The League succeeded in attracting large numbers of working men, including trade unionists, former Chartists, members of the newly-formed International Working Men's Association and the London Trades Council. It also received support and guidance from a number of Positivist Liberal intellectuals and middle-class radicals. For its trade union members, parliamentary reform was an essential preliminary to assaults on the industrial front, which would be facilitated by making politicians more aware of working-class opinion and electing MPs sympathetic to working-class and specifically trade union interests (Gillespie 1927: Ch.9; R. Harrison 1965: 80). The Junta made a significant contribution to the agitation which preceded the passing of the 1867 Reform Bill, at a time when, despite much activity in the provinces, London was once more the centre of working-class radicalism.

However, the Junta's leadership of the trade union movement was challenged by George Potter, leader of the 1859–60 builders' strike and now running the influential *Bee-Hive* newspaper as the voice of organized labour. Demanding a more aggressive policy, Potter argued that the Reform League was too much influenced by middle-class Liberals and was over-anxious not to offend the propertied classes. In 1866, after quarrelling with the Junta over their attitude to the striking Staffordshire miners, Potter was pushed out of the London Trades Council and proceeded to set up the London Working Men's Association to campaign for a radical measure of parliamentary reform, including a lodger franchise.

Industrial unrest after the financial crisis of 1866, together with increasing trade union pressure to change the Master and Servant laws, led to widespread public criticism of trade unions and to the crisis which commenced with the 'Sheffield Outrages'. These marked the climax to a long series of acts of violence against non-unionists in the Sheffield cutlery trades. Public opinion was shocked by the blowing-up of a workman's house with gunpowder in October 1866, a crime which the press depicted as characteristic of trade unions in general, rather than as the result of a specific conflict in Sheffield (Pollard 1959: 152–6). Critics of the unions seized on the Sheffield Outrages in order to demand a full inquiry into trade union activities. The Junta also supported proposals for an inquiry, in order to have the chance to demonstrate that the Outrages were unrepresentative of trade unionism and at the same time to attempt to negate the *Hornby* v. *Close* decision.

In 1867 the Tory government appointed a Royal Commission to inquire into the events at Sheffield and to investigate the role of trade unions in general. The dice were not loaded against the unions, since sympathizers to their cause, like Thomas Hughes, Frederic Harrison and the Earl of Lichfield were appointed to the Commission, while union representatives were invited to attend the proceedings. Applegarth, in close association with Harrison and Hughes, presented an account of the trade union movement which dwelt on the more acceptable features of the amalgamated societies rather than restrictive practices and the violence at Sheffield and Manchester which very much represented 'the other face of respectability'. At a time when the engineers were gaining a nine-hour day and the coalminers were getting their checkweighmen, structural changes in the seasonal and unstable building industry were threatening work-organization and job-control, accompanied by the introduction of non-union labour. Hence the violence, bombings and sabotage which took place at Manchester was a response to a serious threat of proletarianization (McCready 1955; McCready 1956; Harrison 1965; 277–90; Harvie 1976: 148–9; Price 1975).

The Royal Commission reported in 1869, with a majority and a minority report. The latter, signed by Harrison, Hughes and Lichfield, accepted the demands of the union lobby. In the same year the government introduced a Bill to nullify the implications of the *Hornby* v. *Close* decision. Two further Acts were passed in 1871, the first giving trade union funds the same degree of protection as those of friendly societies, the second – the notorious Criminal Law Amendment Act – effectively endorsed existing law, making strikers liable to prosecution for intimidation, molestation and obstruction. Trade union anger with the Gladstone administration was further inflamed by the imprisonment of striking London gas workers for breach of contract. Liberalism's commitment to individualism and property rights and its hostility to collectivism prevented many Liberals from grasping the potential power of labour as a pressure group. It was relatively new in its present form, the size of its following was difficult to assess and its party allegiance was not yet firmly fixed. Working-class disappointment at the failure of Liberal reform to bring about a really substantial improvement in their lot was combined with unprecedented trade union activity during the 1874 general election. The loss of working-class voters by the Liberals, reflected in Tory gains in the large boroughs, was a significant factor in the electorate's rejection of the Gladstone government (Feuchtwanger 1985: 82). As Frederic Harrison commented: 'There *is* a Conservative working man, both a sprinkling of the skilled, and the mass of the unskilled and rough.'[2]

Displaying initial ingratitude for the twenty or so seats which the working-class swing away from the Liberals had brought it, Disraeli's government churlishly failed immediately to repeal the hated Criminal Law Amendment Act. Instead it preferred to appoint a further Royal Commission on the Labour Laws, despite the unwillingness of many trade unions to co-operate. In the event the government, increasingly aware of artisan voting strength, ignored the Commission's recommendation of no substantial change in the law and in 1875 passed the Conspiracy and Protection of Property Act, by which the Criminal Law Amendment Act was repealed and peaceful picketing made legal. Although violence and intimidation remained offences, trade unionists could henceforth not be prosecuted for participating in a conspiracy, or for doing what an individual might lawfully do. In the same year another source of trade union discontent was removed when the Employers and Workmen Act eradicated the remaining inequalities of Master and Servant legislation.

Thus concluded a period of remarkable legislative advance, commencing with the 1867 Reform Act. The legality of trade unions was now finally assured, with their funds protected against theft or embezzlement. Strike action was also much less risky and the unions were in the uniquely privileged position of not being liable for damages. The crisis of the late 1860s and early 1870s had therefore resulted in enhanced status for the trade union movement and a concomitant thawing of official and public attitudes. Ironically, one of the chief results of Conservative legislation to remove labour laws from the arena of political controversy was to facilitate the return of organized labour to the Liberal fold by the time of the general election of 1880 (Hunt 1981: 268; Smith 1967: 213–18).

The most enduring consequence of the increased co-operation between trade unions during the crisis years 1866–75 was the emergence of the Trades Union Congress: an annual meeting of union delegates to discuss issues of common interest and exert political pressure via a small 'Parliamentary Committee' which sat permanently. The TUC had, however, a strictly limited role, in that it refrained from direct intervention in industrial disputes or from organizing joint industrial action. Collective bargaining and strikes remained the prerogative of individual unions.

The TUC was a natural development of the spread of trades councils, some of which had begun to play a national role. The Glasgow Trades Council, for example, had lobbied parliament and called a national conference in 1864 on the Master and Servant laws, while the Sheffield Trades Council in 1866–7 had attempted to create a national network of mutual aid, via trades councils, during lockouts and strikes, in a bid to soften the effects of public hostility following the Sheffield Outrages. The most significant initiative was that of the Manchester and Salford Trades Council in 1868, when it called a congress of trade unions in Manchester, partly in protest at the Junta's willingness to co-operate with the Royal Commission. This congress, a challenge by provincial unionists to the Junta's metropolitan leadership, was sparsely attended. But when a second congress in Birmingham in 1869 was more strongly supported, the Junta reluctantly agreed to make arrangements for a further congress at a time when factional rivalries were being sunk in common opposition to the 1871 Criminal Law Amendment Act. The Junta ceased to operate as a distinct body, although its members remained influential, while the TUC took over as the chief spokesman of organized labour (Lovell and Roberts 1958; Saville 1967).

In 1874 the parliamentary committee of the TUC had directed the trade union campaign which helped to defeat Gladstone's government at the general election. Such trade union political activity was unusual, prompted on this occasion by the direct threat which the Criminal Law Amendment Act posed to essential trade union interests. In general, trade unionists attempted to maintain a non-political attitude, confining themselves almost entirely to trade matters and refusing to entertain social revolutionary ideas. This approach was, of course, a continuation of that of many pre-1850 skilled craft unions. Even the trades councils were only marginally involved in political campaigns not directly concerned with trade issues, although the London Trades Council helped to organize agitation for parliamentary reform, support of the Union in the American Civil War and enthusiastic demonstrations for Italian independence. Certainly the Reform League found it difficult to overcome 'the indifference of organized trade unionism', not so much among the leaders as among the rank-and-file who regarded politics as of comparatively little relevance to their bread-and-butter trade interests (Leventhal 1971: 64–5). Such indifference was overcome only when legal threats to trade unionism appeared in 1866–7. Even then, labour politics remained constitutional and non-revolutionary, firmly in the Paineite non-socialist tradition which remained dominant in working-class radicalism until the 1880s (Thompson 1968 edn: 104–5).

A 'LABOUR ARISTOCRACY'?

Historians puzzled, or even disappointed, by the gradualism and lack of revolutionary consciousness among the English working classes after 1850, a puzzlement which frequently originates in exaggeration of widespread revolutionary aspirations during the 1830s and 1840s, have used the concept of a 'labour aristocracy' to explain both the attainment of a considerable degree of social stability in the mid-Victorian years and the gradualist characteristics of the British labour movement. The existence of a labour aristocracy has also been seen as a major reason why the labour movement failed to develop a coherent analysis of the capitalist relations of production, or to challenge the legitimacy of property ownership. Such historians have followed the comments of Marx and Engels, both of whom were anxious to explain the nature of social stability in mid-Victorian capitalist society and the reason why most workers came to terms with its basic institutions (Gray 1981: 10).

There is certainly a good deal of contemporary evidence referring to 'an aristocracy of the working classes', distinguished from other workers by their way of life, values and attitudes, as well as by their superior economic position. According to the *Bradford Observer* in 1851:

> There is a schism among the unenfranchised – a schism which, though inarticulate, is beyond the hope of immediate reconciliation. The hewers of wood and drawers of water are widely separated in sentiment and interest from the educated, intelligent and not infrequently refined fellow-labourer, who is as certain of bettering his condition as the ignorant and immoral are for ever flourishing in the mire, although men and gods decreed that they should rise.[3]

The existence of a distinct upper stratum among the working classes has been stressed by a number of historians dissatisfied with the overall explanatory power of 'improvement', starting with Hobsbawm who, in his classic 1954 essay, defined the labour aristocracy as essentially: 'the man who earned a good regular wage ... who put enough by to avoid the Poor Law, to live outside the worst slum areas, to be treated with some respect and dignity by employers and to have some freedom of choice in his job, to give his children a chance of a better education, and so on' (Hobsbawm 1954: 273). Thirty years later, he still emphasized wage levels as the key qualification for membership of the labour aristocracy: 'Only men who could expect a certain level of wages, which in the nineteenth century indicated relative scarcity in a free market, however this was obtained, could enjoy the lifestyles and develop the tastes and characteristic activities of the labour aristocracy' (Hobsbawm 1984: 220). The existence and expansion of the labour aristocracy has been regarded as a powerful moderating influence on the politics of popular protest, helping to stabilize political and social relationships between classes as it contributed to the mid-century disintegration of Chartism.

For Marxist–Leninist historians, the labour aristocracy was basically a slavish creation of capitalist class dominance and bourgeois ideological hegemony. John Foster, for example, attributed the erosion of 'revolutionary consciousness' in Oldham after 1850 partly to the emergence of a new 'tame' stratum of skilled men willing to collaborate with their masters. Authority at work, rather than high wages, was the distinguishing feature of these collaborators:

> Both [the cotton and engineering] industries show the development of a stratum of production workers exercising authority on behalf of the management. By the 1860s about one-third of all workers in engineering and about one-third of all *male* workers in cotton were acting as pacemakers over the rest, and in so doing made a decisive break with all previous traditions of skilled activity (Foster 1974: 237).

Royden Harrison, referring to the 'altered mood and reduced ambitions' of the labour movement after 1850, stresses the exclusiveness of the New Model Unions, separated from the mass of 'inferior' workers, so that 'if the thesis concerning the "two working class movements" contains a considerable exaggeration, it is not so extravagant that it can be dismissed out of hand' (Harrison 1965: 19, 21). Less tentatively, Keith Burgess asserts that:

> The economics of working-class differentiation created, therefore, a mechanism for transmitting a negotiated version of the dominant ideology to a privileged elite of labour during the third quarter of the nineteenth century ... The fact that the widening wage differentials obtained during these years by a privileged minority of workers were won as a result of playing the capitalist rules of the game was just one aspect of the legitimacy this gave to the dominant ideology ... A striking characteristic of labour utilization in this period was the extent to which authority and responsibility were delegated to key workers who were often sub-contractors in their own right ... the extent to which sub-contracting involved the delegation of the authority of the capitalist to a small elite in the labour force, who consequently enjoyed a comparatively privileged position, was part of the wider hegemony established by the industrial bourgeoisie during the mid-Victorian period (Burgess 1980: 20–2).

Inevitably, there has been considerable debate about the labour aristocracy thesis, given the hard fact that the working class was not a uniform, homogeneous social entity, with a fixed, unchanging identity, and that neither supporters nor opponents of the concept agree among themselves on what exactly the existence of a labour aristocracy explains. Indeed, one scholar goes so far as to dismiss the theory of the labour aristocracy as 'unclear, confused and contradictory' (Gray 1981: 9–10; Moorhouse 1978). Considerable doubt has been cast on the simple view that improved economic conditions for particular sections of the working class led to their social separation from other workers and their adoption of the dominant ideology of capitalist society. While sharp contrasts certainly existed in the economic experience and standards of living of different working-class groups, it has already been noted that even well-paid skilled workers were often only at a precarious distance from subsistence level. Even in well-organized trades, unions could be destroyed by systematic lock-outs and victimization, with wages subsequently forced down. And of course, the enormous diversity of the later nineteenth-century workforce makes all generalization hazardous. In any case, it may be questioned whether a unified working class has ever been other than a theoretical possibility (Dunn 1984: 24–7).

If Joyce sees the concept of a reformist labour aristocracy choking back the revolutionary class-conscious potential of the majority as irrelevant in the case of northern textile workers, where labour aristocrats were always in the forefront of radicals politics, as Pelling pointed out long ago, then the concept has also been seen as essential for explaining the moderation of the flint-glass workers of Stourbridge (Joyce 1980: xiv–xv; Pelling 1968: 56–7; Matsamura 1983). Some historians, notably Foster – the only historian who believes that working-class reformism can be adequately explained by the existence of a labour aristocracy – emphasize the significance of changes in industrial structures. Attention is focused on the system of authority in the workplace, where pieceworkers in engineering, male spinners in cotton and checkweighmen in coalmining acted as agents of capitalism in supervision, pace-setting and disciplining the rest of the workforce.

Others claim that the shift after 1850 to a more stable industrial capitalism, with an expanding sector of mechanized production, involved the adaptation of *all* sections of the labour force to the effective capitalist control of production (Reid 1978; Stedman Jones 1983: 62–75). Richard Price argues that a degree of balance between capital and labour, between the economic pressures of dependence and independence, was achieved in the 1850–80 period within a context of the paternalist model of the social hierarchy, with many craft workers retaining a considerable degree of independence in the workplace (Price 1986: 71–83). The lack of revolutionary potential among the working class and the mid-Victorian decline in political radicalism are perhaps better explained by the failure of Chartism and some improvement in real wages after 1860, than by the influence of a labour aristocracy.

Some recent exponents of the notion of the labour aristocracy have combined the economic approach with the idea of ideological hegemony, where skilled workers shared a common culture, values and lifestyles. Studies of Edinburgh and Kentish London point to the existence of an 'artisan elite', where social institutions drew together men from different trades, setting them apart from the less well-paid and secure sections of the labour force (Gray 1976; Crossick 1978). The skilled trades were disproportionately represented in trade unions, friendly societies, churches, co-operative societies, sports clubs, savings banks and so on. Such membership helped to confer a sense of separate social identity. Yet this was hardly a new development after 1850, since traditional crafts like building, tailoring and shoemaking had always tended to be sectional and exclusive. On the other hand, greater craft wage differentials after mid-century may have rendered a working-class elite more visible.

Such 'cultural' approaches to the concept of the labour aristocracy reflect a broader appraisal of class as an historical category, placing more emphasis on the cultural and political constituents of class consciousness. Exclusive values, social aspirations and patterns of behaviour may be as necessary as economic security for distinguishing a social stratum. According to Crossick: 'there is no necessary reason why high wage-earners should form an exclusive social group with aspirations and values distinct from others' (Crossick 1978: 19).

Yet the pattern of relationships between skilled and unskilled men varied according to occupation and locality. For example, many, if not all, of the Lancashire cotton towns were unified culturally by the effects of family employment and acceptance of the social leadership of employers. But at Coatbridge, on the Lanarkshire coalfield, the growing number of Irish immigrants led to frequent clashes between Orangemen and Roman Catholics, so that divisions within the working class ran mainly on religious and sectarian lines. Moreover, in most occupations there were numerous workers of a social status somewhere between labour aristocrats and unskilled men, while in high-wage areas many non-unionized, semi-skilled workers earned more than labour aristocrats elsewhere (Joyce 1975; Campbell 1978: 82–97).

It is always relatively easy to find evidence of degrees of difference between workers. The problem is how to assess and quantify such differences, whether they involve inter-marriage, residential separation, use of language, or some other distinguishing characteristic. The concept of 'respectability', for example, is a particularly slippery one. Respectability was certainly as central a value to the Victorian working class as it was to the middle classes, even if conventions of respectability varied from place to place, group to group and social level to social level. It has been argued that the social divisions between those who were and those who were not 'respectable' was the most important of all social divisions: 'a sharper line by far than that between rich and poor, employer and employee, or capitalist and proletarian' (Best 1971: 260).

The concept of respectability was closely bound up with that of independence, which involved the ability to make choices, to provide for oneself and one's family in the style appropriate to a specific social level. To attain a degree of respectability within the working class might well require regular earnings, as well as a significant degree of craft-control in the workplace. It is, however, no longer possible to regard working-class aspirations towards respectability and independence as merely imitating the middle classes, induced by passive reception of bourgeois indoctrination through such instruments of 'social control' as schools, churches, police forces, magistrates' courts, Sunday schools, adult education classes and factory discipline (Stedman Jones 1977; F. M. L. Thompson 1981; Burgess 1980: 29–31; Kirk 1985: 207–31).

Traditional orthodoxy holds that, as the elite of skilled workers achieved relatively higher incomes and living standards, so it assumed aspirations and values that were characteristically middle-class, beginning to act exclusively and hold moderate social and political views (Perkin 1969: 340–7). But there is considerable evidence to demonstrate that the ethic of respectability was something more than a crude weapon of social control in the hands of the employing class, for it functioned simultaneously as an instrument of working-class liberation. Self-respect, independence, emancipation from poverty, illiteracy and drunkenness were essential for the creation of working-class political consciousness and the training or working-class leaders in the organization of men and money. Crossick's study of the skilled workers of Deptford, Greenwich and Woolwich and their trade unions, friendly societies, co-operatives and building societies, reveals that their concern for respectability and independence and their rejection of patronage from above were designed for the purpose of obtaining status within the working-class community rather than aspiring to leave it and become middle class: 'occupational change that took a man out of the working class was not the general aim'.

Although the artisan elite of Kentish London was willing to accept a good deal of social and political class collaboration, while at the same time being anxious to distance itself residentially from the 'rough' streets of the old central working-class areas, members of the elite were not tame captives of bourgeois ideology, even if they did demonstrate 'an acceptance of the broad contours of the political economy in which they lived'. Their self-help was collective rather than individualist, while their organizations and attitudes were staunchly independent responses to the facts of social and economic life in their south-east London communities, rather than being imposed by middle-class ideology and capitalist employers (Crossick 1976; Crossick 1978: 19; Reid 1976: 282–3).

Similarly in Edinburgh, the labour aristocracy's claim to 'respectability' must 'be set in the context of a strong sense of class pride ... a claim to status recognition and citizenship on behalf of the skilled workers as a corporate group'. It is significant that in many places the skilled workers and craftsmen, the groups most capable of adopting the values and behaviour fostered by middle-class reformers – values like self-education, self-restraint, thrift and temperance – should have been the section of the working class most insistent on its own identity, constantly suspicious of middle-class patronage and guidance (Gray 1976: 139; Kirk 1985: 144). This remains true even if a degree of collaboration is acknowledged, in that proliferating working-class institutions like friendly societies, co-operatives and working-men's clubs were welcome to bourgeois elites, since they frequently rested on a narrower social base than before 1850, placing greater emphasis in financial stability. The wider aspects of co-operation, for example, tended to become submerged under an increasing focus on retailing, keeping the books straight and individual self-help rather than community-building (Pollard 1960; Yeo 1976: 283–9; Kirk 1985: 156–9).

The traditional stereotype of a deferential and thoroughly indoctrinated labour aristocracy has therefore been undermined. Beneath the aspirations of the skilled artisans to respectability, independence and status, there still lay assertive class pride and a distinctive radical ideology which continued to draw on the Paineite, Owenite and Chartist tradition. Even co-operators, despite increasing preoccupation with 'the divi', retained some element of idealism and collective commitment. And while contemporaries sometimes classified artisans among the lower middle classes, the social proximity between the upper strata of the working class and the lower strata of the middle class still involved separation rather than fusion (Tholfsen 1976: 83–121; Gray 1981: 42). It was workers' children, frequently entering lower middle-class employment direct from school, especially after 1870, who left their class, rather than the skilled workers themselves. Therefore, despite the growth of savings banks, building societies, temperance groups and adult education among the skilled artisans, there still persisted considerable class tension during the 'age of equipoise'. Coercive institutions such as the labour laws, the system of poor relief and police forces were enough to prevent the working class retaining any illusions about the limits of middle-class benevolence (Tholfsen 1976: 179–95; Storch 1975).

Bourgeois fear of the working classes still persisted. Hence the determined attempt by urban middle-class elites in the 1850s and 1860s to exert cultural control over the working class (Foster 1974: 187–93; Tholfsen 1976: 126–54). In 1855 the Rochdale Working Men's Educational Institution was founded under the auspices of the local clergy and Tory establishment 'for the purpose of preventing demagogues attaining ascendancy over the popular mind'.[4] Especially alarming was the continued prevalence among the 'lower orders', especially the mass of casual unemployed workers in the cities, of such 'unrespectable' activities as heavy social drinking, street rowdiness, gambling, frequenting brothels and 'low' entertainments. Bourgeois distaste was expressed, for example, by the middle-class Liberal *Leeds Mercury* in 1863:

> On Saturday night, if a foreigner had chanced to pass near the cattle market, he would have seen a sight after which all stories of English virtue and morality would have fallen upon his ears in vain. Crowds of men and women ... drunk, surging up and down the streets, gurgling round the entrance of the ... beershops; pickpockets ... unfortunate women ... children struggling through the crowded booths ... witnesses of all the disgusting immorality, the ribald jesting, the cursing and profanity ... and other nameless things in which these fairs and feasts abound.

At Ilkley Feast in the 1870s there were frightening annual scenes, as trains brought in pleasure-seekers from Leeds and Bradford, filling the streets with drunken, disorderly men, women and children. A small police force, operating from a station which lacked a Bridewell, had no chance of maintaining order (Storch 1982: 1).

Popular rioting remained endemic until late in the century, most notably the metropolitan Sunday trading riots in 1855, Reform riots in Hyde Park in 1866 and the riots of the unemployed in 1886–7. The anti-Irish riots at Ashton-under-Lyne in May 1868, inspired by the rabid rabble-rouser William Murphy, resulted in a Protestant armed mob ransacking the Irish quarter of the town, demolishing two chapels, one hall, one school and over 110 houses and shops, besides severely injuring numerous Irish residents (Richter 1981: 41). Such events helped to perpetuate deep-rooted fears of a working class which retained its own identity and its own popular culture, especially the section of the working class relatively impervious to concepts of 'improvement', focussing instead on the public house 'where no free-born Englishman need call any man his master' (Foster 1974: 238). It was the existence of a large 'residuum' of unskilled labourers who formed the riotous mobs and hedonistic patrons of fairs, low taverns and brothels, which hardened even radical Liberal opinion, including many of the labour aristocracy, against granting genuine universal manhood suffrage.

POPULAR ELECTORAL POLITICS AND THE SECOND REFORM ACT

The influence of working-class voters in the 1860s and 1870s remained remarkably slight in a country more industrialized and mechanized than any other. One reason, of course, was the restricted franchise. Even by the mid-1860s, when increased incomes and property values had enfranchised many artisans and skilled operatives, the proportion of the electorate which could be termed working class remained low. According to a parliamentary return of 1866, working men accounted for 27 per cent of the parliamentary electorate in Manchester, 21 per cent in Bolton, 14 per cent in Oldham, 10 per cent in Halifax and a mere 7 per cent in Leeds. As Derek Fraser has pointed out: 'within this exclusive and shrunken electorate, the opportunities for working-class participation were severely limited' (Fraser 1976: 222–3; Vincent 1967: 26–32; Nossiter 1975: 174).

Even after the 1867 Reform Act, which doubled the electorate and permitted one adult male in every three in Britain (apart from Ireland) to vote, including about 47 per cent of male occupiers in the boroughs, there was relatively little independent working-class political activity. Prior to 1874 there were no working men in the House of Commons, but at the 1874 election Alexander Macdonald and Thomas Burt were elected as 'Lib-Labs' to bring into parliament the voice of an unheard class, having been given a free run against the Conservatives by the Liberals of Stafford and Morpeth. Macdonald, president of the Miners' National Association and chairman of the TUC Parliamentary Committee, was also a shrewd investor and speculator in mining shares. 'Almost a parable of Victorian thrift, diligence and self-help', he financed his entry to Glasgow University by working extra-long hours in especially dangerous conditions underground. No uncouth agitator, Macdonald wrote elegantly and spoke impressively, being much more an orthodox Liberal than a Socialist (Wilson 1982). Those labour candidates who stood independently of the Liberal electoral machine in 1874 were defeated, despite the efforts of the TUC's Labour

Representation League, founded in 1869 after a handful of working-class candidates had been beaten at the 1868 election.

At a time when the conflict between labour and capital was not seen as central in politics, as opposed to the shopfloor, working-class electors remained firmly attached to the traditional parties, especially the 'advanced' wing of the Liberal party. Both parties courted working-class electors, while the Liberal electoral associations were prepared to allow working men some influence in the selection of candidates. If relatively few working men held any concept of a 'class war', then the traditional parties had much to offer. It has to be borne in mind that, in the majority of pre-1867 boroughs, the electorate disproportionately reflected pre-industrial society; working-class voters were mainly skilled craftsmen like tailors and shoemakers. Many of them were self-employed and owned small property, or had become retailers and members of the 'shopocracy'. They tended to regard property rights as unquestioned, with Socialism viewed as a somewhat outlandish Continental doctrine. Radical Liberalism held strong appeal for these working-class electors for the same reason as it appealed to many of the middle classes: the undisputed benefits of free trade, of independence and self-improvement, of the concern for individual rights and hostility to large landlords and aristocratic rural values, and above all for its alliance with militant Nonconformity, temperance and an expanding daily press, especially the development of the penny daily newspaper, as well as its commitment to extension of the franchise and redistribution of seats. Men who were strong upholders of collective values in industrial relations, were often thorough-going individualists at parliamentary elections. In the boroughs of the North East, for example, it was the shopocracy and skilled craftsmen who formed the backbone of popular radical Liberalism (Nossiter 1975: 147–60).

Although the mass of workers in large industrial towns failed to attend a place of worship, apart from Irish Roman Catholics, they were still deeply affected by sectarian rivalries. In any case, large industrial towns formed only a small proportion of parliamentary boroughs. In the more typical county, market and cathedral towns, working-class craftsmen were as likely to vote according to denominational loyalties as were their social superiors. And Liberalism's emphasis on moral issues, economy in expenditure, dignity, restraint and self-improvement had wide appeal. For many working-class electors, then, Liberalism represented, in Vincent's phrase, 'their domestic morality writ large', at a time when the darker side of Liberalism – its association with property and capitalism, its emphasis on the individual and distrust of the communal and the collective – remained relatively unexposed.

Toryism, on the other hand, appealed to those working men who were not usually members of trade unions, who were keen on their daily beer and gamble and who thought little of Victorian sexual morality, mechanics' institutes, mutual improvement societies or debating clubs.

They preferred the sporting to the political press and admired qualities like honour and 'pluck' rather than respectability, independence, prudence and perseverance. Not for nothing was the gamecock the symbol of urban Toryism, the politics of beer and Britannia, in many areas. Members of the Liberal rank-and-file would never have dreamed of calling John Bright 'Johnny'. In 1870 the trade union and Reform League leader George Howell told William Rathbone, Liberal MP for Liverpool, that the Liberals failed to gain the support of many working men because 'their economics are considered harsh and partial' and their behaviour lacked 'geniality and bonhomie' (Vincent 1966: 79–81; Vincent 1967: 20; Joyce 1975; Waller 1981: 16).

For many of the lower working class, most of whom stood well outside all working-class movements and rarely supported Radical candidates, elections offered the pleasures of free food and beer and, not infrequently, a saturnalia of mob violence. In Blackburn on the day before the 1868 municipal election rival mobs, well lubricated by open treating, fought in the streets and destroyed the committee-rooms of each candidate. The *Annual Register* described the scene the following day at the Trinity Ward polling station:

> A cart of stones was kept in readiness by the blue and orange [Tory] party, and a crowd of women kept supplying them with missiles. Most of the rioters were armed with picking sticks about two feet in length and 1½ inches thick at the head ... All along the pavement streams of blood were flowing, and the sickening sight of men with blood flowing from their heads and faces met one at every turn. The police charged the mob with drawn cutlasses and truncheons, committing great havoc; but they did not succeed in restoring even comparative quiet for a long time ... Business was interrupted at the polls for hours.

Blackburn's schools were turned into hospitals to accommodate the injured.

At Bradford, a town which epitomized progressive radical Liberalism and the spirit of improvement, as well as being eventually the cradle of the Independent Labour Party, elections between 1867 and 1869 were distinguished by similar scenes of riot, bloodshed, police and military charges (Richter 1981: 64; Wright 1979: 52, 56–7). Like Victorian trade unionism, elections had more than one face of respectability, with the politics of influence and the market threatening to overwhelm the politics of conscience even in progressive Liberal industrial boroughs which prided themselves on being centres of religious Nonconformity and moral uplift.

The politics of deference and influence were certainly not confined to the rural county constituencies so meticulously dissected by D. C. Moore. In a pioneering article, Patrick Joyce demonstrated that in Blackburn in 1868, where a substantial working-class electorate had been created by the 1867 Reform Act, voters living in streets around large cotton mills tended to vote the same way as the millowners. In such factory 'townlet' communities, employer paternalism was exercised through ownership of workers' housing, through promotion or demotion in the factory, through the control exercised by supervisory workers, through dinners, treats, festivals and extensive patronage; all reinforced by factory-owner control of churches, chapels and schools. Such factory paternalism, together with denominational allegiance and ethnic loyalties, constituted a powerful determinant of working-class voting behaviour. In the North Durham county constituency in 1868, industrial influence had replaced that of the landowners, so that mine and factory owners brought their employees to the polls after paying them £3 per voter (Joyce 1975; Joyce 1980: 158–221; Nossiter 1975: 79). Although there was always a substantial minority of working-class Conservative voters, especially in Lancashire, where popular Toryism was largely an ethnic vote based on hostility to Irish immigrants and Liberal attempts to conciliate Irish nationalism, the majority of working-class votes went to the Liberal party. After the labour legislation of 1875, the alliance between Liberalism and organized labour was rapidly re-cemented and remained in being until at least the end of the century.

Not until the mid-1860s was there anything like a sustained campaign for a further Reform Bill. During the previous decade there was little prospect of effective independent working-class initiatives. One reason for this was the rapid demise of Chartism after 1848. Only in one or two areas, like Halifax, Bradford and the Black Country, did Chartist organizations manage to persist during the 1850s, and then on a much-reduced scale (Tiller 1982: 311–44; Wright 1982: 165–98; Barnsby 1971: 93–114). In both Halifax and Bradford, middle-class radical Non-conformist Liberal employers sought to wean working men away from Chartism ('demagoguery') in favour of a programme of household suffrage at the very most. In both towns they met resistance. Halifax retained a special relationship with Ernest Jones, who in his various publications, particularly his *Notes to the People* (1851–2), emerged as the leading ideologist and strategist of the working-class radical movement. At the 1847 general election he obtained 280 votes at Halifax, but only 28 when he stood again in 1852. Like O'Connor, he regarded temperance, co-operative associations and middle-class radical overtures as so many distractions from the main aim of striving to secure political power for the working man. Yet his efforts to revive Chartism as a mass movement came to nothing and in 1858 he bowed to the inevitable, calling a conference to promote co-operation with middle-class radicals in a broadly-based Reform movement (Saville 1952: 66–9).

The political dialogue at Halifax remained a two-way one between working-class and middle-class Reformers, so that the transition from Chartism to popular Liberalism was never smooth prior to 1874. There was similar resistance to middle-class Reformers in Bradford, a town which had risen three times for the Charter between 1840 and 1848 and where a hard core of former Chartists refused to support household suffrage, standing firm for manhood suffrage and the ballot. At the Leeds Northern Reform Conference, called in February 1864 to support a £6 borough franchise, it was the Bradford working-class radical leaders who provided the most vehement opposition to anything short of manhood suffrage. After much acrimony, a *modus vivendi* between working-class Reformers and 'Advanced Liberals' was eventually worked out, whereby wealthy members of the local branch of the National Reform Union, committed to household suffrage, agreed to subsidize the local National Reform League and its programme of manhood suffrage and the ballot.

If it proved difficult to launch a mass campaign for extension of the suffrage before 1864 in so radical a town as Bradford, a major centre of popular Liberalism and funds for the national party, there was little hope for the rest of the country. There was still the major obstacle of widespread working-class apathy after the trauma of the failure of Chartism, besides the fact that a significant proportion of the skilled workers were not seriously dissatisfied with the pace of material and political advance, preferring to concentrate on trade and craft issues. And if further extension of the franchise demanded a Reform coalition between working- and middle-class groups, there was relatively little middle-class enthusiasm for further parliamentary reform during the early 1850s. John Bright, for example, imagined that Manchester merchants and manufacturers would be willing to lead a Reform agitation on the lines of the Anti-Corn Law League, but Cobden realized that by the early 1850s Manchester had become too prosperous and conservative (Read 1967: 154).

On the other hand, many of the labour aristocracy came to desire the status which the right to vote conferred in Victorian England (Hunt 1981: 278; Crossick 1978: 215). Most of the politically active working class supported the Liberal Party because it represented the qualities of respectability and dignity, if not the collective aspirations, so admired by the skilled artisans. As Vincent has pointed out: 'For the nineteenth century man the mark or note of being fully human was that he should provide for his own family, have his own religion or politics, and call no man master. It is as a mode of entry into this full humanity that the Gladstonian Liberal Party most claims our respect' (Vincent 1966: xiii).

Yet even skilled working men in parliamentary boroughs only got the vote as householders in 1867, apart from the minority who qualified under the 1832 £10 franchise. The northern industrialists and New Model employers who desired suffrage extension in order to push through their own programme of strengthening Nonconformity at the expense of the established church and the landed gentry found it difficult during the 1850s to rally support from their own class. Increasing prosperity and the greater stability of the economic system helped consolidate a 'balance of interests' between the various dominant elites: large landowners, rentiers concentrated in London and the south of England, the industrial capitalists mainly located north of the Trent, and the intellectuals who were closely aligned with the landowners and rentier middle classes, often serving the state in an administrative capacity (Harvie 1976: 11–49). Such a balance did not mean total absence of conflict, for example on religious issues, parliamentary reform and education; but the Nonconformist radicals were genuinely willing to accept the continued political dominance and social status of the landed classes, which Corn Law repeal in 1846, like the Reform Act of 1832, had been designed to perpetuate (Moore 1965). In mid-Victorian England the traditional landed class still ruled. Fewer than 25 per cent of MPs were manufacturers, merchant bankers and the like, the vast majority consisting of relatives, descendants or dependants of the landed aristocracy and gentry, a predominance which persisted to the end of the century. Cabinets, as well as county and small rural borough constituencies, remained under the control of the landed elite (Guttsman 1965: 41).

While the provincial, urban industrial elites in northern and Midland cities had no wish to control central, as opposed to local, government, sources of tension between them and the landed classes existed on questions like disestablishment of the Church, land reform, the game laws, 'aggressive' foreign policy, a reformed army and civil service and the franchise issue. There was also a good deal of provincial exasperation at the frequency with which landed parliaments emasculated local improvement bills (Garrard 1983: 100–3). During the 1850s a small but influential group of radical businessmen, including John Bright, Samuel Morley and W. E. Forster, attempted to launch a major campaign for household suffrage. It proved difficult, however, to make much impression on the House of Commons, dominated as it was by the Palmerstonian coalition, or to rouse mass support in the country, especially as many working-class radicals and former Chartists regarded household suffrage as a device for rewarding only the 'respectable' skilled sections of the working class deemed 'worthy' of the franchise, rather than conferring the vote as a democratic right.

So valued was the suffrage, however, as a symbolic mark of status, a test of the 'manliness' and 'independence' inherent in popular Liberal ideology, that there were eventually substantial numbers of working men willing to compromise over household suffrage and join middle-class Radicals in a major campaign for a further Reform Bill in the late 1860s, at a time when working-class votes accounted for something like 26 per cent of the total (Smith 1966: 21). Yet this not inconsiderable working-class voting power remained largely submerged through not being organized to support specific working-class programmes or candidates.

During the 1860s, Russell and Gladstone became convinced that efficient government required the stimulus of a wider electorate, though one stopping well short of manhood suffrage. Gladstone was particularly impressed by the 'respectable' artisan elite, which deserved votes as a reward for good behaviour and for embracing such individualist qualities as thrift, self-reliance, sexual 'prudence' and self-improvement (Shannon 1982: 506–8). Such qualities, argued middle-class Reformers, meant that these men could be entrusted with votes, since they were likely to defer to social superiors and reject 'socialist' notions. Not even John Bright, who coined the term 'residuum', wished to enfranchise unskilled labourers: those regarded by the propertied classes as corrupt, irresponsible, immoral and liable to support extremist assaults on the sacred rights of property and the divinely-ordained laws of the free market (Robbins: 1979: 184; Arblaster 1984: 264–83).

What middle-class Reformers really wanted was an enfranchised working-class elite which would serve as crucial reinforcement in a campaign to push the Palmerstonian Whig–Liberal coalition in a radical direction, in order to attack the privileged social position of the landed classes and their associated institutions. Without the status symbol of the franchise, the labour aristocracy might be tempted to act as the vanguard for a frontal assault on the capitalist system, an assault which would involve increased trade union activity and strike action. Many leading provincial Reformers were also employers, and could hardly help viewing parliamentary reform as one means of nipping in the bud any incipient anti-capitalist movement. They had therefore no wish to encourage manhood suffrage, or to subscribe to theories which held that working men should possess the vote as a natural right.

Before 1865 the chances of a successful Reform Bill were very slim. With the passing of Chartism, the working-class political movement had become fragmented. Among the fissiparous tendencies were the growing differential between skilled and unskilled workers, the lack of a political philosophy ascribing to working men a clear and independent political function, and the seduction of many prosperous workers by middle-class movements and institutions, even if the numbers involved and the extent of the seduction have been exaggerated. In the economic sphere, there was a good deal of militant trade unionism and a reluctance to swallow the message contained in vulgarized tracts of political economy written for literate working men. But the political legacy of Chartism was soon spent, so that, according to Bagehot in 1869: 'the mass of the people yield obedience to a select few'. Even in radical industrial cities, the politics of deference and paternalism were often able to flourish (Joyce 1980: 134–54; Gillespie 1927: Ch.7).

A succession of Reform Bills in the 1850s and early 1860s came to grief in a House of Commons composed largely of landowners and Churchmen who cared little either for democracy or for the aspirations of middle-class Nonconformists. The seventy or so radicals on the fringes of the Palmerstonian coalition were able to make little impression. What really made a major Reform campaign in the country a feasible proposition was the American Civil War, seen by many in England as the testing time for democracy in the West. If the 'Great Experiment' survived and the Union won the war, then democracy was demonstrably both stable and efficient. Meetings held throughout industrial England in support of the North after the Emancipation Proclamation of January 1863 eroded a good deal of popular pro-Confederate sympathy, which had flourished even in Lancashire, and created renewed enthusiasm for democracy and antagonism towards those landed gentry who persisted in supporting the Southern states. Such enthusiasm and antagonism helped to push working-class and middle-class Reformers together in a combined campaign (Harrison 1965: 40–69; Wright 1969a; Wright 1974).

Both the middle-class National Reform Union and the largely working-class Reform League were founded before the end of the Civil War. Although relations between the two were acrimonious in some places, they became closer once the 1866 Reform Bill had been introduced, even though trade union members of the Reform League saw parliamentary reform as an essential preliminary to major advance on the industrial front, not least in trade union law. Such advance would certainly not be universally welcome among the employers who formed the hard core of the National Reform Union, although there were some enlightened Liberal employers like A. J. Mundella, M. T. Bass and Samuel Morley who were strong supporters of trade unionism, the co-operative movement and the principle of arbitration in industrial disputes (Harrison 1965: 273–90; Bradley 1980: 169).

The actual passage of the Reform Bill of 1867, which conferred the borough vote on householders with twelve months residence and on £10 lodgers, also with a year's residence, as well as on £5 property owners and £12 occupiers in the counties, was the result of a complex series of parliamentary manoeuvres. Russell's 1866 Bill, whose main proposal was a £7 rental borough franchise, split the parliamentary Liberal party and was defeated in June. When Russell resigned office, Derby and Disraeli formed a minority government. Disraeli now seized the chance to bring in a Tory Reform Bill, which opened the prospect of a Conservative majority government for the first time since 1846 and the consolidation of his own rather precarious position in the party. In order to further these aims, Disraeli proved willing to accept Radical amendments to the Bill, aimed at conferring household suffrage in the boroughs. It eventually passed, with Radical Liberal support (Smith 1966; Blake 1966: Ch. 21; Cowling 1967; Briggs 1965; Chs 8, 10).

Although Royden Harrison has argued that the passing of the Second Reform Act was dictated by the ruling class's perception of 'the proximity to revolutionary situations' and by fear of working-class anger after the Hyde Park demonstration of May 1867, there is considerable evidence to suggest that, in contrast to 1831–2, agitation outside parliament was a relatively minor factor in the passing of the 1867 Act (Harrison 1965: 78–136). John Bright, leader of the Radical Liberal agitation, admitted privately in 1866 that 'the organization of the multitude is not complete enough to enable them to make a very effective demonstration of strength', while the Reform League planned open-air meetings in support of manhood suffrage with little genuine confidence (Robbins 1979: 182; Leventhal 1971: Ch. 4). Harrison's basic argument is that political leaders and men of property became willing to grant concessions on the franchise in order to break up the public agitation, headed by the Reform League and reaching a climax at Hyde Park. By doing so, they avoided having manhood suffrage thrust upon them in the near future. The popular agitation allegedly pushed both Gladstone and Disraeli in a more radical direction than they would otherwise have taken.

But Harrison's claims, recently dismissed as 'heroically wrong-headed', have received little support from historians who have closely studied the 1866–7 Reform crisis (Evans 1983: 346). There is no evidence that either the agitation in general or the Hyde Park riots in particular influenced Disraeli, who was almost entirely motivated by party and personal ambitions, as well as by intense dislike of Gladstone, whom he sought to isolate by means of a drastic Reform measure which would also keep the Liberal Party divided and ensure his own leadership in the Commons. According to Disraeli's secretary, Mrs Disraeli 'sympathized with the crowd', while Lord Stanley, son of Prime Minister Derby, wrote in his journal on 24 July 1866 that 'there was more mischief than malice in the [Hyde Park] affair, and much more of mere larking than either'.[5] Maurice Cowling, writing from a high-Tory viewpoint, goes so far as to claim that politicians were playing a cynical, self-seeking, unprincipled game, which they indulged in purely for personal and party advantage, with public opinion dismissed as largely irrelevant. If some timid Liberals, like Lowe and Horsman, feared 'the mob', Disraeli and the Conservative leaders certainly did not (Cowling 1967; Gash 1986: 57–8).

There is no denying, however, the reality of working-class pressure for Reform. Although the May 1867 Hyde Park demonstration was a peaceful one, even if it were held in defiance of the Home Secretary's ban, that of July 1866 after the defeat of the Liberal Bill resulted in skirmishing between police and sections of the crowd, following an intense crush when dilapidated railings collapsed. Despite the alacrity with which Reform League leaders condemned the violence, besides the fact that a potentially revolutionary situation clearly failed to develop, the riots being more a protest against social exclusion than a manifestation of class warfare, the Hyde Park affair caused considerable fear of social disorder, both in the Carlton Club and in the influential person of Matthew Arnold, who voiced his somewhat hysterical anxieties in *Culture and Anarchy* (1868) (Smith 1966: 231–2; Richter 1981: 51–61).

If working-class pressure, exerted through the Reform League, failed to stampede reluctant politicians towards Reform, given that the League failed to transform the London crowd into a genuine political force, then it certainly played a part in keeping the issue on the boil. This was especially the case after the defeat of the 1866 Bill, when a series of impressive demonstrations, inspired by Bright and Forster, were held in the north of England. Nevertheless, the Reform League never posed much of a revolutionary threat, for its working-class leaders, members of the New Model Unions, were closely linked intellectually to the Liberal Party. At the same time they heavily depended for their finances on rich Nonconformist industrial magnates in the National Reform Union like Samuel Morley and Titus Salt (Reynolds 1983: 213). Neither had the League any intention of seeking the enfranchisement of casual unskilled labourers or the vagrant population of the teeming cities, being as repelled by the drunken crowds as was the *Leeds Mercury* in 1863. As Marx sardonically noted, its demand for manhood suffrage was carefully qualified by the key adjectives 'registered' and 'residential'. Even the Hyde Park demonstration of 1867, ostensibly held in defiance of the Home Office, followed some last-minute collaboration with the Tory Cabinet.

Under the 1867 Reform Act about 30 per cent of adult males in urban working-class constituencies were enfranchised, while in the counties the new property-owning and occupier franchises did nothing to undermine the influence of the landed interest in deference communities, particularly when the redistribution clauses of the Act still left rural areas considerably over-represented (Seymour 1915: 280–350; Moorhouse 1973). In the short run, the 1867 Act did little to modify the mid-Victorian structure of political power. The subsequent rise in electoral costs, necessary to manage an enlarged electorate, gave effective control of local politics to electoral agents and registration bodies financed by either the Liberals or the Tories. A proposal to defray election expenses from the rates was firmly rejected, while parliament continued its opposition to the payment of MPs for another forty years. Thus there was little chance in the immediate future for working men to enter parliament entirely free to pursue the interests of their class, as opposed to sitting as relatively innocuous 'Lib-Labs'.

It was not, however, entirely a matter of objective constraints, for working-class leaders lacked the desire to found a Labour Party. During the 1868 election, for example, Liberal agents were surprised by the limited ambitions of George Howell and other labour leaders in the Reform League, and by their readiness to work in an unequal partnership for the election of Liberal candidates. This partnership marked the real beginning of the Lib-Lab era in working-class politics, which was to last beyond the formation of the Labour Representation

Committee in 1900. The Liberals gave £2,000 to the Reform League during the 1868 campaign in order to supply men to tour the country addressing working-men's clubs and unions, without however encouraging working-class candidates. Only three working men went to the polls. At Birmingham, G. J. Holyoake, a former Owenite and Chartist but now a leader of the co-operative movement, stood on an orthodox Liberal programme, extolling the virtues of Gladstone and his fellow Liberal candidates. His £50 campaign fund was provided by the Birmingham Liberal Electoral Association (Harrison 1965: 209; Leventhal 1971: Ch.5; Grugel 1976: 122–3).

John Vincent has persuasively argued that there was really very little to stop the working class forming its own political party had it genuinely wished to do so, along the lines of the separatist working-class religious denominations like the Primitive Methodists. While there were some industrial boroughs where very few working men possessed votes, there were others in which it might well have been possible to elect working-class candidates. In Leicester, for example, 40 per cent of the voters were working-class before the 1867 Act; in Nottingham the percentage was 39 and in Manchester 27. At the latter in 1868, Ernest Jones, now reduced to standing as a Lib-Lab, polled over 10,000 votes. At Merthyr Tydfil the miners were instrumental in defeating H. A. Bruce, a long-established Liberal MP, on strictly working-class and industrial issues. It was therefore possible to organize working-class votes and it could have been done on a nationwide basis. The large amalgamated unions possessed the funds and managerial experience; the Reform League at its peak, with its hundreds of local branches, 'could get hundreds of thousands of people on to the streets with a drill and discipline unsurpassed in English history'. Local leaders, trained in chapels, co-ops and temperance societies, were readily available. But 'there was no questioning of the doctrines of property and no sense of the essential injustice of the rich existing at all ... still less did any argue that the richness of the rich created the poverty of the poor'. As it was, the bulk of working-class electors remained wedded to Gladstonian Liberalism. The remarkable willingness of the government to enact the labour legislation of the early 1870s, in the face of substantial opposition from employers, is therefore hardly surprising (Vincent 1966: 77–80; Kirk 1985: 70, 161; Jones 1961; Burgess 1975: 38, 112–27).

POST-1867 PARTIES AND THE WORKING-CLASS VOTE

After 1867 both the Liberals and Conservatives made determined and successful attempts to capture the working-class vote, despite gloomy prognostications of political barbarism by leading literary figures like Matthew Arnold, Thomas Carlyle and George Eliot (Wolff 1965; Williams 1961: 85–98, 133–4; Myers 1971: 105–28). Even before 1867 the Liberals had begun recruiting working-class electors on electoral associations and ward committees. The Tories, in their turn, had established popular Conservative Associations in northern cities as a response to the National Reform Union and the Reform League. This process of integrating the working class into the existing system was continued after 1867 under J. E. Gorst, when the Nation Union of Conservative and Constitutional Associations was founded. Yet it received little encouragement from the party leadership. Too many wealthy Conservatives feared allowing the working class genuine influence on party policy. Artisan Tories were permitted only a strictly limited role at grass-roots level: assisting with electioneering, canvassing and propaganda.

Hence Popular Conservative Associations tended to attract only deferential working men, content with the politics of beer and Britannia and the somewhat condescending patronage of their betters. Those working men anxious to further specific working-class interests and seek genuine political status, generally voted Liberal. Only in south-east Lancashire and in sectarian Liverpool – England's Belfast – where popular Orangeism and racial hostility towards immigrant Irish Catholics, as well as Tory factory paternalism, was very powerful, did the Conservatives gain a mass working-class following outside the capital (Feuchtwanger 1959; Feuchtwanger 1968; Kirk 1985: 310–42; Greenall 1974).

Liberals had always tended to view the franchise as a privilege rather than as a right, and by the late 1860s conceded that the behaviour and attitudes of 'respectable' working men had earned them the privilege. The franchise, it was assumed, would improve the moral and intellectual qualities of the recipients. After the passing of the 1867 Reform Act, the Liberal philosopher T. H. Green echoed J. S. Mill when he wrote:

> We who were reformers from the beginning always said that the enfranchisement of the people was an end in itself. We said, and we were much derided for it, that citizenship makes the moral man; that citizenship only gives that self-respect which is the true basis of respect for others, and without which there is no lasting order or real morality.[6]

Nonetheless, during the years following the Reform Act neither of the major parties was in practice willing to accept that possession of the franchise automatically led to immediate improvement in human nature and firm attachment to the institutions of the country.

In Salford, for example, both Conservatives and Liberals after 1867 set out to manage the new electorate in a predominantly working-class city. According to John Garrard, this represented 'an attempt to ensure that the new proletarian entrants to the political system did not disrupt either that system, or the society which it controlled'. Salford Conservative Association, open to working-class members, was founded in January 1867 and Salford Liberal Association in January 1869. By the mid-1870s both parties had created a network of political clubs throughout the city, where working-class members were subjected to strenuous programmes of 'improvement', designed to ensure the 'fitness' of working men for political participation. In the words of the middle-class leaders of the clubs, their aim was 'to make people competent for the wise control by their votes of the public business of the country . . . . Those who formed the great masses of the people should be intelligent and well-educated . . . should be able to think clearly on all subjects'. Clubs were 'places where you shall improve yourselves . . . of material value in increasing the intelligence of the working classes, in promoting orderly habits'.

Neither party in Salford between 1868 and 1914 seriously contemplated nominating a single working-class candidate, the issue only being raised for the first time in the late 1880s. The Salford Conservatives and Liberals, whose middle-class leaders retained firm control over the political associations and clubs, aimed to provide for the new voters a 'total' environment akin to that created by the Social Democratic Party in Germany for its members. Hence the programmes of lectures, the libraries and billiard rooms, the facilities for card games, draughts, chess and bagatelle, with the annual outing and picnic proving the high point of the social round. It was, therefore, by a combination of social activities and rigorous political indoctrination that the new householder voters in Salford, as in many other places, were incorporated into the political system by a process of skilled and intensive political socialization (Garrard 1977).

On the eve of the First World War, the House of Commons had still not been taken over by the working class, who since the Third Reform Act of 1884 had constituted the majority of the electorate, even though 40 per cent of adult males were still effectively disfranchised (Matthew 1976). Only in the 1880s did the idea of a separate working-class party make any substantial progress, despite the existence of such parties on the Continent, most notably the German SPD. The Liberal creed of independence, individualism and the ability to stand on one's own feet, blended well with the outlook of the politically conscious artisans, whose attitudes were often shaped as much by Nonconformist religious beliefs as by class consciousness.

Even more remarkably, Conservatism continued to appeal to a sizeable section of the working class in an age of imperialism. Such appeal was based on a mixture of patriotism, deference and religious allegiance, much assisted by the influence of Anglican elementary day schools and Sunday Schools, as well as by organizations like the Primrose League. For example, the 6,000 paid-up members of the Primrose League in Bolton in 1900 exactly matched the number of members of the Independent Labour Party over the whole country. It is evident from enlistment records after August 1914 that a powerful sense of working-class identity and patriotism were complementary, rather than antagonistic, sentiments in Edwardian Britain. Far from aiming to disrupt the social order, men whose lives were stunted by class subordination and horrific living conditions proved willing in 1914–18 to fight in a cause which had no intention of changing their condition (Winter 1986: 19–20).

Popular Conservatism also owed something to hostility felt by more hedonistic working men, many of them from the unskilled *lumpen-proletariat*, towards relatively prosperous, upright, sober, puritan and rather priggish working-class Liberals, bent on self-improvement and the avoidance of four-letter swearwords. It was an appeal which, despite the rise of the Labour Party after 1893, was to persist through the twentieth century, long after working-class Liberalism had become virtually extinct.

NOTES AND REFERENCES

1. *Annual Register* 1864: 49–50.
2. Frederic Harrison to John Morley, 10 February 1974. Harrison Papers, London School of Economics.
3. *Bradford Observer* 21 November 1861.
4. *Rochdale Observer* 26 April 1856. I owe this reference to Mrs Helen Gill.
5. J. Vincent, ed., *Derby and the Conservative Party: The Political Journals of Lord Stanley 1849–69*, 1978: 261.
6. R. L. Nettleship, ed., *The Works of Thomas Hill Green*, 1888, iii, cxviii.

Chapter 8
CONCLUSION

The introductory chapter of this book reviewed the intense and wide-ranging debate which has taken place on how far there existed in the nineteenth century a working class conscious of possessing an identity and interests separate from, and often antagonistic towards, those of the propertied classes. The difficulty of arriving at firm conclusions concerning the existence of a unified working class, or widespread class consciousness, was emphasized. The structure and attitudes of the working class before 1850, let alone between 1850 and 1880, were complex and difficult for the historian to interpret. Much of the pre-industrial structure and kinship patterns survived to mid century and beyond; as did increasingly outmoded political ideas and attitudes, the preoccupation with 'Old Corruption' furnishing an outstanding example. Relatively quantifiable factors like wages, incomes and consumption patterns differed widely between industries and between one region and another. Less quantifiable aspects of working-class life, like political attitudes and degrees of class consciousness are even more difficult to encompass within the historian's necessary generalizations. One sympathizes with Michael Rose's remark that: 'Like the Cheshire Cat, the working class is rarely visible as a complete whole in this period' (Rose 1981: 266).

The argument of this book is that working-class consciousness certainly existed, most notably in the industrial areas deeply affected by economic change, new technology and the intensification of capitalist control of industry. At the same time, there is no denying the development of a vigorous working-class radical movement from the 1790s, sometimes operating in alliance with middle-class radical groups, or even with sympathizers from the landed gentry; sometimes acting alone, as in 1815–19 and 1839–40. On the other hand, it seems clear that attempts to demonstrate revolutionary class consciousness, except among small minorities of workers, are misguided. The mass of workers, even in the most class-conscious and radical areas like south Lancashire, West Yorkshire and the industrial Midlands, aimed at manhood suffrage not insurrection. General revolutionary conscious-ness, aimed at the overthrow of the state and transformation of the social order, existed only briefly in south Wales in the autumn of 1839. Otherwise, those committed to insurrectionary politics, whether between 1795 and 1812, or immediately after the peace of 1815, remained relatively isolated, unable to gain mass support from their fellow-workers. During the war years, loyalist propaganda and organization attracted the support of many wage-earners and, combined with government repression, was easily able to resist and crush any domestic revolutionary threat. After 1815 the fears of the property-owning classes, including the majority of middle-class Nonconformist radicals in the provinces, prevented them offering the working-class radical movement any significant degree of support. At no time since the days of the United Irishmen and United Englishmen had a confident, stable government any compunction about repressing violence.

Edward Thompson and his followers have exaggerated the extent, if not the existence, of revolutionary class consciousness bent on overthrowing the authority of the state between 1792 and 1832. Proletarian revolution in England was never a real possibility on any scale at any time, despite occasional fear and panic among the propertied elites. Neither was the manhood suffrage which the vast majority of working-class radicals desired and which, in 1830–2 and again between 1838 and 1842, invoked genuine mass support. Yet the 1830–2 Reform campaign marked a major defeat for the working-class radical movement, while also sharpening class antagonisms. Working-class pressure helped to launch the Reform movement, but it soon escaped their control. The Reform Act itself drove a wedge between middle-class and working-class radicalism; for popular radical leaders like Bronterre O'Brien, it was a 'betrayal' from the very first. Manhood suffrage was firmly rejected and had no chance of being enacted during the remainder of the century. Working-class representation increased either through slow incremental additions under the £10 householder franchise, or when the political elites decided, as in 1867, that working men had displayed sufficient evidence of good behaviour and loyalty to the existing order. Votes were privileges to be earned, not rights to be claimed.

Working-class radicalism and the working-class consciousness which lay behind it reached their climax in the Chartist movement before becoming relatively muted and fragmented during the mid-Victorian decades. Yet the evidence for widespread working-class consciousness and a substantial commitment to 'physical force' tactics has been challenged. According to Dorothy Thompson: 'Chartism was pervaded by a sense of class – both a positive sense of identification and a negative hostility to superior classes – which was stronger than perhaps existed at any other point in the nineteenth century' (D. Thompson 1971: 14). But it has been frequently pointed out that the working class which Chartism represented by no means corresponded with the category of propertyless wage-earners, while attracting no support from the agricultural labourers, unskilled casual workers and the permanently destitute. If the Chartist movement embraced a substantial minority of workers, a minority is still less than half. David Goodway has demonstrated how the fragmented labour force in London – Britain's biggest industrial city – was overcome only after 1839, the peak year of Chartist activity. In some parts of the provinces, a mass movement of workers in the dominant industry depended for leadership on members of other occupational groups. In Leicestershire for example, the framework knitters followed the political leadership of artisans, tradesmen and small masters, rather than members of their own order (Prothero 1971; Harrison 1959: 99–146).

Even if it is accepted that Chartists were clearly in conflict with both the entrenched aristocracy and many of the entrepreneurial middle classes, not only because of their exclusion from the franchise after 1832 and resentment of Whig 'class legislation', but also because of changed and often deteriorating working conditions under capitalism, there is truth in Mather's view that 'Chartism was not ... the homogeneous, razor-sharp instrument of class warfare identified in Marxian analysis (Mather 1980: 32). It did not even represent the entire labour movement if one allows for the degree of divergence between the industrial and political wings of the movement. Although more trade unions established close links with the Chartists than once believed, the more prosperous and exclusive craft societies, for example in south Lancashire and Sheffield, tended to remain preoccupied with basic shop-floor issues concerning wages, control of entry to the trade and general working conditions; and were therefore wary of political campaigning (Reid and Reid 1979; Smith 1982: 84). Within the Chartist movement itself there was no coherent and consistent ideology. Aspirations towards Owenite-inspired total reconstruction of society existed alongside individualistic schemes of self-help and self-education. There was no agreement on what might be the role of the state in the reformation of society, a lack of agreement which partly originated in the failure to identify a specific class enemy. Was it the traditional 'parasitic' landed elite, or the new enemy in the shape of manufacturers and middlemen squeezing fat profits from the sweat of the workers' brows? In practice, the middle class tended to be opposed less consistently than the aristocracy and gentry, since there was always some ambition to recruit as allies the more radical sections of the urban bourgeoisie.

Chartism certainly marked the peak of working-class radicalism in England. But it was never a genuine mass revolutionary movement, in the absence of a general willingness to lead one and the swiftness of governments to repress violence by mass arrests. The traditional broad division between 'moral force' and 'physical force' advocates depicted by earlier historians has now been replaced by more complex pattern groupings, classified according to the degree of pressure they were willing to exert on local magistrates and central government. Feargus O'Connor and Bronterre O'Brien, long regarded as the supposed leaders of the physical-force faction, relied in fact on the threat of force to carry the Charter, rather than taking unambiguous steps towards violence. Even threats of future violence were more often than not diluted by appeals to remain within the law for the time being and avoid 'premature outbreaks' (Kemnitz 1973). There were certainly those like G. J. Harney, Peter Bussey and Dr John Taylor who at one time or another actively encouraged armed insurrection. However, excepting Newport in 1839, the numbers involved in riots were relatively insignificant, while the outbreaks themselves tended to take place during the autumn and winter of 1839–40, or between June and August 1848; in other words, after the major outbursts of enthusiasm for the Charter had faded away. Moreover, 'physical force' extremism caused many to desert the movement and deterred others from joining.

A strong sense of class consciousness certainly existed in the manufacturing districts of northern England, if not in many other places, not only during the Chartist years, but also the previous two decades. In towns like Barnsley, Bradford, Ashton-under-Lyne, Stalybridge, Oldham, Stockport and Halifax, Chartism was a mass movement, distinguished by class conflict and threatened insurrection (D. Thompson 1982: 124). By 1839 south Lancashire, Cheshire and the West Riding of Yorkshire were highly-politicized areas, containing networks of popular political and trade organizations dating back to at least the immediate post-war years and developed through radical trade unionism, agitation for the 1832 Reform Bill, mass opposition to the 1834 Poor Law, vocal support for factory legislation and the unstamped press, as well as general contempt for the 'truths' of orthodox political economy. Here Chartism developed its mass following in a context of single-industry dominance, with large cotton mills controlled by a relatively small number of owners. The behaviour and values of the working classes were therefore largely conditioned by the existence of highly visible and relatively unified wealthy industrial elites who subscribed to values directly contrary to those of the cotton workers. Militant mass Chartism in south Lancashire and Cheshire was able to attract not only artisans, tradesmen and workers in domestic industry, but also spinners, weavers and other sections of the factory population (Sykes 1982: 152–5). All these occupations were experiencing threats to their status, independence, security, wage levels and control over the work process, which helped to fuel their political grievances and motivated large numbers of workers, otherwise differentiated in terms of occupation, incomes and levels of skill, to develop a strong sense of class consciousness and join the Chartist ranks.

In these northern manufacturing areas, where industrial capitalism and the factory system were most advanced, there took place polarization in the Marxist sense. Popular anger here was directed not only against the traditional 'idlers' and 'parasites', but also against the factory owners or 'steamlords'. 'The people' increasingly came to mean the manual working class, as there developed growing condemnation of those sections of the middle classes which operated and extolled the capitalist system and who, by supporting the Whig administration before 1841, had joined the 'army of oppressors'. Shopkeepers and tradesmen, themselves often dependent on working-class custom, could frequently be won over to the side of the workers and become members of 'the people' (Epstein 1982: 274; Sykes 1980; Stedman Jones 1983: 150–3). Class tensions were exacerbated by Chartist mistrust of middle-class reformers, who not only opposed physical force Chartism but who were all too often the magistrates who arrested Chartist activists.

While it is difficult to deny that Chartism in the northern manufacturing districts between 1839 and 1842 exhibited a highly-developed class consciousness, relatively few displayed revolutionary consciousness. Like working-class radical movements from the later eighteenth century, all but a tiny majority steered clear of insurrection and sought manhood suffrage by peaceful means, even if such means involved a combination of the politics of the mass platform and attempts to intimidate the authorities and political elites. No section of Chartism subscribed to socialism before 1850, or developed a theory of inherent exploitation within industrial capitalism. Chartists aimed at neither the overthrow of the state nor the expropriation of the capitalist system (Stedman Jones 1983: 57–59). Manhood suffrage was sought for a variety of reasons: the desire to attain full citizenship and due recognition of the moral worth of labouring men; the hope that increased political influence in an overwhelmingly working-class electorate would lead to full recognition of trade unions, factory regulation, repeal of the 1834 Poor Law and a more equitable distribution of property, wealth and taxation. Behind these various aims, moreover, lay a vision of a more egalitarian alternative social order. The industrious would be rewarded, the grosser inequalities between capital and labour diminished, with units of co-operative production reflecting popular principles of mutuality and independence. While property was still accepted as a natural right, such popular aspirations clearly posed a genuine threat to existing social and economic relationships (Joyce 1980: 313–14).

It remains true, however, that these aspirations and visions affected only a minority of the working population as a whole. In terms of the country and its economy in general, the northern textile areas were untypical. Even there, much of this manifest class consciousness failed to persist in any coherent fashion after the setbacks of 1842 and 1848. After 1850 popular radicalism was necessarily diminished in scope and obliged to change tactics. Chartism had been beaten down by state repression, involving mass arrests, imprisonment and even transportation. The movement was never able to shake the essential stability of the British state; none of the political elites was as nervous of Chartism as they had been during the 1830–2 Reform crisis. During the mid-Victorian decades an increasingly fragmented working class proved able to make piecemeal gains within a more settled capitalist system whose broad features they came to accept, even if it did not become incorporated, collaborationist or deferential. Chartism was replaced by moderate reformism. The mid-Victorian boom enabled many large leading employers to adopt a paternalistic approach and gain the loyalty of many of their workers by promoting outings, dinners and celebrations, gaining in return testimonials from loyal employees. Population growth from migration diminished and the resulting more settled communities and family patterns helped to reduce overt class conflict.

Growing working-class institutions like friendly societies, co-operatives, building societies and trade unions were able to achieve gains within the system, despite the bulk of working-class families remaining economically insecure during the mid-Victorian decades. Working-class leaders were obliged to change their perceptions once it became apparent that England was now too well-policed for a repeat of anything like the Chartist movement. Many working-class activists recognized that the way ahead lay through gradual improvement by means of teetotalism, education and respectability, combined with support for the popular Liberal party. Such an approach was infinitely preferable to the propertied middle classes than militant Chartism and its predecessors. The working class proved unable and unwilling to launch further massive campaigns for suffrage extension, while parliamentary elections continued to reflect religious or ethnic divisions, rather than class polarization; that is, where they did not simply reflect deference, treating and thinly disguised bribery.

So far as trade unions and industrial relations were concerned, however, the mid-Victorian working class was less willing to compromise with existing patterns and structures. Trade unions were still regarded by employers, the judiciary and political economists as threatening to undermine the rights of property, as well as challenging natural economic laws. Unions came to be tolerated only when they engaged in intense confrontation and conflict by means of major strikes. Concessions were made from above to prevent wider attacks on property. Hence dramatic improvement in the legal status of trade unions was the major feature and achievement of working-class radicalism between 1850 and 1880, though only after a prolonged and often bitter struggle. Simultaneously with the trade union campaign for legal recognition and status, the mid-Victorian pattern of productive relations allowed many skilled workers a considerable degree of independence, initiative and control in the workplace. The desire for political influence through the electoral system was therefore less pressing than before 1850. Significant piecemeal gains equally meant a lack of pressure for a separate political party representing labour.

With the exception of the successful campaign for improvement in the legal position of trade unions in the 1860s and 1870s, working-class radical pressure achieved very little between 1780 and 1880. Both the Reform Acts of 1832 and 1867 owed as much to middle-class radical pressure as to that of the working class. Delay in the implementation of the New Poor Law in many industrial regions again depended on considerable assistance from middle-class property owners. As early as 1842 it became clear to many working-class radical leaders that political objectives, though not manhood suffrage, could be achieved only by co-operation with middle-class radical organizations, as happened during the Reform agitation of the 1860s, leading to the Second Reform Act. Acting on their own, working-class radicals achieved next to nothing in terms of specific objectives, although they certainly made the 'working class presence' felt and attracted some sympathy from the government and propertied classes about the urban slums and deteriorating environment in industrial cities. In any direct confrontation with the state, the government, military, magistrates and police won hands down. There were simply not enough working-class radicals prepared to engage in the wholesale mass killing which a successful revolution requires. Henceforth the aim had to be reformism: attempting to gain concessions within the system rather than seeking to destroy the system itself. Even the fiery Ernest Jones was obliged to become a Liberal by 1868.

The pattern of working-class reformism, fragmentation and lack of independent labour electoral politics persisted until the 1880s and very different conditions. The 'Great Depression' of 1873–96, exacerbated by more intense international competition, involved falling profitability, an inexorable reduction in prices, and employers anxious to cut the costs of labour. Such a major change in the economic environment began to undermine the privileged position of labour aristocrats and skilled men who had always been in the forefront of both popular radicalism and trade union activity. The greater social division of labour, closer supervision in the workplace, the intensification of the work process, downward pressure on wages and piece rates, as well as further technological change, helped to push many skilled men down to the ranks of the unskilled as wage differentials were narrowed. Such changes provoked enhanced industrial conflict. In this transformed context, social relationships began to be conceived and organized around the concept of class, as localism and sectionalism commenced a slow decline. This process was assisted by urban demolition, commercial development and suburbanization, leading to the consolidation of working-class residential districts, which in large cities became virtually self-contained communities with heightened class feelings and antagonisms.

At the same time, the 1880s saw the beginnings of a fundamental shift in politics, as the paternal basis of political activity in many regions began to be eroded. The Ballot Act of 1871 meant that men could no longer be marched to the polls by the mining and iron masters as they had been at the 1868 North Durham election. An intellectual revival of socialism and the increasing strength of popular Conservativism each reflected the new vulnerability of the central certainties of classical liberalism, with the Liberal party itself in disarray after the Home Rule crisis of 1886. The foundation of the Independent Labour Party in 1893 and the Labour Representation Committee in 1900 was a response to these changes, as well as to attacks on trade union rights and legal status by employers' organizations and the law courts. The creation of a working-class political party was to place popular radicalism on a new footing, as class polarization came to dominate politics over the next forty years.

BIBLIOGRAPHY

ABBREVIATIONS

BIHR	*Bulletin of the Institute of Historical Research*
BSSLH	*Bulletin of the Society for the Study of Labour History*
EHR	*English Historical Review*
Ec.HR	*Economic History Review*
HJ	*The Historical Journal*
HWJ	*History Workshop Journal*
IRSH	*International Review of Social History*
JBS	*Journal of British Studies*
JMH	*Journal of Modern History*
NH	*Northern History*
P and P	*Past and Present*
SH	*Social History*
TRHS	*Transactions of the Royal Historical Society*
VS	*Victorian Studies*

Where applicable, unpublished and contemporary printed sources have been cited in the footnote references (Chs 3,4,5,6,7).

PUBLISHED WORKS

(*Place of publication is London unless otherwise stated*)

Anon., 1969. 'And that's how classes were born', *Times Literary Supplement*, 17 April 1969.

Anderson, M., 1971. *Family Structure in Nineteenth Century Lancashire.* Cambridge UP.

Angelsey, Marquess of, 1963. *One-Leg.*

Apfel, W. and Dunkley, P., 1985. 'English rural society and the New Poor Law: Bedfordshire 1834–47', *SH*, **10**, 1, 1985.

Arblaster, A., 1984. *The Rise and Decline of Western Liberalism.* Oxford.

Ashforth, D., 1976. 'The Urban Poor Law', in Fraser, D. (ed), *The New Poor Law in the Nineteenth Century.*

Aspinall, A., 1949. *The Early English Trade Unions.*

Bamford, S., 1844. *Autobiography, vol. ii, Passages in the Life of a Radical.*

Barnsby, G. T., 1971. 'The standard of living in the Black Country during the nineteenth century', *Ec.HR,* 2nd ser. xxiv, 2, 1971.

Barnsby, G. T., 1971. 'Chartism in the Black Country 1850–60' in Munby, L. M. (ed), *The Luddites and other Essays.*

Barnsby, G. T., 1977. *The Working Class Movement in the Black Country.* Wolverhampton.

Baxter, J. L., 1974. 'The Great Yorkshire Revival 1792–96', in Hill, M. (ed), *A Sociological Yearbook of Religion in Britain, 7.*

Baxter, J. L., 1976. 'Early Chartism and labour class struggle: South Yorkshire 1837–40', in Pollard, S. and Holmes, C. (eds), *Essays in the Economic and Social History of South Yorkshire.* Sheffield.

Baxter, J. L. and Donnelly, F. K., 1974. 'The revolutionary "underground" in the West Riding: myth or reality?' *P and P,* **64,** 1974.

Behagg, C., 1982. 'An alliance with the middle class: the Birmingham Political Union and early Chartism', in Epstein, J. and Thompson, D. (eds), *The Chartist Experience.*

Behagg, C., 1982. 'Secrecy, ritual and folk violence', in Storch, R., (ed), *Popular Culture and Custom in Nineteenth-Century England.*

Belchem, J., 1978. 'Henry Hunt and the evolution of the mass platform', *EHR,* xcliii, 1978.

Belchem, J., 1981. 'Republicanism, constitutionalism and the radical platform in early nineteenth-century England', *SH,* **6,** 1, 1981.

Belchem, J., 1982. '1848: Feargus O'Connor and the collapse of the mass platform', in Epstein, J. and Thompson, D. (eds), *The Chartist Experience.*

Beloff, M., 1949. *The Debate on the American Revolution.*

Bennett, J., 1982. 'The London Democratic Association 1837–41', in Epstein, J. and Thompson, D. (eds), *The Chartist Experience.*

Bentley, M., 1984. *Politics Without Democracy 1815–1914.*

Berg, M., 1980. *The Machinery Question and the Making of Political Economy 1815–1848.* Cambridge UP.

Berg, M., 1985. *The Age of Manufactures.*

Berlin, I., 1969. *Four Essays on Liberty.* Oxford UP.

Best, G., 1971. *Mid-Victorian Britain 1851–1875.*

Bohstedt, J., 1983. *Riots and Community Politics in England and Wales 1790–1810.* Harvard UP, Camb., Mass..

Bonwick, C., 1977. *English Radicals and the American Revolution.* N. Carolina UP, Chapel Hill.

Booth, A., 1983. 'Popular loyalism and public violence in the north-west of England 1790–1800', *SH,* **8,** 3, 1983.

Boyson, R., 1960. 'The New Poor Law in North-East Lancashire 1834–71', *Transactions of the Lancashire and Cheshire Antiquarian Society,* lxx, 1960.

Blake, R., 1966. *Disraeli.*

Bradley, I., 1980. *The Optimists: Themes and Personalities in Victorian Liberalism.*

Brewer, J., 1976. *Party Ideology and Popular Politics at the Accession of George III.* Cambridge UP.

Brewer, J., 1982. 'Commercialization and politics', in McKendrick, N., Brewer, J. and Plumb, J. H. (eds), *The Birth of a Consumer Society*.

Brewer, J., 1984. 'John Bull s'en va t'en guerre', *London Review of Books*, 5 May 1984.

Briggs, A., 1952. 'The background of the parliamentary reform movement in three English cities', *Cambridge Historical Journal*, **10**, 1952.

Briggs, A. (ed), 1959. *Chartist Studies*.

Briggs, A., 1959. *The Age of Improvement*.

Briggs, A., 1960. 'The language of "class" in early nineteenth century England', in Briggs, A. and Saville, J. (eds), *Essays in Labour History*.

Briggs, A., 1954. *Victorian People*.

Briggs, A., 1963. *Victorian Cities*.

Brock, M., 1973. *The Great Reform Act*.

Brown, L., 1959. 'The Chartists and the Anti-Corn Law League', in Briggs, A. (ed), 1959. *Chartist Studies*.

Burgess, K., 1975. *The Origins of British Industrial Relations*.

Burgess, K., 1980. *The Challenge of Labour*.

Butler, J. R. M., 1914. *The Passing of the Great Reform Bill*.

Butler, M., 1984. *Burke, Paine, Godwin and the Revolution Controversy*. Cambridge UP.

Bythell, D., 1969. *The Handloom Weavers*. Cambridge UP.

Bythell, D., 1978. *The Sweated Trades*.

Calhoun, C., 1982. *The Question of Class Struggle*. Oxford.

Campbell, A., 1978. 'Honourable men and degraded slaves', in Harrison, R. (ed), *Independent Collier*. Harvester, Hassocks.

Cannon, J., 1964. *The Chartists in Bristol*. (Historical Association) Bristol.

Cannon, J., 1973. *Parliamentary Reform 1640–1832*. Cambridge UP.

Challenor, R. and Ripley, B., 1968. *The Miners' Association*.

Chambers, J. D., 1961. *The Workshop of the World*. Oxford UP.

Chambers, J. D. and Mingay, G. E., 1966. *The Agricultural Revolution*.

Checkland, S. G., 1964. *The Rise of Industrial Society in England*.

Christie, I. R., 1958. *The End of North's Ministry 1780–1782*.

Christie, I. R., 1962. *Wilkes, Wyvill and Reform*.

Christie, I. R., 1982. *Wars and Revolutions*.

Christie, I. R., 1984. *Stress and Stability in Late Eighteenth Century Britain*. Oxford UP.

Church, R. A. and Chapman, S. D., 1967. 'Gravener Henson and the making of the English working class', in Jones, E. L. and Mingay, G. E. (eds), *Land, Labour and Population in the Industrial Revolution*.

Church, R. A., 1975. *The Great Victorian Boom 1850–73*.

Citrine, W. M. (ed), 1934. *The Book of the Martyrs of Tolpuddle*.

Clark, G. Kitson, 1953. 'Hunger and Politics in 1842', *JMH*, xxv, 4, 1953.

Clark, G. Kitson, 1962. *The Making of Victorian England*.

Clark, J. C. D., 1985. *English Society 1688–1832*. Cambridge UP.

Clark, P. (ed), 1985. *The Transformation of English Provincial Towns*.

Clements, R. V., 1961. 'British trade unions and popular political economy 1850–75', *EcHR*, 2nd ser., xiv, i, 1961.

Clinton, A., 1974. 'The history of trades councils', *BSSLH*, **29**, 1974.

Cobban, A., 1950. *The Debate on the French Revolution*.

Cole, G. D. H., 1941. *Chartist Portraits*.

Cole, G. D. H. and Postgate, R., 1946. *The Common People 1746–1946*. 1961 ed.

Colley, L., 1981. 'Eighteenth century English radicalism before Wilkes', *TRHS*, 5th ser., **31,** 1981.

Colley, L., 1984. 'The apotheosis of George III', *P and P,* **102,** 1984.

Colley, L., 1986. 'Whose nation? Class and national consciousness in Britain 1750–1830', *P and P,* **113,** 1986.

Cookson, J. E., 1975. *Lord Liverpool's Administration.* Edinburgh UP.

Cookson, J. E., 1982. *The Friends of Peace.* Cambridge UP.

Cowling, M., 1967. *1867: Disraeli, Gladstone and Revolution.* Cambridge UP.

Crafts, N. F. R., 1985. *British Economic Growth during the Industrial Revolution.* Oxford UP.

Crossick, G., 1976. 'The Labour aristocracy and its values: a study of mid-Victorian Kentish London', *VS,* xix, 3, 1976.

Crossick, G., 1978. *An Artisan Elite in Victorian Society.*

Crowther, M. A., 1983. *The Workhouse System 1834–1929.*

Crouzet, M., 1982. *The Victorian Economy.*

Cunningham, H., 1981. 'The language of patriotism', *HWJ,* **12,** 1981.

Cunningham, H., 1982. 'Will the real John Bull stand up, please', *The Times Higher Education Supplement,* 19 February 1982.

Curran, J., 1978. 'The press as an agency of social control' in Boyce, G., Curran J. and Wingate, P. (eds), *Newspaper History.*

Darvall, F. O., 1934. *Popular Disturbances and Public Order in Regency England.* 1969 edn. Oxford UP.

Davis, R. W., 1976. 'Deference and aristocracy in the time of the Great Reform Act', *American Historical Review,* **81,** 1976.

Deane, P., 1965. *The First Industrial Revolution.* Cambridge UP.

Dickinson, H. T., 1976. 'Party, principle and public opinion in eighteenth-century politics', *History,* **61,** 202, 1976.

Dickinson, H. T., 1977. *Liberty and Property.*

Dickinson, H. T. (ed), 1982. *The Political Works of Thomas Spence.* Newcastle upon Tyne.

Dickinson, H. T., 1985. *British Radicalism and the French Revolution.* Oxford.

Dickinson, H. T., 1986. *Caricatures and the Constitution.* Cambridge.

Digby, A., 1976. 'The rural Poor Law' in Fraser, D. (ed), *The New Poor Law in the Nineteenth Century.*

Digby, A., 1982. *The Poor Law in Nineteenth-Century England and Wales.*

Dinwiddy, J. R., 1974. 'The "Black Lamp" in Yorkshire 1801–1802', *P and P,* **64,** 1974.

Dinwiddy, J. R., 1976. 'Charles Hall, early English socialist', *IRSH,* **21,** 1976.

Dinwiddy, J. R., 1979. 'Luddism and politics in the Northern Counties', *SH,* **4,** 1979.

Dinwiddy, J. R., 1980. 'Sir Francis Burdett and Burdettite radicalism', *History,* **65,** 1980.

Dinwiddy, J. R., 1982. 'The early nineteenth-century campaign against flogging in the army', *EHR,* xcvii, 1982.

Dobrée, G. and Mainwairing, G. E., 1935. *The Floating Republic.*

Dobson, C. R., 1980. *Masters and Journeymen.*

Donnelly, F. K. and Baxter, J. L., 1975. 'Sheffield and the English revolutionary tradition', *IRSH,* **20,** 1975.

Donnelly, F. K., 1976. 'Ideology and early English working-class history: Edward Thompson and his critics', *SH,* **2,** 1976.

Dozier, R. R., 1983. *For King, Country and Constitution.* Kentucky UP, Lexington.

Driver, C., 1946. *Tory Radical. The Life of Richard Oastler.* Oxford UP, New York.

Dunkley, P., 1974. 'The "Hungry Forties" and the New Poor Law: A case study', *HJ,* **17,** 2, 1984.

Dunn, J., 1984. *The Politics of Socialism.* Cambridge UP.

Dutton, H. I. and King, J. E., 1982. 'The limits of paternalism: the cotton tyrants of North Lancashire 1836–54', *SH,* **7,** 1982.

Edsall, N. C., 1971. *The Anti-Poor Law Movement 1834–1844.* Manchester UP.

Elliott, M., 1977. 'The "Despard Conspiracy" reconsidered', *P and P,* **75,** 1977.

Elliott, M., 1982. *Partners in Revolution: The United Irishmen and France.* Yale UP, New Haven and London.

Elliott, M., 1983. 'French subversion in Britain in the French Revolution', in Jones, C. (ed), *Britain and Revolutionary France.* Exeter UP.

Elster, J., 1985. *Making Sense of Marx.* Cambridge UP.

Emsley, C., 1978. 'The London "Insurrection" of December 1792: fact, fiction or fantasy?', *JBS,* **17,** 1978.

Emsley, C., 1979a. *British Society and the French Wars 1793–1815.*

Emsley, C., 1979b. 'The Home Office and its sources of information and investigation 1791–1801', *EHR,* xciv, 1979.

Emsley, C., 1981. 'An aspect of Pitt's "Terror": prosecutions for sedition during the 1790s', *SH,* **6,** 1981.

Emsley, C., 1983. *Policing and its Context 1750–1870.*

Engels, F., 1969. *The Condition of the Working Class in England* [1845]

Epstein, J., 1976. 'Feargus O'Connor and the *Northern Star*', *IRSH,* xxi, 1976.

Epstein, J., 1982a. *The Lion of Freedom: Feargus O'Connor and the Chartist Movement 1832–1842.*

Epstein, J., 1982b. 'Some organizational and cultural aspects of the Chartist movement in Nottingham', in Epstein, J. and Thompson, D. (eds), *The Chartist Experience.*

Evans, E. J., 1983. *The Forging of the Modern State 1783–1870.*

Fennessy, R. R., 1963. *Burke, Paine and the Rights of Man.* Nijhoff, The Hague.

Feuchtwanger, E. J., 1959. 'The Conservative Party under the impact of the Second Reform Act', *VS,* iii, **4,** 1959.

Feuchtwanger, E. J., 1968. *Disraeli, Democracy and the Tory Party.* Oxford UP.

Feuchtwanger, E. J., 1985. *Democracy and Empire.*

Finlayson, G. B. A. M., 1969. *England in the Eighteen Thirties.*

Flick, C., 1978. *The Birmingham Political Union and the Movement for Reform in Britain 1830–1839.* Dawson, Folkestone.

Flynn, M. W., 1974. 'Trends in real wages 1750–1850', *EcHR,* 2nd ser. xxvii, 1974.

Forrest, A., 1981. *The French Revolution and the Poor.* Oxford UP.

Foster, J., 1974. *Class Struggle in the Industrial Revolution.*

Fraser, D., 1970. 'The agitation for parliamentary reform' in Ward, J. T. (ed), *Popular Movements c.1830–1850.*

Fraser, D., 1976. *Urban Politics in Victorian England.* Leicester UP.

Fraser, D., 1979a. 'Politics and the Victorian city', *Urban History Yearbook.* 1979. Leicester UP.

Fraser, D., 1979b. *Power and Authority in the Victorian City.* Oxford.

Fraser, D. (ed), 1980. *A History of Modern Leeds.* Manchester UP.

Fraser, P., 1961. 'Public petitioning and Parliament before 1832', *History,* **46,** 1961.

Fraser, W. H., 1970. 'Trade Unionism', in Ward, J. T. (ed), *Popular Movements c.1830–1850.*

Fraser, W. H., 1974. *Trade Unions and Society.*

Gadian, D. S., 1978. 'Class consciousness in Oldham and other north-west industrial towns 1830–1850', *HJ,* **21,** 1978.

Gammage, R. G., 1854, *History of the Chartist Movement 1837–1854.* 1894 edn.

Garrard, J. A., 1977. 'Parties, members and voters after 1867: a local study', *HJ,* **20,** 1, 1977.

Garrard, J. A., 1983. *Leadership and Power in Victorian Industrial Towns 1830– 80.* Manchester UP.

Gash, N., 1953. *Politics in the Age of Peel.*

Gash, N., 1979. *Aristocracy and People.*

Gash, N., 1986. *Pillars of Government.*

Geary, D., 1981. *European Labour Protest 1848–1939.*

Giddens, A., 1981. *The Class Structure of Advanced Societies.* 2nd edn.

Gillespie, F. E., 1927. *Labor and Politics in England 1850–67.* Duke UP, Durham, N. Carolina.

Ginter, D. E., 1966. 'The Loyalist Association Movement of 1792–93 and British public opinion', *HJ,* **9,** 1966.

Glen, R., 1984. *Urban Workers in the Early Industrial Revolution.*

Godfrey, C., 1979. 'The Chartist Prisoners 1839–41', *IRSH,* xxiii, 1979.

Goodway, D., 1970. 'Chartism in London', *BSSLH,* **20,** 1970.

Goodway, D., 1982. *London Chartism 1838–1848.* Cambridge UP.

Goodwin, A., 1979. *The Friends of Liberty.*

Gray, R. Q., 1976. *The Labour Aristocracy in Victorian Edinburgh.* Oxford UP.

Gray, R., 1981. *The Aristocracy of Labour in Nineteenth-Century Britain c.1850–1900.*

Greenall, R., 1974. 'Popular Conservatism in Salford 1868–1886', *NH,* ix, 1974.

Grugel, L. E., 1976. *George Jacob Holyoake.* Porcupine Press, Philadelphia.

Guttsman, W. L., 1965. *The British Political Elite.* Newton Abbot.

Hadfield, A. M., 1970. *The Chartist Land Company.*

Hamburger, J., 1963. *James Mill and the Art of Revolution.* Yale UP.

Hammond, J. L. and Hammond, B., 1911. *The Village Labourer.* 1978 edn.

Hammond, J. L. and Hammond, B., 1919. *The Skilled Labourer.* 1979 edn.

Handforth, P., 1956. 'Manchester Radical Politics 1789–1794', *Transactions of the Lancashire and Cheshire Antiquarian Society,* **66,** 1956.

Hardy, D., 1979. *Alternative Communities in Nineteenth Century England.*

Hardy, T., 1832. *The Memoirs of Thomas Hardy.*

Harrison, B. and Hollis, P., 1967. 'Chartism, Liberalism and the life of Robert Lowery', *EHR,* lxxxii, 1967.

Harrison, B., 1973. 'Teetotal Chartism', *History,* **58,** 1973.

Harrison, B. and Hollis, P., 1979. *Robert Lowery: Radical and Chartist.*

Harrison, J. F. C., 1958. 'Chartism's successors', *Manchester Guardian,* 23 November 1958.

Harrison, J. F. C., 1959. 'Chartism in Leeds' and 'Chartism in Leicester', in Briggs, A. (ed), *Chartist Studies.*

Harrison, J. F. C., 1961. *Learning and Living 1790–1960.*

Harrison, J. F. C., 1979. *The Second Coming.*

Harrison, R., 1965. *Before the Socialists.*

Harvey, A. D., 1978. *Britain in the Early Nineteenth Century.*

Harvie, C., 1976. *The Lights of Liberalism.*

Hay, D., 1975. 'Property, authority and the criminal law', in Hay, D. (ed), *Albion's Fatal Tree.*

Hempton, D., 1984. *Methodism and Politics in British Society 1750-1850.*

Henriques, U. R. Q., 1968. 'How cruel was the Victorian Poor Law?', *HJ,* **11,** 1968.

Henriques, U. R. Q., 1979. *Before the Welfare State.*

Hill, B. W., 1985. *British Parliamentary Parties 1742-1832.*

Hill, C., 1958. *Puritanism and Revolution.*

Hilton, B., 1977. *Corn, Cash, Commerce: the Economic Policies of the Tory Governments 1815-1830.* Oxford UP.

Hirst, D., 1975. *The Representation of the People? Voters and Voting in England under the Early Stuarts.* Cambridge UP.

Hobsbawm, E. J., 1948. *Labour's Turning-Point 1880-1900.*

Hobsbawm, E. J., 1952. 'Economic Fluctuations and some social movements since 1800', reprinted in *Labouring Men,* 1964.

Hobsbawm, E. J., 1954. 'The Labour aristocracy in nineteenth-century Britain', reprinted in *Labouring Men,* 1964.

Hobsbawm, E. J., 1959. *Primitive Rebels.* Manchester UP.

Hobsbawm, E. J., 1962. *The Age of Revolution: Europe 1789-1848.*

Hobsbawm, E. J. and Rudé, G., 1969. *Captain Swing.*

Hobsbawm, E. J., 1984. *Worlds of Labour.*

Hole, R., 1983. 'British counter-revolutionary propaganda in the 1790s', in Jones, C. (ed), *Britain and Revolutionary France.* Exeter UP.

Hollis, P., 1970. *The Pauper Press.* Oxford UP.

Hollis, P., 1973. *Class and Conflict in Nineteenth Century England 1815-50.*

Hone, J. A., 1982. *For the Cause of Truth: Radicalism in London 1796-1821.* Oxford UP.

Hopkins, E., 1979. *A Social History of the English Working Classes.*

Hopkins, E., 1982. 'Working hours and conditions during the Industrial Revolution: a re-appraisal'. *EcHR,* 2nd ser., xxxv, 1982.

Hovell, M., 1918. *The Chartist Movement.* 1966 edn. Manchester UP.

Hunt, E. H., 1973. *Regional Wage Variations in Britain 1850-1914.* Oxford UP.

Hunt, E. H., 1981. *British Labour History 1815-1914.*

Hunt, L., 1984. *Politics, Culture and Class in the French Revolution.* 1986 paperback edn.

Ignatieff, M., 1984. *The Needs of Strangers.*

Jenkin, A., 1971. 'Chartism and the trade unions' in Munby, L. M. (ed), *The Luddites and Other Essays.*

Jenkins, D. T. and Ponting, K. G., 1982. *The British Wool Textile Industry 1770-1914.*

Jenkins, M., 1980. *The General Strike of 1842.*

Jewson, C. B., 1975. *The Jacobin City.* Glasgow.

Johnson, R., 1979. 'Really useful knowledge: radical education and working-class culture 1790-1848', in Clark, J., Critcher, C. and Johnson, R. (eds), *Working Class Culture; Studies in History and Theory.*

Jones, D., 1975. *Chartism and the Chartists.*

Jones, D., 1983. 'Women and Chartism', *History,* **68,** 1983.

Jones, D. J. V., 1985. *The Last Rising. The Newport Insurrection of 1839.* Oxford UP.

Jones, G. Stedman, 1971. *Outcast London.* 1976 Penguin edn.

Jones, G. Stedman, 1977. 'Class expression versus social control', *HWJ,* **4,** 1977.

Jones, G. Stedman, 1975. 'England's first proletariat', *New Left Review,* **90,** 1975.

Jones, G. Stedman, 1982. 'The language of Chartism', in Epstein, J. and Thompson, D. (eds), *The Chartist Experience.*

Jones, G. Stedman, 1983. *Languages of Class.* Cambridge UP.

Jones, I. G., 1961. 'The election of 1868 in Merthyr Tydfil', *JMH,* xxxiii, 3, 1961.

Joyce, P., 1975. 'The factory politics of Lancashire in the later nineteenth century', *HJ,* **18,** 3, 1975.

Joyce, P., 1980. *Work, Society and Politics.* Harvester, Hassocks.

Judge, K., 1975. 'Early Chartist organization and the Convention of 1839', *IRSH,* xx, 1975.

Kelly, P., 1972. 'Radicalism and public opinion in the general election of 1784', *BIHR,* xlv, 1972.

Kemnitz, J. M., 1973. 'Approaches to the Chartist Movement: Feargus O'Connor and Chartist Strategy', *Albion,* v, 1973.

Kemnitz, J. M., 1978. 'The Chartist Convention of 1839', *Albion,* x, 1978.

King, J. E., 1981. *Richard Marsden and the Preston Chartists 1837–1848.* Lancaster UP.

Kirby, R. G. and Musson, A. E., 1975. *The Voice of the People: John Doherty 1785–1854.* Manchester UP.

Kirk, N., 1985. *The Growth of Working-Class Reformism in Mid-Victorian England.*

Kirk, N., 1986. 'The myth of class? Workers and the industrial revolution in Stockport', *BSSLH,* **51,** part i, 1986.

Knox, T. R., 1977. 'Thomas Spence: The Trumpet of Jubilee', *P and P,* **76,** 1977.

Kovalev, Y. V., 1971. 'Chartist literature', in Munby L. M. (ed), *The Luddites and Other Essays.*

Large, D., 1974. 'William Lovett', in Hollis, P. (ed), *Pressure From Without.*

Laslett, P., 1971. *The World We Have Lost.*

Lewis, M., 1960. *A Social History of the Navy 1793–1815.*

Leventhal, F. M., 1971. *Respectable Radical: George Howell and Victorian Working Class Politics.*

Levine, D., 1985. 'Industrialization and the proletarian family in England', *P and P,* **107,** 1985.

Lindert, P. and Williamson, J. G., 1983. 'English workers' Living standards during the Industrial Revolution: a new look', *EcHR,* 2nd ser., xxxvi, 1983.

Lloyd, C., 1970. *The British Seaman.*

Lovell, J. and Roberts, B. C., 1958. *A Short History of the T.U.C.*

Lovell, J., 1969. *Stevedores and Dockers.*

Lyons, F. S. L., 1973. *Ireland since the Famine.*

MacAskill, J., 1959. 'The Chartist land plan', in Briggs, A. (ed), *Chartist Studies.*

Macfarlane, A., 1978. *The Origins of English Individualism.* Oxford.

Manning, B., 1976. *The English People and the English Revolution.*

Marlow, J., 1972. *The Tolpuddle Martyrs.*

Mather, F. C., 1959a. *Public Order in the Age of the Chartists.* Manchester UP.

Mather, F. C., 1959b. 'The Government and the Chartists', in Briggs, A. (ed), *Chartist Studies*.

Mather, F. C., 1965. *Chartism*. Historical Association.

Mather, F. C., 1974. 'The General Strike of 1842' in Quinault, R. and Stevenson, J. (eds), *Popular Protest and Public Order*.

Mather, F. C., 1980. *Chartism and Society*.

Matsamura, T., 1983. *The Labour Aristocracy Revisited*. Manchester UP.

Matthew, H. C. G. *et al*, 1976. 'The franchise factor in the rise of the Labour Party', *EHR*, xci, 1976.

McCabe, A. T., 1974. 'The standard of living on Merseyside 1850–75', in Bell, S. P. (ed), *Victorian Lancashire*. Newton Abbot.

McCloskey, D., 1981. 'The Industrial Revolution 1780–1860', in Floud, R. and McCloskey, D. (eds), *The Economic History of Britain since 1700: 1. 1700–1860*. Cambridge UP.

McCord, N., 1958. *The Anti-Corn Law League*.

McCord, N., 1967. 'Some difficulties of parliamentary reform', *HJ*, **10**, 1967.

McCord, N. and Brewster, D. E., 1968. 'Some labour troubles of the 1790s in North East England', *IRSH*, xiii, 1968.

McCord, N., 1969. 'The implementation of the Poor Law Amendment Act on Tyneside', *IRSH*, xiv, 1969.

McCord, N., 1979. *North East England*.

McCord, N., 1985. 'Adding a touch of class', *History*, **70**, 1985.

McCready, H. W., 1955. 'British Labour and the Royal Commission on Trade Unions 1867–69', *University of Toronto Quarterly*, xxiv, 1955.

McCready, H. W., 1956. 'British Labour's Lobby 1867–75', *Canadian Journal of Economics and Political Science*, xxii, 1956.

Miller, N. C., 1968. 'John Cartwright and radical parliamentary reform 1809–19', *EHR*, lxxxiii, 1968.

Milton-Smith, J., 1972. 'Earl Grey's Cabinet and the objects of parliamentary reform', *HJ*, **15**, 1972.

Mingay, G. E., 1963. *English Landed Society in the Eighteenth Century*.

Mingay, G. E., 1977. *Rural Life in Victorian England*.

Mitchell, A. V., 1961. 'The Association Movement of 1792–93', *HJ*, **4**, 1961.

Mitchell, A. V., 1967. *The Whigs in Opposition 1815–30*. Oxford UP.

Money, J., 1971. 'Taverns, coffee houses and class: local politics and popular articulacy in the Birmingham area in the age of the American Revolution', *HJ*, **16**, 1971.

Money, J., 1977. *Experience and Identity: Birmingham and the West Midlands 1760–1800*. Manchester UP.

Moore, D. C., 1965. 'The Corn Laws and High Farming', *EcHR*, 2nd ser., xviii, 1965.

Moore, D. C., 1966. 'Concession or cure: the sociological premises of the First Reform Act', *HJ*, **9**, 1966.

Moore, D. C., 1976. *The Politics of Deference*. Harvester, Hassocks.

Moorhouse, H. J., 1973. 'The political incorporation of the British working class: an interpretation', *Sociology*, **7**, 1973.

Moorhouse, H. J., 1978. 'The Marxist theory of the Labour Aristocracy', *SH*, **3**, 1, 1978.

Morris, R. J., 1976. *Cholera 1832*.

Morris, R. J., 1979. *Class and Class-Consciousness in the Industrial Revolution 1780–1850*.

Murphy, P. J., 1978. 'The origins of the 1852 lock-out in the British engineering industry reconsidered', *IRSH*, xxiii, 1978.

Musson, A. E., 1962. 'The Webbs and their phasing of trade union development between the 1830s and the 1860s', *BSSLH*, **4**, 1962.

Musson, A. E., 1972. *British Trade Unions 1800–1875*.

Musson, A. E., 1976. 'Industrial motive power in the United Kingdom 1800–1870', *EcHR*, 2nd ser., xxix, 1976.

Musson, A. E., 1976. 'Class struggle and the labour aristocracy 1830–1860', *SH*, **3**, 1976.

Musson, A. E., 1978. *The Growth of British Industry*.

Myers, W., 1971. 'George Eliot: politics and personality', in Lucas, J. (ed), *Literature and Politics in the Nineteenth Century*.

Neale, R. S., 1972. *Class and Ideology in the Nineteenth Century*.

Neale, R. S., 1981. *Class in English History 1680–1850*. Oxford.

Nossiter, T. J., 1975. *Influence, Opinion and Political Idioms in Reformed England*. Harvester, Hassocks.

O'Boyle, L., 1967. 'The image of the journalist in France, Germany and England 1815–48', *Comparative Studies in History and Society*, x, 1967–8.

O'Brien, D. P., 1975. *The Classical Economists*. Oxford UP.

O'Gorman, F., 1982. *The Emergence of the British Two-Party System*.

O'Gorman, F., 1986. 'The unreformed electorate of Hanoverian England, *SH*, **11**, 1, 1986.

O'Higgins, R., 1961. 'The Irish influence in the Chartist Movement', *P and P*, **20**, 1961.

Oliver, W. H., 1964. 'The Consolidated Trades Union of 1834', *EcHR*, 2nd ser., xvii, 1964.

O'Neill, M. and Martin, G., 1980. 'A Back-bencher on Parliamentary Reform 1831–32', *HJ*, **23**, 1980.

Osborne, J. W., 1972. *John Cartwright*. Cambridge UP.

Parsinnen, T. M., 1972. 'The Revolutionary Party in London', *BIHR*, **45**, 1972.

Parsinnen, T. M., 1973a. 'Spence on the English Land Question', *Journal of the History of Ideas*, 34, 1973.

Parsinnen, T. M., 1973b. 'Association, Convention and Anti-Parliament in British radical politics 1771–1848', *EHR*, **88**, 1973.

Patterson, A. T., 1954. *Radical Leicester*. Leicester UP.

Peacock, A. J., 1965. *Bread or Blood: The Agrarian Riots in East Anglia 1816*.

Peacock, A. J., 1969. *Bradford Chartism 1838–1840*. Borthwick Institute, York.

Peel, F., 1880. *The Risings of the Luddites, Chartists and Plug-drawers*. 1968 edn. Introduction by Thompson, E. P. Kelley, New York.

Pelling, H., 1963. *A History of British Trade Unionism*.

Pelling, H., 1968. *Popular Politics and Society in Late Victorian England*. Macmillan, London.

Perkin, H., 1969. *The Origins of Modern English Society 1780–1880*.

Philips, D., 1974. 'Riots and public order in the Black Country 1835–1860', in Quinault, R. and Stevenson, J. (eds), *Popular Protest and Public Order*.

Pickering, P. A., 1986. 'Class without words: symbolic communication in the Chartist Movement', *P and P*, **112**, 1986.

Plumb, J. H., 1967. *The Growth of Political Stability in England*.

Plumb, J. H., 1969. 'The growth of the electorate in England from 1600 to 1715', *P and P*, **45**, 1969.

Plummer, A., 1971. *Bronterre.*

Pollard, S., 1959. *A History of Labour in Sheffield.* Liverpool UP.

Pollard, S., 1960. 'Nineteenth century co-operation: from community-building to shopkeeping', in Briggs, A. and Saville, J. (eds), *Essays in Labour History.*

Pollard, S., 1981. *Peaceful Conquest: the industrialization of Europe 1760–1970.* Oxford UP.

Porter, R., 1982. *English Society in the Eighteenth Century.*

Porter, R., 1986. 'Prinney, Boney, Boot: the English satirical print 1660–1832', *London Review of Books,* 20 March 1986.

Price, R. N., 1975. 'The other face of respectability: violence in the Manchester brick-making trade 1859–1870', *P and P,* **66,** 1975.

Price, R., 1986. *Labour in British Society.*

Prochaska, F. K., 1973. 'English state trials in the 1790s', *JBS,* **13,** 1973.

Prothero, I. G., 1969. 'Chartism in London', *P and P,* **44,** 1969.

Prothero, I. G., 1971. 'London Chartism and the Trades', *EcHR,* 2nd ser., xxiv, 2, 1971.

Prothero, I. G., 1974. 'William Benbow and the concept of the general strike', *P and P,* **63,** 1974.

Prothero, I., 1981. *Artisans and Politics in Early Nineteenth Century London.* Folkestone/London.

Randall, A. J., 1982. 'The Shearmen and the Wiltshire outrages of 1802', *SH,* **7,** 3, 1982.

Read, D., 1958. *Peterloo: the massacre and its background.* Manchester UP.

Read, D., 1959. 'Chartism in Manchester' in Briggs, A. (ed), *Chartist Studies.*

Read, D., 1961. *Press and People 1790–1850.*

Read, D. and Glasgow, E., 1961. *Feargus O'Connor.*

Read, D., 1964. *The English Provinces c.1760–1960.*

Read, D., 1967. *Cobden and Bright.*

Reid, A., 1978. 'Politics and economics in the formation of the British working class', *SH,* **3,** 3, 1978.

Reid, C., 1976. 'Middle class values and working class culture in nineteenth century Sheffield: the pursuit of respectability', in Pollard, S. and Holmes, C. (eds), *Essays in the Economic and Social History of South Yorkshire.* Sheffield.

Reid, T. D. W. and Reid, N., 1979. 'The 1842 "Plug Plot" in Stockport', *IRSH,* xxiv, 1979.

Reynolds, J., 1983. *The Great Paternalist. Titus Salt and the growth of nineteenth century Bradford.*

Richter, M., 1981. *Riotous Victorians.* Ohio UP, Athens, Ohio.

Robbins, K. G., 1979. *John Bright.*

Roberts, D., 1979. *Paternalism in early Victorian England.*

Rose, A. G., 1957. 'The Plug Riots of 1842 In Lancashire and Cheshire', *Transactions of the Lancashire and Cheshire Antiquarian Society,* lxvii, 1957.

Rose, M. E., 1966. 'The Anti-Poor Law Movement in the North of England', *NH,* i, 1966.

Rose, M. E., 1970. 'The Anti-Poor Law agitation', in Ward, J. T. (ed), *Popular Movements c.1830–1850.*

Rose, M. E., 1971. *The English Poor Law 1780–1830.* Newton Abbot.

Rose, M. E., 1981. 'Social change in the Industrial Revolution', in Floud, R. and McCloskey, D. (eds), *The Economic History of Britain since 1700: 1. 1700–1860.* Cambridge UP.

Rose, R. B., 1960. 'The Priestley Riots of 1791', *P and P*, **18**, 1960.

Rostow, W. W., 1948. *British Economy of the Nineteenth Century*. Oxford UP.

Rowe, D. J., 1967. 'The London Working Men's Association and the People's Charter', *P and P*, **36**, 1967.

Rowe, D. J., 1977. 'London radicalism in the era of the Great Reform Bill', in Stevenson, J. (ed), *London in the Age of Reform*. Oxford.

Rowe, D. J., 1977. 'Tyneside Chartism', in McCord, N. (ed), *Essays in Tyneside Labour History*. Newcastle upon Tyne.

Royle, E., 1971. *Radical Politics 1790–1900: Religion and Unbelief.*

Royle, E., 1974. *Victorian Infidels*. Manchester UP.

Royle, E., 1980. *Chartism.*

Royle, E. and Walvin, J., 1982. *English Radicals and Reformers 1760–1848.* Harvester, Hassocks.

Rudé, G., 1956. 'The Gordon Riots', *TRHS*, 5th ser., **6**, 1956.

Rudé, G., 1962. *Wilkes and Liberty*. Oxford UP.

Rudé, G., 1964. *The Crowd in History 1730–1848*. John Wiley, New York.

Rudé, G., 1967. 'English rural and urban disturbances on the eve of the First Reform Bill 1830–31', *P and P*, 37, 1967.

Rule, J., 1971. 'Methodism and Chartism among the Cornish miners', *BSSLH*, **22**, 1971.

Rule, J., 1981. *The Experience of Labour in Eighteenth Century Industry.*

Rule, J., 1986. *The Labouring Classes in Early Industrial England.*

Ruter, A. J. C., 1936. 'Benbow's Grand National Holiday', *IRSH*, i, 1936.

Salt, J., 1967. *Chartism in South Yorkshire*. Sheffield UP.

Salt, J., 1972. 'Experiments in anarchism', *Transactions of the Hunter Archaeological Society,* 1972.

Samuel, R., 1977. 'The Workshop of the World: steam-power and hand technology in mid-Victorian Britain', *HWJ*, **3**, 1977.

Saville, J., 1952. *Ernest Jones: Chartist.*

Saville, J., 1967. 'Trades councils and the Labour Movement to 1900', *BSSLH*, 14, 1967.

Schoyen, A. R., 1958. *The Chartist Challenge.*

Searby, P., 1964. *Coventry Politics in the Age of the Chartists*. Coventry.

Seymour, C., 1915. *Electoral Reform in England and Wales*. 1970 edn. Newton Abbot.

Shannon, R., 1982. *Gladstone. vol. i, 1809–65.*

Simon, D., 1954. 'Master and servant', in Saville, J. (ed), *Democracy and the Labour Movement.*

Smith, D., 1982. *Conflict and Compromise: Class Formation in English Society 1830–1914.*

Smith, F. B., 1966. *The Making of the Second Reform Bill*. Cambridge UP.

Smith, F. B., 1979. *The People's Health 1830–1910.*

Smith, P., 1967. *Disraelian Conservatism and Social Reform.*

Soffer, R. N., 1965. 'Attitudes and allegiances in the unskilled North 1830–1850', *IRSH*, x, 1965.

Speck, W. A., 1977. *Stability and Strife.*

Steiner, E. E., 1983. 'Separating the soldier from the citizen', *SH*, **8**, 1, 1983.

Stevenson, J., 1974. 'Food riots in England 1792–1818', in Quinault, R. and Stevenson, J. (eds), *Popular Protest and Public Order.*

Stevenson, J., 1977. 'The Queen Caroline Affair', in Stevenson, J. (ed), *London in the Age of Reform*. Oxford.

Stevenson, J., 1979. *Popular Disturbances in England 1700–1870*.

Stewart, R., 1986. *Henry Brougham: His Public Career 1778–1968*.

Stigant, P., 1971. 'Wesleyan Methodism and working-class radicalism in the North', *NH,* vi, 1971.

Stone, L., 1969. 'Literacy and education', *P and P,* **42,** 1969.

Storch, R. D., 1975. 'The Plague of Blue Locusts', *IRSH,* xx, 1975.

Storch, R. D. (ed), 1982. *Popular Culture and Custom in Nineteenth Century England.*

Sutherland, L. S., 1959. 'The City of London in eighteenth century politics', in Pares, R. and Taylor, A. J. P. (eds), *Essays Presented to Sir Lewis Namier.*

Sykes, R., 1980. 'Some aspects of working-class consciousness in Oldham 1830–42', *HJ,* **23,** 1980.

Sykes, R., 1982. 'Early Chartism and trade unionism in south-east Lancashire', in Epstein, J. and Thompson, D. (eds), *The Chartist Experience.*

Sykes, R., 1985. 'Physical-force Chartism: the cotton district and the Chartist crisis of 1839', *IRSH,* xx, 2, 1985.

Taylor, B., 1983. *Eve and the New Jerusalem.*

Thale, M. (ed), 1972. *The Autobiography of Francis Place.* Cambridge UP.

Thale, M. (ed), 1983. *Selections from the Papers of the London Corresponding Society.* Cambridge UP.

Tholfsen, T. R., 1976. *Working Class Radicalism in Mid-Victorian England.*

Thomas, W. E. S., 1962. 'Francis Place and working class history', *HJ,* **5,** 1962.

Thomis, M. I., 1969. *Politics and Society in Nottingham 1785–1835.* Oxford UP.

Thomis, M. I., 1970. *The Luddites.* Newton Abbot.

Thomis, M. I., 1974. 'Jeremiah Brandreth and Pentrich', in *Popular Politics 1750–1870.* Open University Course Unit. Milton Keynes.

Thomis, M. I. and Holt, P., 1977. *Threats of Revolution in Britain.*

Thomis, M. I., 1983. 'The Dilemma of Colonel Brereton: Bristol 1831', *Australian Journal of Politics and History,* **29,** 2, 1983.

Thomis, M. I. and Grimmett, J., 1983. *Women in Protest 1800–1850.*

Thompson, B., 1982. 'Public provision and private neglect: public health', in Wright, D. G. and Jowitt, J. A. (eds), *Victorian Bradford.* Bradford.

Thompson, D., 1970. 'Chartism as a historical subject', *BSSLH,* **20,** 1970.

Thompson, D., 1971. *The Early Chartists.*

Thompson, D., 1977. 'Radicals and their historians', *Literature and History,* **5,** 1977.

Thompson, D., 1982. 'Ireland and the Irish in English radicalism', in Epstein, J. and Thompson, D. (eds), *The Chartist Experience.*

Thompson, D., 1984. *The Chartists.*

Thompson, E. P., 1968 edn. *The Making of the English Working Class.* Penguin edn. (originally published in 1963).

Thompson, E. P., 1971. 'The moral economy of the English Crowd in the eighteenth century', *P and P,* **50,** 1971.

Thompson, E. P., 1974. 'Testing Class Struggle', *The Times Higher Education Supplement,* 8 March 1974.

Thompson, E. P., 1975. 'The crime of anonymity', in Hay, D. (ed), *Albions Fatal Tree.*

Thompson, F. M. L., 1981. 'Social control in Victorian Britain', *EcHR,* 2nd ser., xxxiv, 1981.

Thompson, N. W., 1984. *The People's Science.* Cambridge UP.

Tiller, K., 1982. 'Late Chartism: Halifax, 1847–58', in Epstein, J. and Thompson, D. (eds), *The Chartist Experience.*

Treble, J. H., 1971. 'The social and economic thought of Robert Owen', in Butt, J. (ed), *Robert Owen: Prince of Cotton Spinners.* Newton Abbot.

Treble, J. H., 1973. 'O'Connor, O'Connell and the attitudes of Irish immigrants towards Chartism in the North of England 1838–1848', in Butt, J. and Clarke, I. F. (eds), *The Victorians and Social Protest.* Newton Abbot.

Turner, H. A., 1962. *Trade Union Growth, Structure and Policy.*

Turner, M. 1984. *Enclosures in Britain.*

Veitch, G. S., 1913. *The Genesis of Parliamentary Reform.*

Vincent, J. R., 1966. *The Formation of the Liberal Party 1857–1868.*

Vincent, J. R., 1967. *Poll Books: How Victorians Voted.* Cambridge UP.

Wallas, G., 1898. *The Life of Francis Place.*

Waller, P. J., 1981. *Democracy and Sectarianism: A political and social history of Liverpool 1868–1939.* Liverpool UP.

Walmsley, R., 1969. *Peterloo: The Case Reopened.* Manchester UP.

Ward, J. T., 1962. *The Factory Movement 1830–1855.*

Ward, J. T., 1967. *Sir James Graham.*

Ward, J. T., 1970. 'The Factory Movement', in Ward, J. T. (ed), *Popular Movements c.1830–1850.*

Ward, J. T., 1973. *Chartism.*

Webb, R. K., 1957. 'The Victorian reading public', *Universities Quarterly,* **12,** 1957–58.

Webb, S. and Webb, B., 1911. *The History of Trade Unionism.* 1911 edn.

Wells, R., 1977. *Dearth and Distress in Yorkshire 1793–1802.* Borthwick Institute, York.

Wells, R., 1983. *Insurrection: the British Experience: 1795–1803.* Gloucester.

Wells, R. A. E., 1979. 'The development of the English rural proletariat and social protest, 1700–1850', *Journal of Peasant Studies,* **6,** 1979.

West, J., 1920. *A History of the Chartist Movement.*

Western, J. R., 1956. 'The Volunteer Movement as an anti-revolutionary force 1793–1801', *EHR,* lxxi, 1956.

White, R. J., 1957. *Waterloo to Peterloo.*

White, R. J., 1965. *Radicalism and its Results.* Historical Association.

Wickwar, W. H., 1928. *The Struggle for the Freedom of the Press 1819–32.*

Wiener, J. H., 1969. *The War of the Unstamped.* Cornell UP, New York.

Wiener, J. H., 1983. *Radicalism and Free Thought in nineteenth-century Great Britain: The Life of Richard Carlile.* Greenwood Press, Westport, Conn..

Wilks, I., 1984. *South Wales and the Rising of 1839.*

Williams, D., 1939. *John Frost: A Study in Chartism.*

Williams, D., 1959. 'Chartism in Wales', in Briggs, A. (ed), *Chartist Studies.*

Williams, G. A., 1968. *Artisans and Sans-Culottes.*

Williams, G. A., 1978. *The Merthyr Rising.*

Williams, R., 1961. *Culture and Society 1780–1950.* Penguin edn.

Wilson, A., 1959. 'Chartism in Glasgow', in Briggs, A. (ed), *Chartist Studies.*

Wilson, A., 1974. 'The Suffrage Movement', in Hollis, P. (ed), *Pressure From Without.*

Wilson, B., 1887. *The Struggles of an Old Chartist.* Reprinted in Vincent, D., 1977. *Testaments of Radicalism.*

Wilson, G. M., 1982. *Alexander MacDonald: Leader of the Miners.* Aberdeen UP.

Winter, J., 1986. *The Great War and the British People.* Oxford UP.

Wolff, M., 1965. 'The uses of context: aspects of the 1860s', *VS,* ix, supplement, 1965.

Wright, D. G., 1969a. 'Bradford and the American Civil War', *JBS,* viii, 1969.

Wright, D. G., 1969b. 'A Radical Borough 1832–41', *NH,* iv, 1969.

Wright, D. G., 1970. *Democracy and Reform 1815–1885.*

Wright, D. G., 1974. 'Leeds politics and the American Civil War', *NH,* ix, 1974.

Wright, D. G., 1979. 'The Bradford Election of 1874', in Jowitt, J. A. and Taylor, R. K. S. (eds), *Nineteenth Century Bradford Elections.* Leeds UP.

Wright, D. G., 1982. 'The Second Reform Agitation', in Wright, D. G. and Jowitt, J. A. (eds), *Victorian Bradford.* Bradford.

Wright, D. G., 1986a. *The Chartist Risings in Bradford.* Bradford.

Wright, T. R., 1986b. *The Religion of Humanity: The impact of Comtean Positivism on Victorian Britain.* Cambridge UP.

Yeo, E., 1971. 'Robert Owen and radical culture', in Pollard, S. and Salt, J. (eds), *Robert Owen: Prophet of the Poor.*

Yeo, E., 1981. 'Christianity in Chartist Struggle 1838–42', *P and P,* **91,** 1981.

Yeo, E., 1982. 'Some Practices and Problems of Chartist Democracy', in Epstein J. and Thompson, D. (eds), *The Chartist Experience.*

Yeo, S., 1976. *Religion and Voluntary Organizations in Crisis.*

Ziegler, P., 1976. *Melbourne.*

Index